AF885410

THE ULTIMATE COMMON SENSE OF THE WORLD:

EMBRACE IT OR GO EXTINCT

EZZRATH BAHT SHEM

GLOBAL CITIZENS UNITE FOR COMMON SENSE

ezzrath@gmail.com

(312) 597-4877

Cover design: Concept by Ezzrath Baht Shem, the cover is a statement of how complacent and happy we behave accepting five thousand years of bondage of the masses while the puppet judges/politicians/corporation distribute the rations; and the puppeteer global elite hoard the wealth of earth all setup and designed by the gods that created the human body a hybrid of god/animal as slaves to mine the gold for Nibiru until this very day.

Interior design and edit: by Ezzrath Baht Shem

Paperback edition

First printing May, 2026

Published by Global Citizens Unite for Common Sense, a nonprofit entity organizing the first socialization of human beings FOR human beings.

COMMON SENSE OF THE WORLD: EMBRACE IT OR GO EXTINCT

"We must learn to live together as brothers or perish together as fools," by Dr. Martin Luther King Jr.

"Alone we can do so little; together we can do so much," by Helen Keller

"There is no power greater than a community discovering what it cares about," by Margaret Wheatley

"Individually, we are one drop of the ocean. Together we are an ocean." by Ryunosuke Satoro

"There is beauty and POWER in UNITY. We must be united in heart and mind. One world, one people." by Lailah Gifty Akita

"Greyhounds soar at racing, hunting, and affection; German Shepherds excel at training, guarding, and protecting; hounds, beagles, labradors, Golden retrievers are great at hunting, service animals, and loyalty; while ALL dogs if socialized are perfect for families… human beings, TODAY are not socialized to perform at their top potential and loved no MATTER WHAT… thus, today human beings' WORTH on earth is less than DOGS' and our societies expose this harsh reality with the very lives we live." BY EZZRATH BAHT SHEM

Table of Contents

FORETHOUGHT

The Ultimate Common Sense of the world is the most disregarded abandoned way of human life. Almost everyone on earth would agree that we human beings should focus the greatest priority on the masses and conservation of our habitat. The Welfare of the most important people on earth belongs to the 99%, which is Mandatory and undisputable, equally required to protect earth, and ***ABSOLUTELY not*** the (1) one-percenters' right to hoard wealth/natural resources, power, and destroy our home called earth.

If you see this as ***truth*** and that the powers that be on earth are for the ***few*** and not the masses… ***Yes***? And, if you can have an open mind that no ***individual*** should agree 100% with everything any **one** individual thinks and believes… more importantly, believe that keeping the ***few*** rich people, "rich" and the ***masses*** of poor, "poor" has been the human experience for as long as written history has existed, Yes??? Have you seen it as a fact that for millennia, **martyrs, saviors, leaders have been pushing the concept to give the poor their share within the system, but *never real change*… *A PUSH FOR A NEW PARADIGM*?** Nothing ever changes throughout all recorded history. I PRESENT real change that has NEVER been tried throughout human existence. The WEAK human beings are the most important in society… no one has ever in all of history advocated this premise.

THIS PREMISE REPRESENTS GENUINE CHANGE!

Yes, of course, you won't like to hear this statement, but you can never deny that no society on earth has ever tried it… Not ever. This is genuine change, a society that targets the weak as most important to strive to become their best person, so that the rest of us become our best persons by default, **IT IS A MUST!** Ponder the experience of a society where the masses reign supreme in importance, having all needs fulfilled just as they have air to breathe, to strive their utmost potential, while equally protecting Earth. Interested? Then this book is a must for you to read.

The ultimate common sense is real change that has never ever been practiced throughout written history… the answer for the salvation of humanity. Christ spoke of giving to the poor because the poor are the same as giving to him. This book speaks of setting a NEW PARADIGM, ending poverty forever (every human being on earth gets their needs met without one breath of concern as to how it will happen (just as no one fights over air), practically eliminating the weak and establishing **ALL** of humanity performing at their optimum capability, where society takes full responsibility for any ONE individual fallen or hurt by human actions. There will be absolutely no poverty, and little to no crime, depressed, suicidal people, no drug addiction, no hopelessness, no imprisonment, no police… nothing but a peaceful, harmonious species called mankind that most none on earth believes is remotely possible to exist. Yet, many Christians would claim to believe in Jesus, who said, " Pray, … Thy will be done on earth, **as it is in heaven**. Jesus wasn't stupid. It has taken thousands of years for this one aspect that Christ was asking to take place… that I now come before you to set up the first community of heaven on Earth, in our lifetime, right now... fulfilling Christ's prayer. Now that it is mentioned, it can now become a possibility, even if I die, someone will establish the heaven on earth that Christ prayed for.

SECOND:

Suppose you are an attorney, paralegal, or someone who works with the law. Please look up the case Black v Friedrichsen 1:19-cv-00307-TLS, Ft Wayne, Indiana Northern District Court. See the original lawsuit filed by the judge under 1:19-cv-00222-WCL-SLC, and find the case number for the original lawsuit filed by me in May 2019, I believe on the 24th day, where the federal judge ordered an opinion that I was court-evicted when the order clearly states that the defendants were denied their claim. She, Susan Collins, would later claim that my grandchildren weren't on the lease, though the court order states they were on the lease and names each child, stating their right to live in the unit. But all federal judges and the Supreme Court found it lawful and just that an erroneous claim that put white defendants in the right, falsely overwhelmingly in the right, against a black plaintiff, with overwhelming evidence against the claims of the white litigants. The judges all used JIM CROW from 2019 till 2023 (Nearly four years of trying to force a blatant lie into trial, and the Supreme Court backed them up. They stated that I had practiced judicial misconduct from day one! In other words, they were saying that I was just a nigger (automatically both IN THE WRONG and 2. My overwhelming evidence against whites was not allowed in the US federal court, meaning that Jim Crow was still in effect in 2023 until this very day!

At the state level, before federal court, the landlords began harassing me to the point that my family's lives were in danger, forcing me to give up fighting for my right to live in the home. My son was in the middle of an eviction, so at that time, I would get a legal right to bring him and his new wife and baby in without attack against us by the landlord in exchange for my safety and time to peacefully find a new home. This is crazy, I later found out that by law, a Spouse and baby shouldn't be forced to live separated by law for those on the lease, and it is not an immediate eviction as the landlords. This evil court embraced landlords' attack against their tenants' right to be married without the immediate threat of eviction. Nonetheless, I never moved my son's spouse and child in until I had an agreement from my landlord. My son and his wife lived with her family and friends until I decided someone could get seriously hurt, and I might as well help my son now that I couldn't stay and was being illegally forced out.

Please look at the pleadings from the beginning, referring to the state case Grant Co. 27D03-1706-PL-000014. You will irrefutably find unprecedented intentional bias and criminal perjury by federal judges and the supreme Court to violate the Constitution and the sworn Duty of judges to seek unbiased Justice and to uphold the Supreme, the highest law of the land, the Constitution of the USA. While the law must come before justice… if the evidence shows strong favor to a litigant being harmed, then the judges must diligently use every far extreme right within the bounds of the law, without breaking the law, and a bias to seek justice to render justice under the law. These judges sought how best to render injustice by Jim Crow Law, black person… automatically considered beyond the wrong, thus GUILTY FOR BEING BLACK AGAINST WHITE LITIGANTS. Really look at the court's opinions from the very beginning.

Look at the state-level court order issued June 14, 2017, then look at the federal judge's opinion of my original complaint filed in May of 2019, which was dismissed. Would you dismiss the case because I was evicted? Do you see an order of eviction? Does it seem that the order to deny possession means eviction? Now look at the Federal Court's order to dismiss my complaint because I was evicted through the court, and they have no jurisdiction over the court that wrongly evicted me. Is it genuinely possible for a seasoned, fair, unbiased, competent judge to see an order denying the defendant's possession to rule that the plaintiff was evicted? Is this a dismissal case or a "correct the defects"? Should a new lawsuit be a reconsideration motion or a granted reconsideration? Defendants respond to the so-called lawsuit ordered on my behalf by the magistrate/Judge Lee. The judge's response to the motion for dismissal is denied, see Order ECF 28. However, when you read the response by the judge that Black is at fault, my grandchildren are not on the lease; if it were true, shouldn't it be automatically dismissed? And if not... should it take over three years for a case where the plaintiff is found in the wrong and caused the eviction, continuously in Misconduct from DAY ONE (Ruled also by the Supreme Court, Writ!)

See my Summary Judgment Brief (overwhelming evidence against the defendants' Affirmative Defense. It was filed because I had absolutely no clue that an order would favor me not to dismiss, but the opinion read it should be dismissed by court opinion, but court was so extremely generous to rightly find that the state court was wrong and that I did have unauthorized occupants in my house and the state court was too incompetent to name my grandchildren with a right to live in the home being officially on the lease. Was the unauthorized occupants a merit-worthy complaint filed by the defendants, or was it brought without evidence? Ruling on the evidence found in the court order. Is there any merit, a worthy document above the lease and the state court order that remotely suggests that my grandchildren are not on the lease? Is there any way that the defendants claim that my grandchildren were not on the lease?

If you're seeking truth and you follow the case closely from the evidence, you will conclude that judges are liars by ECF 80 for sure. After CONSIDERING my response to the court to substantiate and to remove erroneous findings in the order. At any time a factual error is found during a case, it cannot be treated as an opinion, as the district court and circuit court treated the evidence. Watch throughout this case at the gross misconduct to rule whites intentionally in the wrong, and if you look at why this was done... It is a Fraudulent crime of federal judges. The Supreme Court ordered that Errors can't be corrected after a certain time, in opposition to the lower Federal District/and Circuit courts that ordered that there were no errors! The order opinion that my request to repair the order is an objection to the court's order, and the objection is denied. At no time did the district or circuit court claim that the error couldn't be removed due to an untimely request to remove it. It was ordered in ECF 80 and timely requested to remove the error from ECF 80, where the court claimed there were no errors. The circuit court claimed the issue of whether or not the lease had my grandchildren on it was a matter of opinion of the district court, and the Circuit Court does not handle matters of opinion where the litigant disagrees with the order. The lease was not a factual document, and therefore the judge had every right to her opinion that the lie was her right to order.

I ask you to send your findings to the Indiana and Chicago bars to report these judges. As I am not an attorney, it's an automatic denial without any consideration. Hell, most attorneys are not heard over a judge's wrong rulings, you know the truth. This is an extreme violation of oath and public transparency. The dire need to cover up judicial corruption proves it is extreme that a black, Pro se litigant with strong evidence and a request has next to zero chance in court against a white litigant. I will be automatically denied with no explanation other than the judges are right, that a fact is actually an opinion, and my objection to the judge's Opinion is denied! No misconduct! Fair ruling as has been ordered throughout four years of lies! Why four years? Why wasn't I dismissed after the ECF 28 Order? I was found automatically in the wrong, right? Jim Crow ruled illegally. I had absolutely no right by law, being a black person, to have a right to my constitutional right to a trial of a jury of my peers, especially with a request for special damages for my people. Therefore, they were working hard for this wrongful misconduct, litigant who refused to go to trial, Ruled by Jim Crow law, falsely in the wrong with no lawyer. Go to trial, for what? My only choice was to reverse the LIE or be found in the wrong by that lie. I couldn't file a brief in the appellate court due to my disability. There was no doubt that I would be denied, and then I'd have to do the work all over again for the writ. I would have died. This is the entire case in a nutshell. For well over three years!!! Court ordered, you remain falsely in the wrong no matter what, go to trial without an attorney. From day one, there is no right to a trial. I had to go to trial falsely in the wrong or stand my ground that judges can't lie regarding a FACT to make white defendants right. I knew I couldn't win black and be falsely in the wrong. I had no choice but to stop the lie. Either way, I would lose. Did I have evidence against my landlords? Did I stand a chance to win with the biased lies of the judges, and no attorney?

ACKNOWLEDGMENTS

1. My parents, George Black and Mildred Barber, are both deceased, my rock.

2. My children, my beloved firstborn, whom I believe wouldn't want her name associated with me, as such, I respect her wishes, Yetunde Ogunbuyide, and Kemuel Shem my beloved.

3. My grandchildren, Chrisdeon Ogunbuyide, Victoria Goree, Isaiah Goree, and Malik Ogunbuyide, my heart.

4. My siblings, George Martin Fitzgerld Black (deceased, age 40, heart attack), and two brothers, whom I believe would prefer to remain nameless.

5. My best friends, Jennifer and Pearl, and my weird friend, I believe he was afraid of retaliation, so he won't be mentioned by name. Jenny, my sis ALWAYS there through the decades, my dear roommate at Tuskegee and BESTIE for life, I pray, I'll be in the place to bless you as much as you have been a blessing to me. Pearl, just a sweet soul never intending to hurt anybody, UNLESS THEY GOT IT COMIN, hehehe, I love you.

6. Desiree Jemison my stepdaughter who has been in my life remembering so many things I'd forgotten. God places special people to be for each other where blood couldn't. I subtract the step, my daughter be blessed and thanks for supporting me and helping me. WE'LL DO THIS!

INTRODUCTION

How is it possible to be the ***wealthiest*** continent in the entire world of raw resources to have the ***poorest suffering*** citizens on planet earth living on it? What continent am I?

U. S. A., the ***great***, owns the most wealth globally, leading by a significant margin in Gross Domestic Product (***GDP***). Her economy is diverse, driven by finance, technology, energy, and consumer spending, and she holds ***the world's reserve currency, the U. S. dollar***, but with all the world's currency and global wealth comes murderous wars, deaths, raping, figuratively speaking, of any and ***every*** human life incapable of defending themselves. Destroying the lives of her citizens, small countries, and with Trump now attacking the ***entire world*** for their wealth through tariffs. Expanding over centuries, ***as the world turns a blind eye***, she arrogantly participates in such utter criminality, warmongering, wickedness that it's as if nothing, absolutely nothing can be done to stop the tyranny. It's so horrific that a woman bold enough to run for president boasted, "***We came, we saw, he died, HAHAHA***" as Americans died also in Libya. They left one of the wealthiest, self-driven nations of Africa in ruins and a shell of the nation it had been to relentlessly cut Africa off from its strong arm (Kwami Nkrumah, Patrice Lumumba, and countless others oust or murdered by design of westerners. Africans cut off at the root forcing African people perpetually poor, destitute, and dying as owners of the world's gold, diamonds, oil, etc.), from uniting and stopping the nation's livelihood and pride in being absent of the dollar. Libya refused to join the world in accepting the dollar cutting off the federal reserve. The westerners manipulate strong countries' citizens to divide thus cutting them off at the root. Forcing African people to be perpetually poor, destitute, and dying as **owners** of the world's wealth; gold, diamonds, oil, etc. Out of 195 nations in the whole world, fewer than ten are reported on Google trading without the dollar. Less than 10 countries are NOT enslaved to the dollar.

We believe that killing AND stealing from the weak; destroying the weak makes us strong, ***but look at us***. ***You are dying proudly*** because at least you get to be white and proud. The bullet meant for blacks also destroys whites. The bullet meant for poor nations of non-whites is also destroying whites by nature. You are being ***targeted as a black person***, but you see white skin in the mirror and fail to see that. Yes, of course, it's blacks more, but whites are not far behind. ***The*** nigger bullet is ***destroying***

our entire human race, yes, blacks more. Why is this cool with you? You, ***yes, you whites***, you can't dodge the bullet meant to destroy nonwhites, and you'd rather ***die*** with us than join us ***for ALL to have a harmonious life***. Is that ultimate common sense? Let me sacrifice my white skin so the ***few whites win***. ***Really?*** The bullet meant for blacks must ***now be targeted for elimination*** so that ***all*** human beings win by default. If poverty is believed to be a black thing, annihilate it! We all win! If drugs and crime are a black thing, eliminate them, not black people! We all win! If everything that hurts mankind, ***by mankind… we attack and destroy the target.*** LET'S ALL WIN *UNITED!*

Did you know according to the internet and documentaries the global white population was 30% and today it's as low as 8% to possibly 12%. This is the frenzy of the LAWLESS USA we see today. It's a fact there will come a day very soon that there will be absolutely no purely white person on earth. Just as it happened ancient times with the Chinese, Indians, Mexicans where ANCIENT whites mixed with ancient blacks, eliminating whites into people of color. With the damage done by whites to nonwhites, THIS IS THE ONLY SOLUTION for whites the day the world's nonwhites are equal power to white people. In our society, whites, as the weaker group of people becoming both minority and no longer with power, whites will be protected as the weak are the most important. By our current dog eat dog world it can't go well at all. We need ALL humanity, an injury to one is an injury to all. THIS SOCIETY IS OF ABSOLUTE necessity for whites in the long run of humanity. Better still, we allow the current society to run its self extinct with business as usual.

We all win! This is the Ultimate Common Sense of the world.

BACKGROUND

I. ***Undermining of America by the one percenters***, The Royal families of earth and the Pope/catholic church. They own and control everything we do for the favor of Western society as they hoard all resources and earthly ancient secrets and goods.

II. ***Who are the one percenters, who are not.*** The wealthy (Trump, Elon Musk, Oprah etc.), corporations, and governments: ***are not*** the one percenters. These are the puppets of the one percenters used to divide and conquer the masses. Notice with all their wealth, ***never a penny*** spent to eradicate systematically keeping the masses poor, enslaved to a system that works against their good establishing ***self-sabotage***.

III. ***The secret head of the one percenters…*** is the gods/ Anunnaki or the Nephilim mentioned in the Bible. We are all under their influence. They are our Father god who bred our hybrid physical bodies into existence. However, the spirit and soul belongs to ***God*** and us. We are their greatest nightmare and the genuine reason for the human race targeted for utter annihilation. They have done all within their power to destroy us off earth and genocide our species. They give their reasoning inside the Bible Genesis 11. Mankind was united as ***one***, building as spaceship that could escape beyond our realm of reality. We were on a scientific breakthrough that even the gods hadn't figured out. There's two ways of escape of our reality, through spiritual travel or through technology. We were the builders of the pyramids on Earth intentionally placed at opposing sides of earth in the middle east and southern America. According to the bible they were building a city, a tower that would reach to heaven.

According to Zacharia Sitchin, the Bible says they were making a name for themselves. The exact translation for "name" was ***shem***. They were making a ship as large as a city for all mankind to escape out of our self-contained aquarium (Earth) that we were and are confined inside of to this very day. God decides to spy and finds the entire human race escaping our habitat and realizes that there's absolutely nothing that our species can't do once ***we***

unite! We are capable of becoming more than the gods, and the thought of losing their slaves and our becoming more than them drove them crazy. They plotted biological warfare against us so that our ***DNA*** was damaged and we no longer ***united as one*** until this very day. Our ancient books tell the stories of who we are and what happened to us. The story of creating a hybrid human being is an impossibility for anyone in 2000 BC to discuss. How was it spoken back then, ***except it truly happened? Wake-up!*** Our only chance at genuine survival, peace, and joy is ***uniting as one*** with all of our focus on the very least of us raising up to full potential and capability of the individual, so that ***we all win by default.*** Imagine a world where a would-be criminal, mentally ill, depressed, and a drug addict is targeted for success and becomes a ***fruitful***, productive citizen like you and me. Isn't it a far better world where all goes to the one percent and produces our society? ***Nobody has ever tried this***, because we believe we ***must*** be enslaved to the system of the wealthy, foremost important, the powerful, foremost important, the socially acceptable, foremost important... Please see this as common sense ***utter stupidity. Why?*** It's our world, we can ***unite*** as one for our own good.

IV. ***The world's greatest endeavor to create a dysfunctional society of mighty power intentionally specifically for the extinction of humanity.***

A. The Nationwide self-annihilation of the American population

i. ***Big pharma***, ***GMOs***,

According to the internet, ***Big pharma*** began in the 1850's, when German and American companies began producing synthetic drugs and establishing research and manufacturing facilities. By the early twentieth century, major pharmaceutical companies such as Bayer, Merck, and Eli Lilly had emerged. The industry grew as the government began pouring funds into the industry for ***research*** and the development of new drugs. Note the research going on in those days using ***human guinea pigs***. As late as 1972, blacks were being experimented on during the syphilis experiment. I remember one of the doctors on Phil Donahue claiming that blacks were no different than animals, therefore had absolutely no remorse for harming black ***human beings***, hence, for racist blacks are not human beings, therefore black lives don't matter.

Today, ***big pharma*** pays doctors, congressmen, and idiots public speakers to push drugs, vaccines, and ***diseases*** to keep their business lucrative. Look at ***AIDs***, ***science*** says a monkey contracted the disease, and all of a sudden, millions of Africans became infected and died. Then, the New York prison started killing off blacks in prison with ***AIDs***, then all of a sudden, in California, ***only gay*** men became infected in June 1981, reported by the ***CDC*** as a rare form of pneumonia, later identified as ***AIDs***, Acquired Immunodeficiency Syndrome in five ***young*** gay ***bisexual*** men in Los Angeles. It became widespread across the gay community, known as ***GRID***, Gay-related immune deficiency. ***Now!!! We all know!*** This is the ***AIDs***, ***HIV*** began amongst all of the hated communities of Charlie Kirk and ***all racists***… But it's not man-made. I am so damned done with this if you want to believe that only ***blacks*** and ***gays*** by the ***millions*** contract ***AIDs***, ***Wtf!*** Leave it right there. The blacks would be wiped out by now because no one would care about the Western racist infecting Africa, but our poor ***beloved*** white gays… ***Now*** it's gotta be remedied. My message to sicko racist, ***You can never get rid of black people because we are in your mitochondria, DNA.***

ii. Environmental pollution and toxins

iii. Causing diseases, mental illness, suicide, drug addiction, and criminal behavior

iv. Division of the people by color, race, sexism, nationalism, financial security, religion, and age.

v. Lobbying for ***control*** over all finances and activities of the people

B. ***Conspiracy dumbing down of Americans,*** - the above violations against humanity, Schools intentionally defunded. Test score requirements were lowered to failing children's performance standards instead of raising children's educational performance. Our acceptance of the failure to educate, more than ever before, proves our society lives by ***the rule, acceptance of the emperor's new clothing effect by a society as a rule.***

(911), Flat Earth, the Moon landing of 1969 that is utterly impossible to send people ***today***, Racism 2026, the present day holocaust of black

America, (brains of 18 year olds can't make right decisions regarding alcohol, but ***far below*** 18, as young as 10-11 years old can decide when to pick up a gun to kill for prison time (target race black, but white children affected), more prison time to stop criminals, but ***all*** societies with less prison time have ***less prisoners*** including ***the America*** (***USA*** of the past) ***with less crime!*** How does more prisons and time make less crime if we look at our past and the countries that actually care more about their citizens than Vengeance? How does it make sense?

C. Misinformation, governmental/corporate, undermines freedom of speech and ***transparency***.

D. ***The unseen hand*** Ultimate Destruction - Anunnaki, same as Nephilim. The patriarchal society ***requires*** that the few receive all of Earth's resources while the majority share leftover crumbs.

E. ***The experimental us citizen was gaslighted for destruction, so dumb downed, blind, and complacent to accept any demise as a necessary evil***

V. What ***must*** happen to save our country and the entire world? ***Most important: Eliminate*** the accepted construct that no country is of concern, but the ***US***, and ***eliminate all*** irrational treatment of ***US*** citizens ***and the citizens of the world!*** Eliminate lobbying for money to be replaced with proposals ***only***. Educate the people about the ***reality*** of the numbers of whites to nonwhite, the black African mother ***Eve*** of us ***all***. The original black ancient society was the ***first*** racist, so dammit ***we are all even*** stop the madness, ***now***. No need for guilt, no fault-blaming for any color within the HUEman race. There's only time for ***uniting as one*** for ***all humanity***. That includes anyone with human ***DNA***, whether mixed with neanderthal, intellectual disability, or the most psychopathic murderer. ***All*** must receive human dignity as best as we, the masses, can deliver. We speak of Human ***rights***, but none exist for the vast majority of the people in the world. ***This must stop!*** The Earth is drowning in our blood and an insane disconnect from each other. ***We are one!*** Absolutely no fear for anyone on Earth of how to get food, shelter, transportation, physical and mental/emotional medical needs provided, and ***education***. The end of money and capitalism, and the ushering in of our ***greatest asset***,
The ***HUEman being***.

CHAPTER ONE

THE LIVING TESTIMONY: EVIDENCE of A LIFE LIVED EXTREMELY UNEQUAL WHILE BLACK IN AMERICA

Historically, we all choose our preferred time in history to begin our story. Some might begin a historical account with the American birth of a nation, some with the dawning of man, some with the dinosaurs, some with earth, the universe, and so forth, but I will choose our beginning with us, the ***hueman*** race… ***mankind*** and our Universe. It is generally scientifically accepted that all human beings descended from one common ancestor, the mother of us all, ***Eve***. All of us share her mitochondria. We all come from Africa. ***We are all black people***. The truth will set us free. I start shaking things up, and getting to the point that everyone's beliefs are going to be seriously challenged and pissed the hell off, good! If you ***love*** our world as it is today, then ***throw this damn book away right now***. There is absolutely nothing here for you to learn or enjoy.

However, if you desire to see a more happier harmonious, healthier, productive, empathetic, caring, peaceful human species on earth, and are willing to cut through the rock-hard challenges of unpleasant reality that you cannot prove wrong to get through to the diamond, then this book is for you. You will ***never*** see our world the same again, that's my promise. There's something here for everyone to take pleasure in hearing. If you have a mind open to truth beyond the tunnel vision of what you were told, you will use common sense ***and see*** the more ***real*** reality. Let's face it, if everything is perfect within our beliefs and societal behavior, everything would be exceptionally pleasant, smooth, ***easy***, but we ***all*** should agree these attributes are the complete opposite of our societal experience. ***It's not*** peachy crème, it's not okay, depending on how you look at it (through the eyes of Palestinians, Syrians, Haitians, Afghanis, most black Africans, and poor African Americans. This cascade of destruction stems from our ignorance of reality and contentment to live as if nothing can be done about this horrid reality will be our undoing. As a matter of fact, a large majority of humanity is brainwashed to believe that poverty is a must-have. In fact, our societies only get worse and worse for the masses living on earth, sharing crumbs as ***the few*** (one percenters) hoard the wealth of raw resources on earth, and by ***design*** of the unseen hand, forcing division against the masses that fuels the destruction of the people at their own hands of ignorance. They use the wealthy, politicians, and officials to divide us against one another. Black against white, Christians against Muslims, women against men, the young against the old, so on and so on, and vice versa. Aren't you ***sick and tired*** of being ***sick and tired***? The answer is:

One: Understanding our history, who are we, how did we get here, why we are here, ***what is here*** (earth/universe)?

Two: Understanding the ***sick game***. ***Divide and conquer!*** Use the few kept in power to keep the masses dumbed down ***utterly*** against their own benefit. Keep all humanity from the ***truth***. The only way humanity survives is to recognize we are only as strong as our weakest link.

You'll hate it (this ***truth***)! ***That's why we're destroyed*** on the path of extinction!

Here it is!!! The most important people on earth are the criminals, addicts, depressed, suicidal, homicidally insane; those we call the monstrous degenerates, and ***filth*** on earth are our most important people. Why? Because if we target the productivity of these people as our ***number one priority***, then all the rest of us will be even more productive by default; We'll be the gods we were created to be and ***envied*** by the gods due to the reality of our ***flesh/spirit/soul*** entity, ***the envy*** of the gods. See the reality of our existence, who we are. (pg.153) We're only as strong as our weakest link. HEY, WE HYBRIDS ARE BRED TO BE MORE THAN OUR PARENTS... part animal, the gift of instincts; part gods, the gift of intellect. Put our creation all together at maximum productivity and you will have THE NEXT WORLD a new dimension, a new existence... the Architect's next creation of many mansions prepared just for us.

I know that this sounds totally insane, but if you're living in insanity with your priority set in societal Mayhem, how can you have sound judgment of sanity? I have lived with nothing but studies and ***life*** spiritual work experiences. There is no other way for mankind, ***this is what Jesus was teaching***. Most of you have no criminal record like me, but please trust me when I say this, it's without doubt not because of your good soul that you have no record. ***We***, you and I, are sent to earth with a special human gift to follow rules, or maybe you're like my brother and have learned how to evade the law over the years of practice. In any case, we all who are empowered on the inside to survive this hellhole system do so ***only*** by the luck of special ***inside wiring***. Being gifted, we ***must*** rewire (rehabilitate and ***prevent all faulty wiring within the network of our human family***) those damaged and/or requiring special needs to perform at their highest potential. ***Let's make it happen***, why not? Who gets hurt by lifting the unfortunate up? Always remember that the number one mandatory human requirement for all is having all survival needs met easily accessible and always striving for peace and ultimately joy through the pursuit of happiness.. Every human being has a right to live with this ***minimum existence requirement*** on earth, all NEEDS met as easily as obtaining air. This means we have a whole lot of work to get done, raising our species. I am giving you an ever so slight glance towards the end of this book of our ***new world***. No governments, no leaders, no money, no suffering at the hands of human greed and hatred. The ***greatest*** amongst us, who get the most of us all, are those who create the avenues to secure this new system. Of course, doctors, actors, engineers, sports stars, etc., doctors, actors, engineers, sports stars, etc. will still shine for our need and enjoyment of life, but those with the best results at cracking the code against depression, disease, criminal mind, and the sort like are our most prestigious and highest rewarded individuals. Those who design the trade system, assuring that the ***least*** among us become the ***greatest*** of our attention and development for productivity. Of course, this goes for standard and geniuses performing at their highest potential. We must have our ***greatest*** focus on achieving successful children operating at their ***maximum*** performance of their soul's desire, knowing they're loved, safe, and happy. You can close the book now. ***And start!*** You have what must happen right there, but you can continue to read to learn more about the man-made suffering, who you are, where you are, and a slight bit more of a glance at what our new world should look like. You have never thought of such ideas because we want change by trusting the same 5000-year-old way of doing things as the absolute only way. Money is not power! It's and an illusion… ***A human being is your greatest asset on earth*** and the ***US*** kills and enables the killings of our ***most valuable asset***. How many geniuses have we murdered because they were born black, in Palestine, in Syria or some other small country that we don't give a damn about? You better bet your sweet bottom; geniuses are not only born among the 8 to 10 percent ***minority*** white persons on earth.

Currently, we are a species of human beings who ***attack*** human beings for being ***human***. Yes, ***we prey on the weak!*** What I am saying is our patriarchal society is, by design, attacking the weak while gifting the most well-off persons on earth. This is equivalent to the snake that feeds on its own tail. It started with the gods (Anunnaki/Nephilim, now exiled off earth), then royalty.

(kings/queens/princes/princesses/dukes/emperors/dictators/rulers).

Today, it's the one percenters/corporations that ***live in glory*** while the masses suffer at their greedy hands, hoarding most of the raw resources and wealth of the earth. For thousands of years, the masses have complained, fought, and ***continue supporting this paradigm of human annihilation***.

Let me give you a more transparent theoretical correlation scenario to our ***game of destruction***, self-annihilation, and the extinction of the species known as mankind. This was written in books that European culture calls a myth. The people themselves called the information ***stories***. If and ***only if*** the word "stories" means a collection of fiction, then the European explanation of the ancients' stories as fiction may possibly be true. However, how dare we ***take our ancestors'*** reporting of their lives' stories, written clearly for adults to read, and make them children's fairy tales or folklore? The Bible was plagiarized from these stories because it tells a lot of the same stories, but the so-called "myths" predate the Bible. Is the Bible a ***myth?*** Hell no, it's a book of stories many Americans believe are inspired by God. Absolutely no sane person can claim that the Bible doesn't exist. Therefore, even if you don't believe a word it says is true, ***you must accept*** that the words were ***indeed written***. Is that a ***fact?*** I say that to say look at the American slavery spoken about in Deuteronomy 28th Chapter. How was slavery written about, and we ***know*** for a fact it happened, but for ***fact*** it ***never*** happened at the time the Bible was written. ***How can you explain this?*** Especially the ***type of slavery*** that ***never ever existed in that lifetime!*** In other words, these people are talking about somethings some things that ***had never been seen*** or written ever before, but it is prophesied to happen in the future. It says that Americans would be a people that Israel nor their fathers knew. That this nation would come from ***far*** from the end of the earth. (Now imagine the trip between America and Africa) How would people describe this distance back then? Then to throw in their symbol… ***as swift as the eagle*** (not a falcon, the most swift bird) ***flieth***, a nation whose tongue you will not understand. Israel understood the Egyptians, Babylonians, and almost all the eastern tongues, but NOT the American language.) A nation of fierce countenance which shall not regard the person of the old nor show favor to the young Deu 28: 48-50

Check this prophecy out. Thy sons and thy daughters shall be given unto another people, and thine eye shall look and fail with longing for them all the day long. And there shall be no might in thine hand. The fruit of thy land (***Africa/Middle East***) and all thy labours (possession that you worked for) shall a nation which ***you do not know***, eat up. So Israel, in fact, didn't know the Americans who, till this very day, destroy Africa and the Middle East. Middle East, where? Africa was one huge continent comprised of Asia and Europe. From the African you know, African, to the east, the Middle East, and to Asia, the ***Far East*** just adds Africa to show you how we are genuinely referencing these continents. It's crazy how today the Middle East isn't a part of the African map because the Nile and miles east of the other side, including Iraq and Iran, were on my map of Africa as a child in the 60s. It was chopped off in the late 70s or early 80's. And thou shalt only be oppressed and crushed always. (hmmm, as is happening to this very day) v33 The LORD and thy king, which thou shalt set over thee to a nation which neither thou nor thy father's have known, and ***there shalt thou serve other gods***, wood/paper, stone/coins, ***money***. V36 Thou shalt become an astonishment and a proverb (good for nothing, lazy people, criminals, monkeys) and a byword, (the n-word, coloreds, coon) among ***all nations*** whither the Lord shall lead thee v37 You shall plant vineyards and dress them, but shall neither drink of the wine nor gather the grapes, for the warms shall eat them. You shall bear sons and daughters, but you shall not enjoy them, for they shall go into captivity. Chapter 28 verse 41

The thousands of years of patriarchal society rule ***of dehumanization*** are undetectable and thus overlooked in this scenario. When you live in dung, you start not to notice the stench as much. It's just the way life is… swallow it. The patriarchal society has massively influenced the human psyche's acceptance and pursuance of self-annihilation. We are misinformed that there is no other way, but our way or a variation of our way, ***but never something***

totally different, in order to experience a change that is totally different from the attack against the weak of humanity.

Look at my mock scenario of what we do, scaled down so you can see, and ***stop the madness!***

The gods (Anunnaki/Nephilim) kidnapped 100 people (human population) and locked them into a single large room (creation of physical man on earth). They (gods) call one person (king) to the side, gifting the king with the knowledge of the gods to ***rule everything*** and to keep the 99% in despair, divided, and ignorant.

The king gets ***ten pizzas*** (representing earth's wealth and resources.

The king follows through with the deception and division of the people to secretly manipulate the 99% (global events) for their (king and three people puppets) own benefit ***at the expense of the 99***. He (king)1%, elects three people (the Oprahs, Bill Gates, Elon Musk, Jeff Bezos as ONE PERSON, the national governments of earth (congress/parliament/FEMA/WHO/CDC…etc.) AS THE SECOND PERSON, and global corporations (banks/big pharma/Monsanto…etc) as the THIRD PERSON to disperse ***one pizza*** for all 99% to share (the 99 never see the king's hand stirring the pot), to pollute the room, to create disease and ignorance by intentional misinformation presented to the 99. The 99 are brainwashed to believe that the minority 8 TO 10% are most important in the room, getting 70% of the ***one pizza***, while the 90% of the 99 people fight for their 30% share of crumbs ***from one pizza***. It's established that only the three people have the privilege to access resources; that are that are available to the king. They get to share nine pizzas with immunity to accountability. The 99% watch that 1% control, so that they can't have any more than one small portion of pizza to share.

Meanwhile, the gods who have set this game in play are gone to other ***rooms*** (planets), wreaking havoc ***everywhere they go***.

This, my fellow human beings, is our social reality!

My question to you is, as ***one person*** of the 99% in this scenario, in this room, do you honestly believe you will see that this is ***just the way things must be?*** Do you think 99 people in the room would knowing allow the one-person keep charge over ten pizzas, sharing one among the 99? If you can see uniting 8 billion human beings on earth against the shenanigans of the one percenters is nothing different than uniting the 99 in the room against the 1% having everything... then you ***must*** join the 99% to say NO MORE acceptance of the lie that we can't do anything. ***Ultimate common sense***, absolutely no way 99 people are going to allow the ***rule of that one destroyer*** of the people in the room. It can NEVER happen. We ***must*** think like a musketeer. ***One for all*** and all for one. The weakest individuals on earth are the extremely ***most*** vulnerable and most important on earth to protect. ***Reverse***, patriarchal societal suffering and ultimately the extinction of humanity. ***Genuine change!***

Three: ***Choose a side intentionally or by omission***

This is a sample explanation. You will, in fact, choose a side to promote no matter what. Your choices are limited to two sides: ***for humanity*** or ***against humanity***.

It's as simple as that. If you do nothing to change our condition, or your ***fight*** to continue in our negatively downward spiraling extinction of humanity, then that's your choice, to destroy humanity.

However, if you choose to be a ***force to be reckoned with***, go to the last chapter and see if you can identify with the suggestions offered there or come up with your own ideas that no longer support destroying weak human beings. (***We***) must do things differently than we have been doing them for the past 5000 years. If so, look for ways to implement these ideas and concepts into reality. When you make this decision final, your choice will be to save (change) humanity. You become the CHRIST, and not the antichrist, the salvation humanity has been seeking for millennia. You discover your purpose... promoting a harmonious existence for ALL mankind. You create heaven on earth as Christians were taught to pray to happen ***because it is possible***, not an impossibility requested by an idiot asking for something that is impossible.

Yes, we really can! Create heaven on earth, but not by continuously doing the same things we have done for the past 5000 years that have ***never ever*** once been successful for the masses of human beings.

1a. ***Who are we:***

The human species, according to Kabballah, began when ***God*** fell 10 consciousnesses from Kether (spirit/heaven) to Malkuth (flesh/earth), ***thus the soul*** of mankind, called the Adam Kaddmon. All over the world, ancient peoples of planet earth told the story of gods making men in their image. It is even told in our ***Bible*** that we accept as Christians as 100% factual. Genesis 1: 26, 27… And gOD said, Let us make man (gods ask the father Anu to allow them to make a man) in ***our*** image, after ***our*** likeness; and let ***them***, mankind, have dominion over the fish of the sea, fowl of the air, and over the cattle and over ***all the earth***… How do we know these are gods and ***not*** God? It's because if anyone studies the Bible and world ***ancient history***, they know that the Bible is simply a copycat version of Babylonian, Assyrian, Sumerian, Yoruba, Ancient American, European, South African, and Egyptian folklore, numerous stories of creation. Most of these stories predate the Bible; therefore, the writers of the bible plagiarized more ancient texts/scrolls. They described using some form of a test tube baby creation, mixing god, sperm DNA with ape, egg DNA, and making man.

First of all, for these ancient books to discuss such an occurrence ***factually*** requires that there was a ***discussion*** of mixing species of gods and apes to make man ***before*** the human race is capable of making test tube babies. So ***how*** can they discuss something that was ***impossible*** to have discussed, as it did not exist in modern science reality at the time? Read the Seven Tablets of Creation, older than the Bible, if the gods can describe a laboratory and mix gods with apes to make man. Then discussing coming back to earth, ***return to earth*** on a cyclic basis to evolve each generation around 3000 years (The extraterrestrials, genocide the inferior race created previously). Just as we breed dogs today, they raised a higher and higher species of man because, ***as they reported***, their younger offspring, called Igigis, rebelled at mining earth's gold for the Anunnaki. Hence, Enki/Ea (part Anunnaki/part snake people) asked the father god to allow him to make man. Enlil, the older brother of the pure Anunnaki, asked Anu for his right to make a man that he made sterile because he hated the beast called man and ordered them not to procreate. Both half-brothers Enki and Enlil's stories are told similarly in our Bible as Esau/Jacob and as Ishmael/Isaac, where the purer-bred younger brother is seen as more worthy or receives the father's inheritance, and it never goes to the firstborn son due to the inferior mother's DNA. Please note this is not my conclusion, but ancient tablets and the Bible. It's pure ***BS*** of the patriarchal society as far as I am concerned, ***this is the***

beginning of separation/division of mankind, separating royalty from the commoner or the one percenters from the 99%. ***This is how it all began, BS.*** The Bible mentioned that Israel was making the greatest mistake to want a king because only ***God*** should rule over the individual person.

Look at the Bible in Job chapter 30. It shows a black man down on his luck. You know he's black because of how he dwelt. He lived in tribes as black Africans live today, and his tormentors, whom he claimed their fathers (**ancient white men**) would be hated to sit next to his dogs, who were people who lived in caves. The Bible is one of the most racist books on earth, ALL BY BLACK PEOPLE. So what the hell do whites need to feel guilty for? The gods gave it to blacks and WE BLACKS gave racism to whites. Whites have absolutely nothing that we didn't give them as they are no different other than their black turned white differently and not before our very eyes. ABSOLUTELY NO DIFFERENCE! Jesus, a black man, forbids a white woman (a Greek) to receive his healing work and explains why. He explains to her that it isn't right to take the food for the children (Israelites, racist god's chosen) and give it to a dog. He literally calls this white woman a dog and refuses to help her. In the end, without lifting one hand for healing, he tells the white woman HER FAITH has granted her the desires she sought after. Matthew 15:21 – 28 and Mark 7:24:30.

When you look at ***black global suffering***, take a look at Africa. We scientifically agree that ***all*** human beings come from one common ancestor, whom they call Eve, who shares mitochondria with ALL human beings today. We all ***know*** it's a ***fact*** that the African continent is the ***most*** abundantly RICH continent in natural resources on the entire planet, with the most POOR people on top of this continent; yet we don't want to recognize the unseen hand stirring dung to make this reality that should be an impossibility. How the hell is the WEALTHIEST continent home to the poorest people, HOW? White supremacy teaches us blacks to hate ourselves, blame ourselves, and to UTTERLY REFUSE to look at how it is possible for our impossible condition to happen.

It's manipulation!!! It's being hoodwinked to believe you are not deserving, you are less than scum as a people, and the only real deserving people... that is the only real deserving race is the white race. We utterly turn a blind eye to how the manipulation, ***lies***, hatred of secret undiscussed attack against a voiceless people has been happening for nearly half a millennium and is being done criminally maliciously ***this very day*** by federal judges, traitors against the constitution that they have SWORN to protect. See my case, the absolute ***only*** case presented ***ever*** where ***all federal judges lie*** that the contents of a housing lease agreement, contents of who is on the lease, is an OPINION of the judge, therefore an opinion can ***not*** be overturned. A lease is a factual document; any judge calling this a lie that places white landlords falsely in the right is using ***Jim Crow*** against me, which says I cannot be black and heard equally against whites, going against constitutional law. Do you really believe that a judge is so ***stupid*** they can't understand that a lease that reads and is signed by parties that grandchildren are on the lease COUPLED with a court order from the state court that reads that the grandchildren are on the lease can genuinely be mistaken or are they purely ***liars***, fraudsters against the truth in protection of white supremacy where if ***black Americans were awarded special damages*** it could be the total downfall of global white supremacy. These liars, Susan Collins, Theresa Springman, and Diane Sykes, to name a few, are ***all*** judges who knew that Collins was protecting white supremacy, and all cosigned the ***lie!*** They all treated me as if I were a nigger of the 60's. They went AGAINST everything modern-day America claims. ***CNN***, FOX, all media outlets, Biden, Obama, Trump, governor of Indiana, State's Attorney, Federal Attorney, ***NAACP***, The ***ACLU***, United Nations ***all cosigned by omission*** the acceptance of judges to LIE against 41 MILLION PEOPLE having their day in court through one personal representative of the group presenting ***EMBEDDED LAW*** a term desired for consideration of a jury of my peers that my life and my evidence shows it factual that black American are specially damaged uniquely far more any race or group of people our size in America. Thus, if our damages are far greater, there is no way to set us equal to minorities to offset the damages LEAVES BLACKS as the ***only citizens in all of America not given equal rights***, which is why a jury should consider my case, my extreme suffering at the hands of whites, and the maliciousness of the white defendants as cause to award ***special damages***. As a matter of fact, a jury has already made such an award, which was pointed out to these judges of 231 million dollars in Diaz v Tesla. The judge in that case ruled that it was an unconstitutional amount to be awarded against the corporation and ***refused*** to consider that it was constitutional to award it SPECIAL DAMAGES to all blacks, by awarding Diaz 15 million and 216 million to black Americans. When I file my civil lawsuit for obstruction of justice, I want the nation and global citizens to stand with me for my constitutional right by law to be heard by a jury of my peers. This time, the criminal judges will ***not*** have the right to use Jim Crow against me. Their ***lie*** is so extremely easy to prove, as it is, whether or not a lease is a factual document or an opinion. Did a person ***under oath*** of the bar participate in the criminal activity?

I will include court documents that I submitted to these criminals who hate blacks so desperately that they turn traitor against the constitution and their sworn oath ***duties***.

Look at what Vladimir Putin says about black ***Africans***...

When an African becomes rich...

His bank accounts are in Switzerland,

He travels to France for medical treatment,

He invests in Germany,

He buys from Dubai,

He consumes Chinese,

He prays in ***Rome*** or ***Mecca***.

His children study in Europe.

He travels to Canada, the USA, and Europe for tourism,

If he dies, he will be buried in his native country...

Africa is just a cemetery for Africans.

How could a cemetery be developed?

Global Black hatred runs amok!

1 B.. HOW DID WE GET HERE?

I did touch on this. The gods bred mankind by using their DNA and ape DNA. However, that only explains our physical bodies. What of our spirit and soul? If you listen to people talk, they use spirit and soul as if the words are synonymous. They aren't. The human spirit, like all spirits, is an entity of a type of existence. Spirits are found in trees, animals, houses, planets, and so forth, but the soul is ***God*** and a rarity of existence. We have a body, spirit, and soul when we transform this existence; instead of separating the body from the soul and spirit, we ***escape*** death. The salvation that Jesus Christ spoke of is that few would find this path, which leads to life. He said if we believe in him, that he ***is the way***, we would ***never*** taste death. He said ***keep my word***, and you shall never see death, but Christians twist Jesus' actual saying to mean you won't feel like you died. ***Just make it up!*** See Luke 9:27, John 11:25-26, John 8-51. Jesus ***never*** once says that death will not feel like death, or you will die, but it won't be as if you died.

1c. ***Why are we here*** – The purpose of mankind is to first find the ***way*** back to Kether (***highest*** consciousness) and then bring the species as well. We all escape death and transfigure off earth instead of laying down the body in death as a state of perpetual reincarnation. We are here on Earth for mere seconds relative to the existence of time; Earth is over a billion years old. How old are you? A tree, a turtle, and birds all outlive human beings only because of our regression as a species. Most of us are a lot better today; we don't become cannibals, sell our children into slavery or prostitution, or own people ***as a wonderful*** way of life. However, the grim reality is that we have barely shifted from a global barbaric state of consciousness. Look at the evidence, ***The world*** watches a lunatic manic break international law, ***blowing up other nationals*** without proper protocol ***required by the world. Wtf!!!*** So, as slightly better morally, you can't see ***long since*** the first blowing up of international people the world should have ***at the very least*** condemned that bastard! You must stand up for the ***weak***, or you are equally just as barbaric as the ***global*** fiend bully narcissist.

We are here to establish harmony and peace on earth for all mankind. Not just for the rule of the one percenters, that 8 to 10 percent get most of the crumbs of the pie we, the masses, share. ***No human beings but the 1*** percenters get to hoard Earth's resources.

1d. ***What is here (the Universe)*** Some call this place hell, but I see it as an aquarium that was designed by an architect to support life and use a self-contained process of regeneration of both biological and ecological self-maintenance.

2. *UNDERSTANDING THE GAME*

The simplest explanation of understanding the game for us all is to genuinely embrace the individual person to ***accept your own inner instinct.***

One thing we all have is instincts to feel when something is not right. There's a huge difference between intellect and instincts. Intellect requires GPS to fly south, where instinct requires inner knowing, and both can possibly get you south; the evidence is the birds and the pilot. These simple ways of thinking are going to be the dawning of ***understanding the game.*** No intellectual will disagree that pilots use technology to fly in the right direction and that birds use instinct to fly in the right direction. However, dealing with instinct requires trusting the universe to move you and guide you in the way that you desire, and that way will end in your satisfaction, your desired outcome. I'm hoping to get your spidey-senses tingling. Because ***you*** already know some things that you are expected to believe are true is pure ***Bs.*** Let's not mention vaccines; I won't touch them. But you know, and you know to keep your mouth shut. We all ***know*** politics and religion are explosive subjects, ***Why?*** Well, this book will put an end to the emperor's new clothes. That peon is as naked as a jaybird, and you're far above his ***way*** of life. That's why you're forced to keep silent and play the game, ***but when is enough, enough?***

HOW DOES ONE KNOW HE/SHE IS LIVING IN TOTAL DELUSION?

Ah ha, see ***your*** reality for what it is, ***yours!*** It's made up of your parents' reality, your community, and the ***society accepted reality*** for the times! Your reality is ***forever*** changing, please own that ***fact***. It's a scientific ***fact*** you can't see or know if you're living in a reality of delusion, a hologram. You can't see if you're being fooled, misguided, hoodwinked, bamboozled, until you do; then you're immediately no longer fooled. It's like night and day. The requirement to live in a delusion is that ***you don't know*** that ***you don't know the truth,*** you genuinely have absolutely no clue because the second you get the clue or thought that something is not as you believed it to be is the very second you are putting an end to the delusion or you make your mind to live in it, but ***you know.***

You and I have been so extremely deceived about our reality, even though we know something is wrong... we feel we must trust authorities after all their children will die in the delusions too. Their kids get charged and fall prey to the system, too, but it's always to a different level. Thus the brain washed idea that officials and the wealthy will always have an upper hand in setting the reality of our lives, society will always, in general accept the emperor's new clothes and the few who buck against societal acceptance of the delusion insisting that the emperor is naked as a jay bird are too few, powerless, and threatened rejects for punishment by the peoples of the society if they dare to speak out.

Let's examine the ***reality you know damn well*** and the masses except the false reality. 1. 911, official narrative: planes crashed into towers. The jet fuel behaved as a fire inferno, behaved as a bomb, and caused the buildings to disintegrate. I challenge ***you***. ***Find one building ever!!!!*** Where a fire and/or bombs are ***not*** intentionally strategically located within the building's foundation joints, and precisely timed detonation so as to bring the building down in a ***controlled*** manner, minimizing damage to the surrounding buildings' infrastructure. ***Name one building,*** where just random bombing and fire can cause such damage!!! ***You can't!*** Because scientifically demolition of buildings fall completely into a disintegration, ***crumbling,*** collapse of a building straight down, and is possible ***only*** by strategic ***intentional*** planning. Thus, the mother nature of random bombs and fire can never imitate a demolition as accepted by the official report and the masses. Scientifically, if it is ***not repeatable, it did not happen.*** The 911 fall of the towers was caused by an expert, intentional, perfectly detailed demolition of the buildings, and everyone watched the emperor's new clothes, ***naked as a jaybird,*** and accepted that demolition as a random bombing by jet fuel and fire. So sad! Okay, show us ***one*** building ever in history that was burned and bombed behaving in this manner. ***Just one!*** Don't forget we watched ***two*** the same day fall as a demolition style crumbling from floor collapse on top of floor crumbling all the way down, ***not blown up.***

2. Every sane adult on planet Earth knows that the wealthy Westerners own the wealth and the power of the earth. ***Just facts!!!*** We all know, any

major asset, raw resource in existence ***must be owned*** or controlled by the Westerners. ***Just facts!*** So… there exists this ***huge*** land mass called the moon where structures can be built for the most luxurious living ever, ***But for some reason… facts,*** the Westerners with their combined TRILLIONS of dollars have no remote intention of inhabiting the moon ever since the so-called moon-landing in 1969. Hmmmmmm? Don't you ever stop to wonder why, given the fact that a driven people, Westerners (generally speaking) on planet earth have zero desire to occupy the moon if for nothing but scavenger hunting raw resources. Why numerous trips to outer space, but zero trips to the moon for nearly 60 years? ***Not one??? Really???*** This makes sense, we go to outer space all the time, but ***Never the moon. Never!!! Why zero interest in going to the moon?***

Because they do not have the technology to get a human body past the Van Allen belts, the Van Allen belts are a doughnut-shaped region of high-energy charged particles of ***radiation*** and intensely ***hot*** with temperatures ranging from 3000 to **35,000** degrees Fahrenheit. ***What suit of armor survives thirty-five thousand degree heat? The most heat a suit can withstand today is 3000 F for seconds. I read that even at 3000 degrees a fireman will burn to death in minute with this suit on.*** So here's the pretense given, like with 911, the radiation particles are so sparse (lol, magical radiation particles) that there's very little mass to transfer heat through the belts. So the heat is nonexistent to spaceships ***and*** human beings due to particles not having mass. Dag gone, just make that shit up. People go to outer space ***all the time! Fly past the belts!*** Dammit! ***It's not hot!*** There's another tale that all the people died who knew how to design and build the ship capable of moving through the Van Allen belts. ONLY IN 1969, are the people intelligent enough to make it to the moon. 1969's people are even beyond AI today we just can't do it. Just make it all up. Then add on the conversation from the moon that was recorded as if the conversation it HAD TO TAKE PLACE within the same country, let alone on the moon, oh, but it was on the moon. OMG, listen to this, there was no technology available for talking from country to country in the 60's, but it was there just for the moon talk. Also talking from the moon is technically easier than sending a high-quality signal through the complex, noisy, and obstructed atmosphere and geography of Earth. DAMN! WOW, thank god we don't go through Earth's atmosphere to get to the moon, lol, we just jump right over it with high power signals that don't exist for country to country in the 1960's.

They will ***never do it (go to the moon),*** because they have never done it and ***cannot find a way to survive it to this very day!*** Reality check, we watched a Hollywood movie and believed it was reality and there is ZERO evidence that I know of to prove it differently other than the emperor's NEW CLOTHING.

The communication from the moon to earth back in 1969, having absolutely no delay, ***as if they were on the phone*** in the same country. In 1969, it is 100% totally impossible to be on the moon and communicate back and forth to Earth without ***serious*** time delays for the sound to travel. The only way that was possible is that there was ***no distance*** between those who were taking in 1969. ***No moon trip.*** In summary, scientifically, they couldn't get past the Van Allen belt, they couldn't talk back and forth without time delay, and ***most important,*** if it was an easy trip, ***common sense…*** trips to the moon would be regular explorations for raw resources and possible inhabitation for the rich white supremacist to claim ownership of the moon, ***simple general facts of our society.*** ABSOLUTELY NO WAY, Westerners abandoned trips to the moon solely due to no dollars and no intellect to make the trip. MAJORITY OF RUSSIANS KNOW THAT THE US NEVER WENT, WHILE 90% OF AMERICANS BELIEVE IT HAPPENED AND JUST MAGICALLY CAN'T HAPPEN AGAIN. Emperors' new clothes, we don't want to see nakedness. Y'all, got to know that Trump and Elon Musk would be up their dividing the moon up charging tariffs, fees, oil ransom for kidnaped country leaders to fly back to earth from the moon. We would be building a huge MOON **BALL ROOM** for them to party in and talking about how nasty that earth has become with all the riff raff down there. We don't want it to be remotely possible that common sense should erase the decades of our truth. Thus the FACT we're incapable of repeating the event more than once and NEVER in the history of mankind have we had the intelligence to advance powerfully **ONCE**, but never again. How is this NOT huge evidence to question the authenticity OF THE CLAIM? NOT A QUESTION? There's **absolutely no question** even for Neil Degrassi I believe to be one of the MOST scientifically intelligent and empathic individuals on earth. But HE SHARED HIS EMBEDDED LAW moment. I believe he was watching Close Encounters of the Fourth Kind, some movie and saw NOTHING, BUT WHITES working the entire project and it was normal, no problem then, he asked how he missed that. Embedded Law forces you to not see problems with black exclusion, IT JUST FEELS

RIGHT so you don't thing anything. My moment happened just a few years ago with a white taxi driver totally out of place, but no problem, but the black one I started to go call the taxi dispatch to confirm and then thumped my head, NO, I DIDN'T CHECK OUT THE WHITE GUY. Keep reading, you'll get what I am talking about later. I'm a true fan of Neil and a libra wondering how he doesn't see our sign of balance, fairness, JUSTICE, indecisiveness, most talkative/weighing all possibilities and still wondering what you missed... more you than any of the other 11 signs. Some people do not fit their signs, but it is rare that I see it happen. It has to do with the planets and other things going on at the time of birth that create additional attributes. I never got that deep off into astrology, but my personality is every bit exactly what a libra is all about to the T.

Science LAW, REQUIRES that experiments are repeatable. If an event CAN'T be repeated, that shot up out of fear that the Russians would beat the US to the moon it's a scientific fact that it **MIGHT** not have ever happened. Jesus hasn't saved mankind yet and God hasn't impregnated another virgin to try to fix us again this is the same sort of event that NEEDS to be repeated if it ever happened, but it is not happening. Russia seriously almost beat the US to the moon using the Soyuz 7K-L1(Zond) space craft, but their massive N1 moon-landing rocket failed (unmanned), like the challenger disaster. Accepted report, In 1959, Russia was the first country to send an unmanned spaceship to the moon. Both countries began competing, sending **unmanned** spacecraft. Russia was more advanced. Magically, the USA, fully manned ships don't burn up human beings and cannot do it today because the people who wove the special designed spacesuits and designed rockets are no longer living. For me that's magical, to claim we were so extremely technically advance then not to burn up traveling to the moon, but totally technologically incapable for decades to this very day makes no sense. Even RUSSIA can **NOT**, CAN **NOT** do it at all. But then the USA, is so extremely moral she would never fake a Hollywood landing on the moon. I asked AI, to list the countries where a country was far advanced ahead of the USA in technology and the USA ended up better by far. THERE IS ONLY ONE TIME GIVEN and you better bet your ass the only one time in history it happened. The moon landing, where in ONE YEAR the USA successful lands mankind on the moon, but NEVER in the history of humanity has any country using its OWN TECHNOLOGY beaten another country that was far more advanced BUT CAN'T EVER DO IT in modern days due to financial and technology incapability. 90% of the American people cannot even fantom the **question** that the USA faked the landing and squash all the BS stories of numerous excuses against the more likely truth, we can't go back to the moon because no human being has ever gone. Gees, you finally figure it out and go in 3000AD, yeah we just thought it was about time. REALLY? We can't stage it today because there is no way to hide from the technology of the masses today. Did you ever stop to think? That's why we can't go today, trying to use their notes of how they went but NEVER WENT. You are on your own and the first INVENTORS to come up with a way to the moon for mankind. Then you might go, but send that monkey first, I'm begging. LOL

CHAPTER TWO

The Evolution of Sandra Black, Part One

THE DELUSIONAL REALITY EXPOSED, RACISM NEVER ENDED

I. GENCORP

When I worked at GenCorp, formerly known as General Tire, in Wabash, Indiana, I was literally tortured similarly to the movie "Men of Honor." If you have never seen it, now is a good time to experience a life similar to mine. This took place from the late 80's to the late 90's, a decade of abuse, harassment, and torture. Individual black life stories like mine ***are never told today!*** Journalism is ***dead.*** No one reports on anything at all that is contrary to what we are ***allowed to see.*** Thus, no local news media, let alone national, would ever report the ***fact*** that most no black in America is allowed to overcome racial discrimination. I nearly lost my life intentionally by my superiors (attempted murder, ***twice***), not workers who work side by side with me, but bosses and bosses of bosses.

Being an individual who believed racism was over, I was flabbergasted, overwhelmed, and totally devastated, knowing that the reality of what was happening to me was absolutely impossible to happen at that time. Living prior to the 60s, black disdain, pure hatred was and pure hatred were the expected way of life. I was totally off guard that something like this was remotely possible, let alone that it could happen to me. I believed that by the time you get grown, every black person knows that an individual will hate you because you're black, but I understood that's not racism, that's prejudice. I could be hated for being fat, too young or old, for the way I talk and think. ***Everyone*** on earth has prejudices, whether it's the preference of an apple over an orange, it's all the same thing, human weakness/sickness. However, racism is a horse of another color that **HIDES** behind hate and prejudice, the ***tools*** used for racism. RACISM is the only word in the English language that we can use as the word that defines *power to permanently oppress/harm* and *block an entire group of people from human rights that are with prejudice* ***by privilege*** *granted to others. Racism is where a group* or *individual is forced without any possibility of escape or genuine retribution and/or reparations for all violated persons* by a different group of people (the racist) who either by direct acts or by omission to act subjects the victims to the oppression AS OBJECTS, NOT EVEN HUMAN (less than animal). This is why all others harmed are owed retribution, but not **THEM THINGS**. Now think about the ***centuries*** that this has been going on. Do you really believe that if it happens for next to forever, nobody who gained from it to this very day shouldn't be held financially responsible? REALLY??? Do you think there's no such thing as ***karma?*** Maybe you might believe that if you pretend it never happened, you get a pass from the Universe. ***Still to this very day, FBA,*** Black Americans are ***targeted to inflict pain*** solely due to their ***color, and there's absolutely no real*** law, agency, department, commission, office ***to stop the cruelty!!!*** All the ones, including the ***EEOC,*** the ***NAACP,*** Human Rights, and Civil Rights commissions, and ***ACLU,*** fight to ensure that no black individual wins. If you don't believe it's true, get the stats on people reporting ***harm*** who are ***black*** actually getting help v. whites. After the Civil Rights Act was put into law, ***they quietly removed it!***

The ***US*** representatives reversed where the law required that the person or corporation accused of discrimination had the burden of proof. This original law of the 60's was the only ***fair*** and true help for blacks, but the racism was so bad that the companies complained that they were going bankrupt. Do you think our representatives came back with instructions such as better train employees, better documenting skilled people to ***prove it a fact*** that you are not discriminating? ***Oh no!*** Our government agreed with the corporations that the burden of proof was too hard for corporations and better ***for the individual.*** In other words, there are no human rights nor civil rights for black people. It doesn't exist, but a white person is many times more likely to win discrimination claims. Proving it a fact that only whites are genuinely discriminated against, ***right? It's unbelievable the craziness one country gets to push down our throats that no other country tolerates.***

I actually believed, until ***Gencorp,*** that laws and institutions were in place so that these sick individuals could never permanently block my right to access the American dream, my piece of the pie that I had worked so hard to obtain. I earned one of the most lucrative degrees that made it apparent that I wasn't lazy, nor was I incapable of above-average intelligence. Only a few can obtain an engineering degree, and I obtained one higher than Civil, Mechanical, and Electrical engineering. ***I am a chemical engineer,*** and absolutely nobody on earth can take that away from me, no matter how I wasn't allowed to use my degree, to work in peace. I would like to give an example of how I nearly lost my life.

While I was working at GenCorp, they had me in a situation where I was hired as what was called a token. I never heard of the word for a human being, ***a token?*** I was just a black girl thankful that racism was over, I was going to be a great engineer, and I would never suffer what my mom and those before her encountered. Every black person has black moments with individuals (hell, black coons are worse than white racists any day) or in the workplace, where you know how to handle the racist. I have done it so many times, I was a pro at it by the time I was an engineer. I did extra work if needed, talked the white girl talk, danced the dance that society (white world) required. I believe it's called being yourself vs. being your public self. Any black who doesn't learn that ***is out the gate screwed*** without any chance. That's racism that I never saw as racism because anything you can overcome being black means, ***no racism.*** I was young and extremely ignorant of what ***racism*** was and that it did still exist. That's not ***racism,*** just because you you're attacked by individual racists for being black, that's personal hatred, bigotry, prejudice. RACISM is that systemic ***monster*** that no matter how you fight or use the system to grant you equal access, ***YOU ARE***

DENIED! Only FEW escape through the cracks and notice they do absolutely nothing to stop it. I genuinely believe if they do, they're warned they will get the "Bill Cosby treatment" and WORSE. Obama, KNEW he better not come out helping black people, WE ALL KNOW IT, let's get real! Had Obama stopped PAID lobbying, ended racism, he'd be dead! Nothing will be done right by politics, only by the people is it possible. Although we don't see it, like the black me who overcomes, by not being black publicly vs. the blacks who are just themselves at all times and will never make it purely due to their persona, speech, nappy hair, blackness. ***They are doomed*** to ***never*** be an Oprah. I was ***so ignorant!*** Why couldn't I see that my need to talk white, get a college education, be twice as good as any white person in my studies and my work, ***and that is the way it had to be combatted, life's norms like being born with a disability or poor, black...*** that's self-inflicted racism EMBEDDED LAW.

I remember when Oprah swore she would never have a nose job because she wanted little black girls to see a big nose, but now she magically has a more European nose swearing that nothing has been done to alter her nose and just like white society has technology to colonize the moon, but just chooses not to have that privilege as white society has never remotely desired privilege so has Oprah's nose never had makeup or surgery to **intentionally** make her nose more European looking it just happened to be the only nose on earth that I know of that gets magically smaller nostrils and thinner bridge. There goes my interview with Oprah, but that's okay. I think Oprah is a wonderful person, no different than I was in my younger days. She just got blessed not to have the physical body that I got. I have a body that non-stop STRESS drives blood pressure up and up to where no medicine will bring it down (**I die!**), while all the required BP medicines have your heart rate at 40bpm and lower. It's so rare that I never met anyone untreatable for BP under continuous stress as it has happened to me. I was diagnosed with stage 1 renal failure at age 28, before it was called out in stages. It was just called bad kidney disease. Today, I have lived with stage 4 kidney failure for over 15 years. I was told in my early 30's that I would never see my 40th birthday if I didn't live a meditative life free of stress, I would be dead before I could turn 40. I'm saying this so that hopefully, though you can never feel what I am feeling, you can possibly try to wonder. What does it feel like to have a burning fire in your gut so bad that while you're in confrontation, you're focused on keeping conscious and not showing your failing health to your adversary? This is my life, my disability, though no doctors have a ***direct*** diagnosis other than Generalized Anxiety with stage 4 kidney failure. This diagnosis leaves out the ***PTSD*** because 1. being almost killed by racism, 2. your son murdered in the womb, 3. losing your career, 4. your mom, your home, stolen away, 5. your children lost to society's ills 6. the landlord moves you into an apartment with black mold tells you to clean it for six years and refuses to pay your deposit due to mold, 7. nearly lost your grandchild in a three year battle against the system all alone, 8. then your next landlord tricks you into an unfinished filthy stinking barn house that ***HUD*** isn't supposed to pass, but Marion, Indiana ***HUD*** always passes stinky, filthy houses of those landlords they like and force black landlords to perfection, 9. you're forced to move to Chicago to get a clean, decent house to live in. 10. your federal court case ***totally lost*** all due to racism, solely because of skin color these things truly happen to you because if your were white you would be welcome as an engineer making 100k today, but there's no black experiences in western diagnosis... ***none of this is real,*** it's all delusional. As a matter of fact, that was a part of my diagnosis. Until I ***forced*** the psychiatrist to prove that what she had heard me talk about was delusional. She told me, "Come on... You claim to have a college education with a degree in chemical engineering and can't work due to racism, you claim to be an author of a book that has sold internationally, you claim to have lived in Africa, all of this is just too big to be real." I told her it was true and that on my next visit, I will bring my certificate from Tuskegee University showing that I graduated from Tuskegee University with a degree in Chemical Engineering, that she should go online now and look up my book, and I will bring my passport showing I lived in Africa from 2003 to 2008. A prior psychiatrist called me delusional, also for claiming that God was black according to the Bible, and for my spiritual beliefs, which were ruled out by an African doctor in the same establishment, who said my beliefs are religious practices in Africa.

Thus in general being DIFFERENT from the standard white culture lifestyle (who writes the diagnosis), whether over performing, author, traveler, degreed engineer or underperforming, no job, no money, a dead child, no church, and/or your beliefs, our god we worship is black in the Bible, Quran, and most ***all*** religions on earth and our god is ***not*** God. He's needy himself, but we ***all*** believe in his help. The difference is I know he's limited, which is why our world is so screwed up. The masses don't know they are asking a deity ***god,*** not ***GOD,*** to help them. I do pray in their names for the vibrational effect, but ***god*** ceases to be ***GOD*** the very moment we place ***GOD*** into our human likeness box, where god has a name, and the highest best life is always good. THIS IS IN OPPOSITION TO GOD, and we all know reality shows it. If GOD is all-powerful and hates sin, pain, suffering, wrongdoers… why create it into existence? For real, you got all the power, are you going to create rape of your mother, sister, brother? Absolutely not. And for you to believe that God has all power, all knowing, and allows such wickedness, this can't be God. The wickedness we see is the severe imbalance and sickness of our society. GOD IS NOT GOOD, GOD IS! Good and bad are the same one thing! It only becomes different due to the human experience. You eat steak, that's good, but what' about the cow's experience? GOD IS RAW ENERGY, VIBRATION, THE ALL, THE NOTHING. We choose this life, and God chooses that we will either learn or become extinct so that a different species gets our opportunity to do good and evolve into a new creation.

This is ***God, all existence, all knowing, all power, everywhere, nowhere,*** and ***everything all at once…*** The omnipotent. When you name God, you lose GOD because God doesn't fit into our religions, our gods, or our beliefs of what GOD is. I believe that we are all gods and have lost knowing who we really are GOD IN FLESH. ***God,*** the omnipotent, is like the ocean, and we are like a drop of ocean water (our spirit). As human beings, we're the only unique creation according to the Persian Sufi poet Rumi… you are not the drop in the ocean, but ***God*** (ocean) living inside the drop, your body. When we discover who we really are, we shall not die. We transfigure into a new living creature, transfiguring body/spirit/soul as ***one,*** never departing the body, never leaving any residue of the ego/self here on earth to return to earth (reincarnate).

Solely all of this, and an old, retired, senile doctor called in to replace the real doctor I was supposed to see once wrote that I said I talked to Indiana Jones… Solely this will get you a diagnosis of schizophrenia and a delusional diagnosis, even though when I was asked if I said it (hence it is not verifiable), and told them I never said that… it wasn't allowed to be removed from my record. Never has anyone out of all the numerous doctors, therapists, psychiatrists ever reported that I talk to Indiana Jones. Nonetheless, Lawyers in Marion, Indiana, who ***know*** my acts and behavior to be normal and court-appropriate as much or more than the average person would have me barred from helping my son due to this information that has been ***ruled out,*** but they use it against me. I'm too crazy to help my son and he's too crazy to know that I am too crazy so by the evil Grant County PUBLIC DEFENDER (the prosecutor in disguise) I can't assist my son nor have his information BACKED BY JUDGE MARK SPITZER IN COURT. So for a year he sit not allowed to speak to an attorney. **THIS IS REAL AMERICA, in general the public defender works for the prosecution, the judge works for the prosecution and the individual has nothing on his side, but words "evidence beyond a reasonable doubt" and most jurors convict solely on "if a person looks guilty" like Darlie Lynn Routier and countless others!** The Bar, the Judicial Commission will only back them up. Seeking help is added support to the injustice department locomotive of destroying the people through NO ACCOUNTABILITY.

One day, I told my therapist/caseworker that being raped once and all the ten years of suffering as a black person at work is not allowable, and that I would gladly trade it. I still say to GOD right now, give me the choice of ***just one rape*** and allow me to perform free from the rape of racism every day of work. I realized that regular workers ***never*** see what a high-performing black person gets. It's not just whites, but nobody who never experiences it gets the gravity of HORROR and TORTURE racism brings to a life. Even when you take the day off, it hurts worrying about the next day coming too and ya can't keep taking days off. When I was a factory worker, waitress, operator, and the sort I rarely ever experienced racism, I WAS IN MY PLACE. I loved working. But out of place, becoming a nigger, the hatred is so great, and the daily dread of another day of torture, they ***never*** get it ***because they never live it.*** CNN, FOX refused to cover it.

So I was told that I was exaggerating by my case worker. There was no way he could imagine a woman choosing a one time rape over racism. If anyone wouldn't they have NOT lived tortured daily by racism. That's an EASY CHOICE. You lose your body one day, most likely in the worst pain ever and emotionally scarred for life... destroyed one day AND YOU GAIN AN ENTIRE LIFE??? I realized that day that no human being can feel it, not even blacks. Damn one ***moment*** in a day of the life's worst possible suffering and free to work without discrimination and hate, free to breathe without that fire raising up your gut day in and day out for years, an entire decade. I swear, I understand why racism is so real... but until you live it, you'll ***never*** know it, as IMPOSSIBLE to survive it. I once had a white friend whom I really enjoyed her friendship. I visited her house, and she visited mine. Just a wonderful, sweet, kind person who suffered from poverty and discrimination, where she filed with the ***EEOC*** and won. She got a letter, a document stating her win. All I got was them being told to knock it off. I knew only because of Curt Reid, who told me he was scared to death of me because of what had been passed around about me. But damn, I ***never*** got any answer from ***EEOC,*** nor do I know any black person ***ever*** to get a positive response in writing. I've heard groups of blacks at Denny's win, but it had to be major in your face for a black person to be documented winning. My friend and I shared all our stories, talked daily until one day she told me, "I never want to see you again." I couldn't believe it. "Why?" "What did I do?" She said it wasn't anything I did; it was the stories that I told. I was like, but you were telling your stories, and I mine, why is it that you ***never*** want to see me again? How does this happen? She told me that it is totally impossible for a human being to suffer all of the atrocities by white people and want to be a true friend to her. To this day, now another pain that I'll never understand. I told her how the hell are you responsible for what a piece of shit did to me. You are a different individual, you have been a friend to me, and I to you. She said that's true, but it's impossible that the friendship ends today, and I ***never*** saw her ever again. So I'm left thinking she believed I would do something to her somehow, or maybe she wanted to do something to me because of those blacks who hurt her, but she had other ***black*** friends, so I'll never understand ending a relationship because her race of people violated me so badly. She's now just as bad, if not worse, because she was a part of my world, my friend; ***they,*** were always the enemy. She saw herself as ***they,*** my enemy, and I hers solely due to how horrible other whites had treated me. I'm clueless, to me it's only about how you are to me and how you treat others. She saw my being mistreated by her people as too damaging for me to love her. FINAL WORD, there was something in her I missed, PERIOD!!!

Lifelong oppression is hard to keep short and in order, but you need to understand that this place ***never*** allowed any type of black professional to work there. Some black workers were allowed, but no managers or engineers. To these people, it was no different than hiring monkeys to get paid better and tell them what to do; in all honesty, I believe a monkey would have been treated better. It was so bad that they spoke openly about it in meetings. Sorry, I AM BACK AT GENCORP, dear readers. I told you, I'm not a good writer, but my story is profound if you bear with me. In a union meeting, I was told that a steward reported that too many niggers were being hired. I had been the only degreed one ever. John Murphy hired me against all backlash, putting his job on the line, and told me that I'd have to stand strong against racism as this company had never hired a black professional and didn't believe it was possible. I'm going to skip over a lot for the sake of time.

I was hired to supervise before working as an engineer so that I could learn the processes throughout the plant. In reality, hindsight, no engineering department would have me. The work, "extrusion rubber parts (look at the rubber seals of your car doors, that's me) and cutting gaskets to size," was run by operators who had years of experience running the machines, in short. It all went to hell, though the plant and workers practically ran themselves. I was written up about two months later in an evaluation that stated I was incapable of doing anything right. I couldn't talk, write, follow instructions, have creative ideas, or get along with anyone. There was absolutely nothing that I did well, ok, or fair. My best was lacking, and the worst was totally incapable of all.

Unlike today, good feedback was all 5's. Then a 5 was the very worst thing you could get with two pages of responsibilities reported and evaluated. I received all 5's with the exception of writing, where they gave me a four, which was my worst subject. Is it really possible for anyone who goes to college, works jobs throughout her entire schooling to pay her way, never ever once get reported as having a bad attitude, incapable of getting along with others, and never ever getting all F's, D's, or C's not even half, failing grades.? ***Damn!!!*** F's and D's at my college, TUSKEGEE, meant that you automatically failed. Your lowest grade possible to pass was a C. Clearly, I ***never*** got marks this bad, even if I got all (4's) D's, I'd never get a degree. So how could it be "totally impossible to understand anything communicated orally or in writing."? You may not agree with me, and I am not a good writer. I am a mathematician and scientist. I'm into spirituality and saving our world. So why the hell is it that my worst subject ever (my writing) is the absolute only category that I did the best? I just figured it out. ***Damn!!!*** I just realized. My writings were documented, they are not a matter of opinion; I should have gotten at least a 2 or 3, no one would argue against the opinion of a 4 after nothing but 5's in everything, WOW. I have been baffled about that for years. I knew it should have been an automatic 5, but why my worst category (writing) got a 4, my best score, I never understood one iota until just now. My writings were documented, and while clearly not the best subject, it was in writing, NOT the worst ever, My lowest school subject was rated my highest performance score because they couldn't possibly hide the fact that I wasn't a 5 and I just figured this one out.

When this happened, my mom told me, "They are setting you up to be fired." I had been removed from supervision to absolutely nothing. John Murphy was demoted from production manager and didn't want to see my face. John didn't write the evaluation; he got one just like mine for hiring me in the first place. The place was a mess. The hateful eyes were all that was seen except for a black lady worker who had been there about 17 years, who had been promoted by time and relationships, no education, no threat, working as a second shift supervisor.

I filed a complaint with the ***EEOC,*** and that halted everything. I showed up for work with no boss, no workplace, no kind face. A black janitor showed me a storage closet with an old desk, junk, and a Christmas tree where I could hang out to pass the time. Mom told me to take books with me to read and make that money girl, this is how it is. After months of walking in the door past white engineers, all inside their nicely lit engineering cubby holes, on my way to my storage closet, ***EEOC*** handed down a verdict, and they were forced to treat me just like the white engineers. I never got anything in writing. I assumed the change occurred because of the change in my working environment. I was going to be working as an engineer, and I was placed in my own office. My new boss was Jim Law. He assigned me to the plant engineer (who got rid of me immediately), who gave me a project to redesign the cooling system for the missile molding press. It was in the 80's, I used to brag about this project, but I barely remember anything but getting a big thumbs up, completing the job before my deadline. The next project he assigned me was to oversee a contractor who would put on a new rubber roof. I had never heard of or seen a rubber roof in my life, but things seem to be going just like my mother instructed me. ***Never*** let them see you down; always greet and keep a smile on your face. They'll break one day. Mom knew because she had already been through it as the first black electrician at RCA. My mama was one bad force to reckon with. I did exactly as I was instructed: read up on rubber roofing to become familiar and get involved with the crew, ask questions, show gratitude, and compliment how well-informed and professional they were. Absolutely no problems!

Every day was like a day of vacation out in the sun with guys who loved sharing information with me and showing me the trade. I was really one of the guys. I suck up information, nowhere near as fast as Johnny 5, but every bit as desperate, even to this day, for knowledge. Nothing goes by me of interest if I don't know, it's googled, and if Google is tripping, it's AI. I trust AI slightly better than I trust the information from my children. In all honesty, when AI plays stupid, I don't go to the library like I used to. But you know you can't trust answers by asking the question differently to make it look like it favors the system, and you'll get closer to the real answer that way.

One important detail the roofing workers told me was that the flashing at the edge of the roof is the most likely area for leaks; the flashing was perfect. They showed me and bragged on me how great it was to see a woman among them comfortably at the edge, just like one of the guys. I told them that's my job; if I'm going to be afraid to do my job, I shouldn't be here. ***Oh,*** I strongly believe that I must be highly qualified because I couldn't live with myself in a job I couldn't do and do well. Every day we were there, I made sure everything was perfectly consistent, no bubbling, puckering, or ***off-line*** installation of rubber. I never did this before, but that made sense, and it was always so not once did I get to find a piece out of place. The contractors were perfection; I was a newbie, and the company needed its own employee in charge. I believe they were so used to this company that only a name was probably used as being over them, because I normally find some sort of mistake, no matter how small. I loved learning, and they appeared to enjoy my inquisitiveness. The flashing was perfect. All was complete. A second job well done, but on this one, I felt it was more for me getting information and working well with the guys than my genuinely being responsible for the outcome. The guy never made one mistake that I could find over that entire roof, and I tried. They were thorough, and I gave my boss my findings of the project.

He told me, " Good job that the fellows had been in to tell him how well I caught on and paid attention to detail. I told him how they explained the flashing at the edge was one of the most important areas to carefully inspect, and that I did. He was happy and told me to report back to Jim Law that his projects were completed. I did. And was assigned to Curt Reid. That guy, without doubt, has to be dead by now; he was so nervous and jumpy, poor fellow. I will end my ongoing story here, but tell you how I almost died or could have been seriously injured on purpose.

One rainy day, shortly after the conclusion of the roofing assignment. About four men, all in business suits, including the plant engineer who brought them to me and told me all, smiling how wonderful my work had been, and how they wanted to see how I would inspect the roofing project. I was so excited to have them all interested in me, and the entire trip up the steps, nearly three stories high, I planned to walk swiftly and confidently to show them how I could bend over the ledge to inspect the flashing. If you're a seasoned engineer and knowledgeable with OSHA, you already ***know*** something is not right. So I'm all pumped up, going to show off how I'm as confident as any man, and begin walking swiftly for the edge of the roof. I've done it many times before. I was at my stopping place to bend over, but though my ***feet stopped... I didn't.*** I kept sliding on the wet roof with no way to stop. A voice in my mind yelled, ***SIT DOWN!*** I did, my feet were dangling over what was meant to be my death, or from a three-story fall, without doubt serious injury, while I heard laughter back at the door entry to the roof. I sat there looking at just death and me until I knew I was alone. They knew I was all pumped up over this flashing. I had no clue about rain and a rubber roof being slick. I found out in about 2016 that it is against OSHA regulations to allow anyone to work on a wet roof. I don't believe they thought I would live to tell my story, but who would believe me? It's just my words. I never reported the incident because I would lose people like Jim Law and the others that I still had to work with, and he was very professional in the way he handled me. I didn't won't that to change. After Curt Reid, I had a few more successful jobs and quit GenCorp due to unequal treatment, and my husband was forced to work separately from me in Chicago, while all white engineers had their spouses working with them there at GenCorp AS A MATTER OF POLICY.

II. E. A. Palmer Co.

Had I been white, I would be the owner of this company, building it into multiple companies. I was fired for being too great at running the company while the pretty blond secretary wanted my job. After only receiving pay raises every few months and never once being written up. I was fired and kept away from my employees because of my boss's fear that they would walk off the job with me. The ***EEOC*** wrongly persuaded me to accept what they called a nuisance pay because the company would be going out of business, and I would get nothing. So take 2000 dollars or get nothing, they told me. It never went bankrupt. It went into my boss's name instead of E.A. Palmer's name, who was dead. Thus, John Skelner Company, continued and got away with wrongful termination with the lie that the company would go bankrupt. I had no representation. ***EEOC is for the corporation to win.*** The only cases I've ever heard of remotely winning are those filed by whites.

III. Chicago Water Department

This would be my third and final try at acceptance into a company, hoping for just a chance at earning a wage for an honest day's work. My dream of being a great person is now understood that it would ***never*** be allowed to happen, considered unacceptable in my society. I believe this was my first statistical defeat, prey to the system, my mind KNEW, you're black, get back. Just show up, do my work, be friendly, no matter how unfair, just try to stay away from trouble was my new understanding of what my career's survival would be. It can ***never*** happen, especially when you land jobs where you have only whites are supervising. The City of Chicago supervisor mentality is that no black person should have the same lucrative opportunity as whites. I was almost killed here, too. I will end up nearly killing these people, as I would ***die*** if I stayed and fought for my right to be there. I was blessed to wake from my dream and to remember that poverty still allows life to continue. I could go without and give my children everything I had. The interview had been forced on these white guys. They obviously were not seeking to know if I was qualified or should remotely be considered. Just awful. I knew that those people interviewing me would never hire me, but I pushed through Commissioner Hurley, who was black. It took forever. In the interview, Phil, I suspect suffering from dementia kept telling me, "you know you must have a bachelor's degree" as they were on a mission for disqualification. They all took turns seeking a way towards disqualification. Then one of them yelled at Phil, "SHE'S GOT A DEGREE, SHE CAN'T MAKE IT TO THE INTERVIEW WITH OUT IT! after his third or fourth time asking me. Then the next guy would ask about how I would be able to carry the 50-pound sampling kit that was required. It was over in less than ten minutes after giving me a problem to solve on chlorination dilution for piping. I asked, "wouldn't you like to know more about why I am the best person for this job." I was told no, they would call. Like damn really, you are letting me know you don't even want to consider me.

I know one hundred percent, if I had the spirituality of that time only and knew what would be the ***actual*** outcome of destruction of my children, my mother, my grandchildren, my life... I would have followed through with my plan to kill both Fred Shutltz and Joe Vencil so that their children, like my children, would suffer without their parents, just as when the cops killed me, my children would suffer. My children could ***never*** have been any worse off, and maybe, just maybe, not seeing all the hard day to day work of my life to only live a hell of an existence that helped to place them into depressed, lost creatures of life. Not one of them lives without depression. If they only knew of my death and mom's success, perhaps somehow the trust in doing right, loving others, helping others not for show, but for your own heart to bless without any expectation of anything in return, that love tingle euphoric feeling of uplifting another, being there for another person. ***They only think of themselves*** and their COMFORT in a world of hopelessness. Any discomfort and they're depressed and lost, life is hopeless. It's so sad that they ***never*** saw me depressed, But couldn't follow my example as I lived life. I've told them that ***depression*** is the utmost worst human weakness on earth because it requires you to be so damned selfish that you can't get out of thinking about yourself, how life is for yourself, how the whole world is just pure shit; when it's so much out there to love, to give yourself to, where you can access bliss. ***Don't get me wrong,*** knowing what I know, I would still live poor instead of taking lives, but I had no idea then how horrible our lives would actually turn out due to my being forced into poverty solely due to the color of my skin. Had I remotely known, this was a possibility, the ***real*** me couldn't have come through to shut down the insane me that the City of Chicago had created. ***All*** I would have seen is horrific gloom and destruction. ***Thank God,*** we can't see the future. My children don't even love themselves enough to give up the selfishness of depression. No one can commit suicide without the worst human weakness, ***depression,*** the denial of ***all*** potential productivity and love you have to give the world, utter hopelessness.

In all honesty, I never saw it remotely possible that the black snare ***trap*** of our system would utterly swallow my children inside and out until they weren't my children at all, ***nothing*** at all of me was left inside them. How I raised them to be, GONE. How I lived my life NEVER allowing the hells of poverty turn me from being dedicated to that which was right. No matter how I may have disagreed with my mother, ***never ever*** did my children see me disrespect her, talk down at her, or physically touch her ever in a demeaning or disrespectful way. I taught by living the life of example. Just as my mother taught me. Children were precious, and she always fed us first, clothed us, kept a roof over our heads, and absolutely nothing did we push and stress that we wanted and needed, did she not get for us. My mother did this to a fault, and I loved her and respected her so deeply, not knowing that kids don't respect such love. Her sons, my three brothers didn't, and not one of my children appreciated what we had to give. I am the same product of both my parents as my three brothers, and not one of them cherished our parents as I did. They made my parents' lives a living hell, ***never*** satisfied, and everything that went wrong in their lives was mom and dad's fault.

My mother ***never ever*** had to lift a finger to clean, cook, or take care of my children while I was in her house. It was always my responsibility to designate chores to my children and me. Dad died an early death at 58, living black. Mom did only as she pleased while I was in the home. She always did the washing because she preferred it, and sometimes cooking a meal if she felt like it. Cooking meals was my daily chore. The worst was when she'd clean and pulled everything out, but eventually, my children and I always helped her get things back in order. I never knew that kids had to be told to do their schoolwork or that kids don't do what you tell them. My kids were teenagers, telling me how they met someone who went to school with me and told them how they my children weren't anything like me. I never ever skipped school; I thought only the weirdos did that, but I found out I was the weirdo. I was the abnormal one. I never lied, cheated, or intentionally did wrong after my conscience grew in between 10 – 12. At ten something happened to me that made it so I **NEVER** lied, next story book.

I learned it later after realizing my children were just like my brothers, not at all like me. I remember almost all my young friends saying they hope they ***never*** have kids who act as they did. At the same time, I'm praying to ***God*** for children to act just like me. Children who, for the most part, try to do good, and as their conscience grows, they always try to do right and their best. I teach my children that doing their best doesn't make them perfect, and no human being should seek perfection because then they will live full of guilt. Being human, sometimes we're too tired, make wrong judgments, but we always do our best, so I ***never*** have any regrets... Being your best self doesn't mean you get everything you have worked for, but it does guarantee that you can get your best life possible. I worked hard for my share of the American pie, ***never*** got it, but the wealth of knowledge, life, and the hope for my generations and species brings gratification that I have lived my best life possible for my condition.

IV. Permanent Disability End of an Engineering Career at 37 Years of Age made it possible for a lifetime of study, meditation, and life's experience ***to find the answers*** that will change our world from this cesspool of hell for the masses if only we try.

Now, I can write a book. I can still be productive. I can teach the world how our religions have deceived us and divided us from the most ancient of times. I can teach how our ancient religions teach us who we are and how we got here. I started in 1998 and self-published it.

V. Writing and Publishing of the Ultimate Deceit of the Human Race: The Ezzrath Theory

CHAPTER THREE

The Evolution, Part Two

MOTHER ENSLAVED: Published a book to document

Dementia: The matriarch leader of our family, ***our backbone***, was doing so many strange things when I returned from Africa in 2008. I got trapped here because Mom no longer had her mental faculties. While work dehumanized me and caused emotional suffering, my mom with dementia changed ***all*** our lives forever. No mother to have my back. She had forgotten my place in her life, but worse, she had forgotten my brother's place in her life and saw Mom's house and money as ***all his***. This ended mom's quality of life as I knew it to be, and our relationship to work together. We were great companions to each other. People began climbing out of the lime work like cockroaches, like predators pouncing on their prey, and my children and I, like the buffalo that could only watch the lions' bloody mouths suck my poor old mama dry. We were helpless because the vultures were in mom's ears to drink her dry, and our only choice was to leave her to the predators because Randall, a police officer, came out, and when he saw my daughter, he chose the wrong side, went against the law. I was paying the internet and water bill ***in my name***, at my mom's house, but Officer Eric Randle told me to get my things as fast as I could and get out. He supported an illegal eviction, with me trying to explain to him that Mom doesn't understand what my brother is doing to her.

My mother was ***never*** allowed to live her life normally, as she had lived it all her years with me, my children, and me. My brother, who came to me desperate for money, was planning to lie that he was hearing voices to get a check. I told him he didn't have to lie; "you don't get along with anyone." My problems were all work-related. Mom and I always got along very well, for decades... ***Nobody*** got along with my brother. I told him that I would be a witness that you are a societal misfit. Don't lie that you're hearing voices. I had him over to take mom fishing and help with dementia, and when he saw what was going on, he decided no, he needed to rent his place out, kick my kids and me out, and take over mom's house. She immediately lost her gaming room and her right to play on the computer. Later, he kicked her out of her bedroom and confined her to an upstairs room with no TV. The solitary confinement made mom eventually snap and start talking to herself for company.

Know this! Courts are not here to find the truth; they are here solely to finalize our lives, like ***God***, and right or wrong, they don't give a damn. The most important thing to them is that, right or wrong, their decision must stick. The same with ***DCS***, that's why children are forced to die and be raped over and over because once there's a bad placement, the caseworker who messed up does everything in their power, no matter how bad their choice was, to force a child to stay in a dangerous placement. They're never wrong, as best as they can. This happened to my grandson, but ***God said no, and I got my grandson***.

The judge claimed that ***DCS and Casa did everything to the*** best of their ability, though the court ***knew*** that they were fighting against me for a person with major problems, no different from my daughter, who was being reported with them refusing to investigate. Even if they investigated for ***three years***, how the hell do you never catch any issue with an addict? How the hell is it the best job they possibly could have done? It's just unbelievable how judges think and run their courts. In the end, the system; courts, departments, agencies, commissions, etc. are not for their ***sworn duty***, but solely for ***their own desires*** and are ***never wrong*** as best as possible. Let us pray that the wrongs of the Federal Court and the Supreme Court are ***exposed*** so that judicial reform takes place and justice happens.

When Mama died, somebody hurt her badly. She had bruises on both shoulders where she seemed to have been held down by hands that were on the front of her shoulders, wrapped around the top of both shoulders, and bruised the back of her shoulder. There was an equal-sized bruising on both shoulders. When I told the funeral director's assistant she said bruising was a natural part of dying, but when I explained how the bruising was on both shoulders, the exact same size, like someone was on top of her holding her down, she came to look, she said bruising was a natural part of dying, but when I explained how the bruising was on both shoulders, the exact same size, like someone was on top of her holding her down, she came to look, and her eyes were wide. I said, " Don't worry, Mom will get in the ground without controversy. No one cared about her, and I had no power to force it while she was alive. Now she's gone, let her be free. Mom was forced to be bedridden on two occasions, which is documented. The first time she was given to me, she strived whenever she was at my home, but it was a nightmare the first day because she happened to come to my house, but she would run straight to bed, talking about *GG* would get her. It would take me a couple of days to get her to understand that she did have to stay in bed with me because *GG* can't come here to get her. As soon as she was starting to get used to being free, they would come and literally ***force*** my mother back to *GG*, with her protesting, not wanting to go there every single week. They would call *GG* to come get her, and he wouldn't come because he knew she'd really protest against him. There was one day mom didn't understand that she was coming to my house and I had to go get her, absolutely ***no problems, but they never*** helped mom to stay with the right person, me. They claimed that Haas didn't want me to have her, and nothing could be done. I was living in one of those types of situations where the child is raped, and you MUST send the child back into it every visit. Months went by with me begging my brother to just let her stay with me; they're forcing mom to have days in her own house, miserable with a person who is miserable to spend quality time with her.

There was no way to stop the abuse, absolutely no end in sight. My BP and kidney function both started becoming uncontrollable. Just like work, I am now in a life-and-death situation. I had to decide never to see Mom again. It took days. This will be your last chance ever. How can I live under such stress of the abuse, and your grandchildren have no one? I must give up, Mom, or my grandchildren will lose a parent. After all, under solitary confinement, my social bird mother wouldn't last a year, I thought. The joke was on me. She not only lasted a year. She survived being starved and without water for at least 5 to 7 days, the doctors said. My brother was on the run, and strangers called me to say that Mom was unresponsive. The doctor told me to take Mom off the ventilator, and she would die tonight. I told the doctor that my brother put her into this situation with no food or water; he will be the only one to make that decision. The next night, GG got the nerve to come see Mom and ordered our local hospital to take Mom to Ft Wayne and not remove her from life support. Mom's condition didn't change, and the Ft Wayne hospital ordered Mom off life support. ***Mom refused to die***. She came home and lived in a vegetated state, strong as an ox if she got hold of your hand and squeezed it, and would laugh at it. ***She was forced into a vegetative state and died a <u>year</u> later because of it***, and 100% if her engineering daughter had been allowed to work as an engineer, Mom would have never been bedridden twice, as she was forced. She may still be alive today at age 87 and I loved taking care of her and making her days fun. I could have afforded a lawyer, and my brother couldn't have gotten away with misleading the court. Her mother, my mom's mother lived to be 88, and Mama was strong as an ox. She would go walking with me, dance and sing with me, but greed and sick family members, along with the court, forced my mother to live a horrid last decade of her 80 years of life, into an early, miserable grave.

Court Ordered mother enslaved = for my health and my grandchildren, I made that hard decision to let mother go. I moved into Hunters Run in 2015. The first week, Naomi Friedrichsen was trying to evict me. She said my dog was an aggressive breed and had to go. I told her that I put on the fact that she was a sixty-pound mutt, but she looks like a pitt bull, and she was bought from the pound as a lab mix. Naomi said it doesn't matter, "Even I can't bring a pitt bull to this community so I then said okay just financially help us move because I can't afford another move. At that time, she said to take it to the vet to get a vet to state if she's aggressive. The vet signed that my dog wasn't aggressive, and that was the first of many attempts at falsely removing me and all people of color with children from our homes.

CHAPTER FOUR

The Evolution, Part Three

State Court Win for ***Sandra Black*** and the ***Unlawful Taking of Hunters Run***

We go to court as Hunters Run, Naomi Friedrichsen tries to illegally evict me for absolutely no reason other than I was the last black family with kids that had to go. She couldn't watch and catch me violating rules, so she FABRICATED A VIOLATION. She and Erika Holiday watched my son and his family walk into my house, not knowing it was my son. My son had totaled his car and was driving a car they didn't know. His 15-year-old wife and daughter, ***both white*** females, were court-ordered into my son's custody to take them to Bloomington, where he attended Indiana University of Bloomington. They (my son, wife to be, and baby) stopped at my house before leaving out, and they (both Naomi and Erika) watched my son with a near bald head, whom they knew to have dreadlocks down to his butt... the white girl and her baby all freely opened my door and walked in my home. Not hours later, I get a 30 day vacate to move out letter for unauthorized occupants (UO) living in my home. They saw these people for an hour or so for the first time ever and were prepared to lie and swear they had been living in my home for weeks, even a couple of months prior. As a matter of fact, both managers have perjured themselves in both state and federal courts. Here's their bad luck.

The several people they claimed to be unauthorized occupants living in my home ***required a court order*** to get a sheriff to remove the 15-year-old daughter/mama and baby from her mama/grandma, who wasn't giving consent to marry. They claim that these people had been seen living there, no pictures, no documentation of any sort as evidence, even their surveillance doesn't capture anyone previously visiting, but I have my son's court order that required a sheriff to get these people away from living in Converse, Indiana.

My family and I lived nearly two years being taunted by Naomi Friedrichsen. I was the only person taking out the dog to make it a ***FACT*** for me that I never once left one dog pile. They couldn't say my family members did it. We lived in emotional turmoil, knowing that they were on the hunt for a way to get rid of us. No black family or Hispanic family that I know of was allowed to stay. Many were here when we first arrived. Issues over maintenance of their old, falling-apart appliances that were failing. There was ***intentional*** refusal to fix the furnace. This will be discussed on pages 38 and 97/98. Many of these issues were discussed throughout this book. The fabricated violations are mentioned in the state court order page 67.

CHAPTER FIVE

The Evolution, Part Four

The Lawsuit Against Hunters Run- Federal Judges Enforce Jim Crow

RACIST LANDLORDS DEMAND THAT BLACKS WITH KIDS MUST GO

I have not had a decent/fair landlord since 2010. Y'all, that's fifteen years! I am the ideal tenant because I have never in my life been late or missed paying my rent. NEVER! I never have a lot of visitors, problems with my neighbors, criminal activity, destruction to property, disrespectful to landlords, until THE VERY END when I JUST DON'T GIVE A DAMN and will no longer kiss their ass any longer. The reason for horrible landlords is the POVERTY of the nation, which demands that tenants MUST live in squalor or no home at all. This is the living conditions of Indiana at the 7.25 minimum wage state requirement. IN INDIANA, SLUM LORDS WANTED! NO JOKE! And HUD will pass the FAVORED landlords while holding the struggling black perhaps poor landlords to a higher degree and refuse them participation.

In my last home in Indiana, I was FORCED by my landlords and HUD to leave the state as they moved my grandchildren and me into a filthy, stank barn, which is supposed to be against HUD guidelines, but HUD allows local offices freedom in their own policies. As such, as I was told by my section 8 after explaining that trees were dying and life threating, the toilet volcano rushes water onto my private areas with flushes from upstairs, there's an animal (not mice/rat) that takes a bowl movement in my kitchen, there's no lock on my bathroom door, the carpet is beyond filthy our cat is permanently stained burnt orange because she can't clean herself and more. I was told to realize that, unfortunately, in this society, those who are in poverty are only allowed the bare minimum. You have running water, a working furnace, and electricity. Then what about a simple lock on my bathroom door? She replied, "That's not a necessity." I told her, "But my five-year-old could come in on my nakedness." And she gives a sigh, but that's not a necessity.

And as far as the trees are concerned, HUD only inspects the home, not the property. My prayers for protection from the trees kept us safe, but the house and electricity got taken out by a tree-sized branch. The Electric company had to shut off the electricity, and professionals were required to restore it. Landlords now decide to fix the problem by trimming trees and cutting one down. The tree specialist saw the branch that hit our house and said that if that had hit a human head, the person would have died. BUT NOBODY CARED, and in the end, I moved because there was no regard for human life or decency as long as you could pretend nothing was wrong. PLEASE UNDERSTAND, when you live in poverty, if you STRIVE, you are among the highest performing individuals because poverty is USED to take out children who become adults so that society can call the impoverished, MONSTERS. Society that INTENTIONALLY causes suffering of those trapped in poverty IS THE TRUE MONSTERS, either by omission or by direct evil action like Trump's EVIL BEAUTIFUL BILL. We're all watching Trump set up the NATION'S TAKE OVER before he can be removed from power. He started day one. He's trying to seize every major municipality in the nation by causing civil unrest that he will claim requires him to remain in power. This same type of power is being used corruptly by the courts, the judicial system that empowers judges as gods over the people, unjustly. This is what this discrimination landlord case is all about. Let's go into detail.

I first began my search for the perfect home to live-out the rest of my days, as the houses in Marion, Indiana, are not kept up as required by HUD. My landlord was forced to let me out of my lease because I recorded everything, and she was refusing to fix items that HUD ordered fixed. She waited until the last day, I was at the bank, and she called me to say that she had to go inside my home and would enter right now without notice. I told her, " Please do not. I will be home in about 30 minutes; you must wait until then. She told me I have no rights, that it's an emergency, and she will enter right now. I warned her that I will get out of my lease because you are breaking the law. You had plenty of notice to fix the house, and you waited until the last day, and you don't want to wait until I get home. I will call HUD. She stated that she would enter. When I reported her, she lied and said she never said anything I said above. I told my manager that I have the recorded statements, and it is just as I said. She listened to the recording and released me from my lease. This time, I'm going to make 100% sure I move into a nice home because I will move into the nicest low-income apartments that I know of. however, the sad part is that I had heard of their reputation as RACISTS. I misjudged them, thinking that I would be treated differently because I don't have the black drama (poverty issues) that blacks are stereotyped to have. Besides, I'm an excellent tenant, so as to be too valuable to want to get rid of. I FORGOT the most important rule ever in dealing with racists. A black person must NEVER outperform whites. What the hell was I thinking?

I filled out the application and was interviewed and initially DENIED. The reason I was denied was .my last landlord stated that she had nothing good to say about me. I put my responses in writing so that they know they are not dealing with total ignorance and explained that I cannot be denied for that cause because I faithfully paid rent on time and yadda yadda yadda EXCELLENT TENANT and can be verified by statements from my last landlord and previous landlord before she refused to complete required repairs. This can also be verified through our local HUD office. See below my landlord recommendations to the court for my case involving my mother being enslaved by the state under Judge Warren Haas. I will point out all of his evil deeds against my family and me prior to this case that began in August, 2010.

Exhibit I

IN THE MATTER OF THE GUARDIANSHIP OF) In the State of Indiana, Grant County

MILDRED C. BARBER) Superior Court 3

AN ADULT) Cause No27DO 3 1008-GU-000185

PETITION TO THE COURTS FOR SANDRA BLACK TO NOT BE DISCRIMINATED AGAINST DUE TO HER DISABILITY/POVERTY

I have known Sandra Black as a renter of my rental property in the past [redacted]2 West 16th Street for a couple of years. I sold my rental property last summer to Fay Baughman. Sandra Black was an excellent renter even to the point that I reduced the rent in order to keep her in the home when she wanted to move to public housing. She is a dependable, kind, and responsible renter. I would recommend her and did recommend her to Faye as an excellent renter. I had no complaints from the neighbors and rarely needed to make repairs in the home as she has maintained the property in good condition during the time that I owned the property. She also has in her custody and on the lease a minor son, Kemuel Shem. Sandra Black is "fit" and responsible at paying rent and maintaining her home. Finally, there was absolutely no detectable "unfit" or abnormal behavior observed in the manner at which Sandra Black operated and functioned in my rental property during the time that I owned it. I believe that she should not be discriminated against for her disability and should be considered fit to care for her elderly mother based on what I have said in this statement

Under the penalties of perjury I, [redacted] state that the above statement is the truth to my knowledge.

Signed: [redacted] Date: 7/24/13

[redacted]4-7671

39

Exhibit H

IN THE MATTER OF THE GUARDIANSHIP OF) In the State of Indiana, Grant County

)

MILDRED C. BARBER) Superior Court 2

)

AN ADULT) Cause No27DO2-1008-GU-000185

PETITION TO THE COURTS FOR SANDRA BLACK TO NOT BE DISCRIMINATED AGAINST DUE TO HER DISABILITY/POVERTY

I have known Sandra Black as a renter of my rental property located at 312 West 16th Street for ~~nearly~~ a year. I purchased my rental property from [redacted] last summer and have been paid my rent in a timely manner without fai[redacted] and Sandra Black had such a great relationship that [redacted] reduced Sandra's rent in order to keep her as a tenant and not lose her to Marion Housing. She is a dependable and responsible renter; I would love to keep her as a renter. I have no complaints from the neighbors and am rarely needed to make repairs in the home as she has maintained the property in good condition. I fully recommend to the best of my knowledge that from firsthand knowledge of Sandra Black as my renter that she does not allow her disability to affect the maintaining and upkeep of her home. She also has in her custody and on the lease a minor son, Kemuel Shem. Sandra Black is "fit" and responsible at paying rent and maintaining her home.

Under the penalties of perjury I, [redacted] state that the above statement is the truth to my knowledge.

Signed: [redacted] Date: 7-25-13

Phone: [redacted]

38

In that case, my mother was forced to live in near solitary confinement without anyone to talk to and share love with her, simply because this was the easiest way out. I had prayed for my brother to expose himself to the court under Dana Kenworthy, who was ATTEMPTING to rule fairly. Her hardship was due to the refusal of appointed guardian ad litem Terry Pollet and the adult protection agency to conduct an investigation of our family. They came out to my mother's home and asked her what she wanted, and asked what my brother wanted, and sealed my mother's fate of doom TO HER DEATH. To this day, our family cannot be sure of the worst of the worst possible happenings that have happened to my mother. The one thing that we are one hundred percent sure of is that my mother was manipulated, neglected, abandoned, and FORCED into being bedridden on TWO OCCASIONS without anything we could do to stop it. The first time she was bedridden solely due to the depression that she had sold herself into doom, she refused to eat or leave her bed. I finally got custody for only 4 days out of the week, and mom started to glow and do so much better, but the abuse was unbearable to watch, and FORCED PARTICIPATION every week. Mom came to life so much that she KNEW she didn't want to go back for 3 days into solitary confinement with a man (her son) that didn't bring any warmth or enjoyment to her life. The court-appointed guardians KNEW my mom was better off and happier with me, but they claimed they couldn't do anything about it because Judge Haas was adamant about keeping me blocked away. I was told the only way I got those 4 days was through the state representatives, forcing the guardians to admit that they couldn't put mom into a nursing home when she had a daughter who could keep her happy and eating. I had heard that my brother was holding off the guardians at gunpoint from trying to put her in a nursing home. She was so depressed, she refused to eat, drink, or leave her bed. The guardians called her bedridden and wanted her placed in a nursing home.

Within one month of visits, Mom never wanted to go back. Future Choices would send their workers who would force mom for an hour, so that she had no choice. Mom would cry, "Mildred don't want to go." It was the most horrible thing to watch. Mom would look for me to save her. I was afraid to tell her to keep fighting them, no matter what till they got tired, because I believed they would stop bringing mom to me and end my visitation. There were a couple of times where they asked my brother to come get mom because it was getting into hours that she wasn't leaving. He refused them, and they kept tormenting Mom that she had no choice. When mom came, she'd be so happy and then would run to her bed. I told mom, "you don't have to go to bed in my house," and she would say, "GG will get me." "He said stay in that bed, that's what he said." And I would say this is a different house, and she would agree, but not understand "We have to have fun, we have to sing or watch TV, but we can't just lie around, Mom, we can't." She would eventually come around, and by the end of the second day, Mom was normal at not running to bed in fear of being in trouble. By the third and fourth day, mom was a regular person freely walking all over the house, even going into the fridge to help herself at times. I would care for mom in panties, but my brother kept her in diapers. I used diapers at night, but Mom never had an accident. When I went to the bathroom, so did Mom. When I ate, so did Mom. When I drank, so did Mom. We did everything together, exercised, walked, danced, and sang together. Her favorite shows for us to watch were BB King, Denise LaSalle, Clarence Carter, Millie Jackson, Mister Ed, Sanford and Son, and The Jeffersons, etc. We had BIG fun together. The funeral picture of her with full-blown dementia, kept under my care, looked better than she had looked for about a decade PRIOR. I tried to find a nice older picture without going back so far, and the only one nicer was back in her 50's, and mom died at 80. It is highly likely that Mom would be living today and enjoying herself, though she wouldn't remember it. The abuse mom spoke of to me and the bitter contesting and refusing to go back **EVERY SINGLE WEEK** was more than I could take. I called my brother, begging him to let Mom go. I called guardians to fix this nightmare. I called an attorney who took my three thousand dollars and did nothing for us. He said there's no way around the judge, and the guardians won't fight because their attorney says nothing can be done. I started failing in health, with my kidneys going down and down. I was in the same condition as when I had to give up my job for my life. I had to give up, Mom. I had her from February until October and had no way to stop the abuse, no way to be healthy living in it. I thought for weeks about how I had to let mom go. How horrible mom's life would be, but I wouldn't be alive much longer if I continued to live in the abuse with my mother. I thought since I pulled mom back from being bedridden that she would simply die within a few months of abuse. I told everyone, including mom, that this would be the last time we would ever see each other. The look in mom's eyes. My God, she understood, it was horrid, this time I joined the demons, sorry, Mom, you really have to go. I want to explain, but no way she'd understand that my keeping her under abuse was going to be the end of me. I wonder how people continue visiting their children forced to keep their children, court-ordered, into rape and child abuse, visiting the spouse. However, I have never lived a life as an adult with kidney failure/BP/anxiety incapable of not dying under nonstop stress. My guts never got a break, BP sky high, from her being forced abused with me seeking a way out every day a fight. I was born to lose, no agility to live under constant stress, forced to acquiesce for a battle another day or lose the war period. I had mom from February to the end of October fighting for a way to get her permanently. How can they watch it every single week? I couldn't do it. I couldn't die because my grandchildren needed me. Next to my son dying, I believe this was my second hardest day ever. She understood that day. It was horrible.

She did nearly die. The doctors wanted to pull the plug and let her die because she hadn't been fed and had no water for at least five days, according to the doctor. My brother was hiding for a while, but we got the message to him that he put her in that condition, so he had to pull the plug. My brother fought Marion General Hospital not to pull the plug, and she was sent to Fort Wayne hospital, I believe Park View. Around about ten days later, the doctors ordered that Mom had to be taken off life support. They said the same thing as MGH had said, but Mom didn't die. **MOM WANTED TO PROVE THAT SHE HAD PLENTY OF LIFE!** That she was robbed of her life prematurely, and as such, she stuck around even through an apparent physical battle with a man or machine of great strength, the mortician's assistant witnessed the aftermath. I said nothing. NOBODY CARED, AND I wanted Mom free of the bickering. Now she's dead, there's nothing to save anymore, but getting her in the ground without a fight. They killed my mom; THE COURTS were the ones who starved her into a vegetative state because they didn't care about us at all. Haas wanted me to be the monster he forced away from my mother. He even stated in court that he couldn't care if I NEVER saw my mother again in life. The words pierced my soul. Then he ordered that I never brought my petition for guardianship over my mother and that I was no longer a person of interest to my mother's matter, and my brother was never a person of interest. He ordered that neither of us could move the court. That completely favored my brother because he did as he pleased, taking over mom's home setup for himself and not as she kept it. The guardians were afraid of him and only laid eyes on Mom every once in a while, back to the landlord case at Hunters Run.

After moving in just one week or less, I was served by Naomi Friedrichsen with a notice to vacate due to owning an aggressive breed of dog. I explained that my dog wasn't aggressive, and I filled out the pet lease honestly. She came back with "EVEN I COULDN'T HAVE A PIT BULL." I told her no problem, but I need my move-in cost because I can't afford a second move. She then told me to take the dog to a vet for a statement that the dog wasn't aggressive. I did so, and it was supposedly all good. But it wasn't. There were VIOLATIONS for the broken pieces of blinds in my window and a sign that only said, www.motherenslaved.com, the sign was a website and a book about my mother being destroyed. She was still alive, and we never know who might be able to get her free. I immediately fixed the blind and called to explain that my website was not for financial gain. I was told it didn't matter, no signs, no matter what, are allowed, and I removed the signs immediately. The very next warning was a fabricated violation, FINAL warning that the landlords made up against me, that I left dog waste without picking it up. I got my neighbors to vouch for me, and the landlords were forced to remove the lie. See the June 14, 2017 state court order pg 7, item F in this book on page 67. I IMMEDIATELY FILED A COMPLAINT with the Indiana Commission of Civil Rights. These places are all fake. EEOC, Human rights, Legal aid, ALL BS. If you are really in trouble with a legitimate complaint and you're black too, FORGET IT. I knew this from my work experience. You guys, Trump thought a civil war was going to break out because he went after taking everything that was supposed to help black people. YOU CAN'T HURT US like whites committing suicide over the stock market in the 30's. Our people are used to abuse, having nothing, and keeping it moving. SO!!!, know this, when you take something from black people that never helped us to any noticeable degree in the first place, like affirmative action, civil rights, EEOC; you'll get more reaction and fight out of taking candy from a baby. Trump and republicans thought they would get their race war they so desperately are fighting for AND YOU CAN TOUCH US! You NEVER DID ANYTHING JUST FOR BLACK PEOPLE! The joke is on you racist. Take our jobs... It's what we're raised to expect. Just like the battered woman syndrome, everything you're doing to us WE ALREADY DONE TO YOU, and Dear God, we're still here. WE ARE EVEN! STOP! Look at how you took civil rights back.

Damn, they took civil rights back??? YES! almost day one, in the seventies. The corporations went to congress belly aching that they were going bankrupt due to discrimination cases. So our wonderfully smart congress agreed with the racist corporations (instead of telling them to stop discriminating then you won't lose so many cases going bankrupt) they agreed that the individual is better equipped, got more money, and more allies to handle the burden of proof. THE BURDEN OF PROOF IS ON THE INDIVIDUAL. This made it next to impossible to prove a discrimination case because corporations have more money, more allies and are far better equipped than the individual. The moment you walk in the door black, you're greeted as if you can't never lose when you show them how strong your evidence is and OR told first thing discrimination is almost impossible to prove, in the end, there's nothing they can do. Sometimes you'll get lucky and before they ever hear your evidence, they start out with "well you know discrimination cases are almost impossible to win". That way you don't waste their time filling out your claim. I won't waste your time talking about the Indiana CRC, CIVIL RIGHTS COMMISSION. I hope they were the first hit hard and removed. They will NOT let you write your complaint in your own words because you are only allowed ABOUT THREE LINES to tell two years of discrimination. If you leave anything out then your story is false or conflicted. Now tell me how you overcome this? I started on December 5, 2016 knowing that my landlord was sitting me up to join all the other nonwhite families out the door, but we argued back and forth over how to get my wording in my voice, my story. It wound up taking until landlords were in final stages of a fabricated eviction when I finally realized that I hadn't a chance to get my statement in and we agreed that I could email my real statement while signing their THREE lines of everything that happened. From December until May, they refused my statement and NEVER allowed it! They forced me to give in to their three-line statement that told the two years of suffering. But the truth is sent to them by email. They sided with the landlords that nothing happened and if I am not mistaken, I believe this is where the mistake/JUDGES lie of my grandkids not being on the lease is first taken. They never investigated anything so I was court evicted because my grandkids were NOT on the lease, according to ICRC. I don't know. I was denied and couldn't go through the details due to my disability. It was exactly what I expected. I couldn't read most of the things liars sent to me. You will find so much more EXTREME injustice against me as I couldn't read it. That's how I keep alive. Better to lose the battle and win the war. I'm sick, in crisis, just quit, leave it; better alive.

I received a 30-day-vacate letter for **SEVERAL** unauthorized occupants living in my home on APRIL 19, 2017. Please check out their blatant lie. **GOD IN HEAVEN SET THESE EVIL RACIST LANDLORDS UP.** He armed me with a COURT ORDER that required a sheriff to take custody of my son's wife to be and his daughter because he couldn't bring her to the court BLOOMINGTON, IN to marry her, as he

REQUIRED a court order to gain custody of the minor wife to be from her mother. REPEAT: My son couldn't get access to the people THEY SAW walking in my house until that DAY the court ORDERED into my son's custody. Normally, it's always your word against theirs, and the system prefers the story of a landlord over a citizen, a cop over a citizen, DCS or ANYONE in power over citizens; so most simply move out.

The idiots had absolutely no idea that the so-called "unauthorized occupants" [UO] they saw walk into my house was my son (totally **UNRECOGNIZABLE AT ALL**), his wife to be, and their baby (she's totally white, but my son couldn't be talked out of signing the birth certificate). They saw THREE people in their minds that they had never EVER seen before in their lives, OPEN MY DOOR and walk right in. They saw some strange black man with a WHITE woman and her white baby all walk into my BLACK HOUSEHOLD. They targeted me for eviction day one. They planned to LIE that they had always been seeing these people never knowing that there was no way to get them without a court order. THEY KNOW they get to make up any story, and routinely (blacks) are done, automatically evicted. What they did not know is that I wasn't the regular black person they could **EASILY** watch and catch a human moment and remove me. They allow almost all black applicants in (this gives the appearance of compliance to Equal Housing Opportunity) and work them (blacks) out day one! This is also done in the work field, but blacks have no voice, not one place on earth that genuinely seeks to stop black discrimination. Sadly, the only person I have ever met personally to win a discrimination claim with EEOC is WHITE!

The landlords have NEVER documented these people visiting or ever entering my home prior to this day. They never warned HUD that they were watching and documenting for eviction, which would have joined them, as HUD has strict requirements that no one can live in the dwelling except those on the lease. They didn't have ONE PICTURE prior to their lie that the UO had been there days, weeks before! Even the surveillance camera of the so-called "burgundy Camero driving recklessly" was MAGICALLY erased at the precise time the car entered, stayed, and left. This was done by Naomi Friedrichsen (the worst racist landlord) because Erika Holiday (the backup racist) showed the video footage voluntarily to both my daughter and me, not knowing that Naomi had erased it. Immediately after receiving the 30-day notice, I went around to all the neighbors showing them what the landlords claimed, and they all signed that they had NEVER seen anyone visit my house other than my daughter, who is the mother of my grandchildren.

See their letter to illegally remove me from my home:

Exhibit F (21)

Fed EXHIBIT 4

64 of 66

Hunter's Run Apartments
717 E. Hunter's Run Drive
Marion, IN 46953
765-677-1701

April 19th, 2017

Sandra Black
655 E. Hunter's Run Drive
Marion, IN 46953

RE: Lease Violation- unauthorized occupants – 30 day notice to vacate

Dear Ms. Black,

I have been witness to your occupant (burgundy colored Camaro) driving recklessly in and out of the parking lot at Hunter's Run Apartments. In addition, several other persons have been witnessed at your apartment and appear to be permanent occupants at Hunters Run and are not on your lease or authorized to be living in your apartment.

At this time, we have reason to believe that you have unauthorized occupants living in your apartment Hunters Run. As a result, you are being provided a 30 day notice to vacate. You will be required to vacate your apartment on or before May 20, 2017 at 4:00 p.m.

We appreciate your cooperation.

Sincerely,

Naomi Friedrichsen
Senior Community Manager
Hunter's Run Apartments

cc: Resident file
Marion Housing Authority

SEE THE COURT ORDER THAT REQUIRED A SHERIFF TO GET THE PEOPLE THEY SAW!

Exhibit G (22)

STATE OF INDIANA)
) SS:
COUNTY OF MONROE)

IN THE MONROE CIRCUIT COURT VIII

CASE NO. 53C08 1703 MI 000630

IN RE THE APPLICATION FOR A
MARRIAGE LICENSE OF:

KEMUEL SHEM and
JACEE BARBER

ORDER TO GRANT COUNTY SHERIFF My son sleeps over

The Court, having held a hearing on April 18, 2017 and issuing an Order to Clerk to Issue Marriage License on the same day NOW FINDS Grant County Sheriff shall release Jacee Barber and her minor child, [redacted] to Kemuel Shem.

* The proble
The problem

SO ORDERED THIS 19th DAY OF APRIL, 2017.

V. Haughton
Valeri Haughton, Judge
Monroe Circuit Court VIII

Distribution:
File
Petitioners
Grant County Sheriff- by fax

Monroe Circuit Court 8

CASE NO: 53C08 1703
MI 000630

When you're black in America, SERIOUS EVIDENCE AGAINST EVIL RACISTS IS NOT ALLOWED IN COURT!!! You will NEVER SEE THIS Monroe County Court **ORDER** RECOGNIZED in either court at the state level or the Federal court. THIS IS JIM CROW because they (JUDGES) have the POWER to lie and TRADITION, illegally, there is absolutely no judge that will overrule a judge, no matter how GREAT THE LIE for a pro se litigant. If a judge is against you and you are pro se, you are AUTOMATICALLY DENIED WITHOUT REVIEW by the Judicial Council at the state level and by the Judicial Council in the Seventh Circuit Court of Appeals for Misconduct, BUT IF YOU ARE BLACK... double whammy hell no, Jim Crow; you do not get your constitutional RIGHTS TO BE HEARD! For pro se black people, a court order in your favor is either INVISIBLE or like the one against the defendants coming up ignored for the fact finding that NO unauthorized occupants were proven to exist, and that my grandchildren are on the lease, so RACIST FEDERAL JUDGES can't make it up that they are not on the lease.

Hell, I guarantee you, if Judge Haas had foreseen this case going to Federal Court, he would have evicted me with a lie, and I would be struggling for housing and most likely lose my Section 8, even though Section 8 KNEW that there was no evidence of [UO]. HUD agreed with me that my landlords failed to establish evidence of [UO]. My evidence was overwhelming against the landlords. Haas and Morris (the landlord's attorney) were in bed together, thus they see their eviction lawsuit as the perfect chance to get even. They golf and work together against the law, entering cases that both of them have decided in their own favor without ever having considered the opposing side. Haas destroyed my mother's life for a DECADE OF TORTURE. Haas or Morris used each other for a ten-year claim filed against me when I lived in Africa, which I had no knowledge of and was not responsible for.

I UTTERLY REFUSED TO PAY. I never paid, and I challenged the judge as a LIAR for claiming that I paid and satisfied the judgment. I was prepared to go to jail! Haas tried to intimidate me that I would pay or go to jail, and continued to reset a hearing until it became evident that this bitch is not going to pay, so he put an ORDER IN THAT I PAID! I MOTIONED THE COURT TO REMOVE THE LIE BECAUSE I DID NOT PAY, he must simply dismiss the case unsatisfied, but judges have all RIGHTS TO UTTER CORRUPTIOIN and I want you to examine your ridiculous judicial system that says powerful great rites of passage called a (judicial CODE) that almost NO JUDGE IS REQUIRED TO FOLLOW unless that judge is utterly lawless or hated, ie (supporting BLACKS, PRO SE, OR RULING FAIRLY against the system for citizens). UNDERSTAND!!! Numerous judges saw this case against the landlords. It's a matter of **FACTS** that judge LIED to place whites falsely in the right, and all judges and lawyers in bad faith LIED in pretense that it was a matter of opinion.

SEE THE CASE FINAL ENTRY

NOTICE

Grant Superior Court 3
101 E. 4th St.
Marion Indiana 46952

City Of Marion V Black — 27D03-0503-SC-000921

To: Sandra Black
210 North G St
Marion, IN 46952

EVENTS

Entry Date	File Stamped / Order Signed	Event and Comments
04/06/2015	04/06/2015	Hearing Journal Entry Parties agree to reset this matter and Court sets this matter for Proceeding Supplemental and will be heard in the Grant Superior Court 3 on Thursday 5-21-15 at 8:15 am. cs
04/06/2015		Hearing Scheduling Activity Proceedings Supplemental scheduled for 05/21/2015 at 8:15 AM.

OTHER PARTY - NOTICED	OTHER PARTY - ENOTICED
N/A	Morris Adin Kelsay (Attorney)

GRANT COUNTY, 2005

27D03-0503-SC-000921

Judge Haas was out to get me in 2015. He looked this case up got his friend Kelsay Morris to come after me. Notice 2005 case in 2015, WHY NOW? THE ANSWER IS WARREN HAAS and tracking my cases!

Petition for Guardianship of Mildred Barber: Cause No: 27D02-1008-GU-000185

Case no: 27D03-1008-GU-000185, Grant County, Superior Court 3, Judge Warren Haas, Petition for Guardianship filed by Sandra Black, August 10, 2010, in Superior Court 2, Judge Dana Kenworthy. Dana was forced off the case with my Motion to Substantiate the order. She recused. Judges don't fix mistakes. My brother was proven to be against my mom, but Kenworthy had mistakenly ruled me unfit due to Terri Pollet's REFUSAL to even interview me and a false diagnosis that had been presented by my bother to the court. I was systematically IGNORED as Terri Pollet, an attorney, falsified that she interviewed me for my side of the story, and Dana took her testimony PERIOD without any evidence, without interviewing me for what I said on my side. What notes had she taken? NONE. Judges, prosecutors, attorneys, police, DCS, and officials **ALWAYS** do all within their power to take the viewpoints of each other, while minimizing at BEST what regular people say. And at worst, they totally ignore or FABRICATE lies for their co-conspirators (officials), that is not supposed to be this way. But having a KNOWN outcome always makes it extremely easy for the OFFICIALS and next to IMPOSSIBLE FOR CITIZENS.

Transparency, honesty, fairness, unbiased, DILIGENTLY seeking justice, all requirements are annihilated! BECAUSE COURTS DO NOT GO SOLELY ON EVIDENCE, BUT FIRST WEIGHING OFFICIALS' POSITION, NEXT WEIGHING SOCIETAL BIAS, AND, in my case, allowing absolutely no evidence to be considered (Jim Crow), though in passing at times slightly barely mentioned. THEY ARE SIMPLY AUTOMATICALLY RIGHT. After my prayers for my brother to expose himself, he asked the court for nearly a QUARTER MILLION DOLLARS for one year caring for my mom. That was when I requested substantiation of the order of how Polett could possibly be right, that my brother would be a good candidate for mom's personal care, and to request the court to rob my mom to pay him. Haas took over and ordered that Kenworthy was right and had no reason to recuse. NO WORK at all! Even Pollet has now changed her testimony against me, but HAAS saw it as too much work and my family as too little value to get it right.

SEE MY BROTHER'S REQUEST FOR MOM'S MONEY, AND HAS FORCED HER TO STICK WITH A PERSON LIKE THIS:

IN THE STATE OF INDIANA
GRANT COUNTY SUPERIOR COURT 2

CAUSE NO.27D02-1008-GU185

In the Matter of the Guardianship of
Mildred C. Barber,

Request for Compensation.

Comes now Elijah Israel and request compensation for 30 months of 24 hour a day in home care provided to Mildred C. Barber. The Court made clear that I wasn't to have one dime of Mildred's Money.

1. Kim Lytle told me that my mother couldn't help me get my dentures as a gift that I had to repay every dime, (which I did) two weeks later Kim Lytle okayed spending more than I needed on a 340.00 collar that broke, for the dóg, (which I would not allow as the true Guardian of my mother)

2. When I asked Kim Lytle about compensating me for my Services rendered to Mildred Daily, she said "I have to check into that because I'm not sure how that works"
it wasn't until a new judge held the hearing for objections to Kim Lytle's report that I learned that I had to file in writing to the Court for my request, so now that I learned how to be compensated for Services Rendered, to a person made a ward of the state, therefore I'm now seeking full compensation with full consideration of my pay history, before Sandra decided to slander my relationship with my Mother because I was Managing my own Business, not laying around my mothers house unemployed.

I can't earn my previous income supported by Exhibits Q and R showing my 20.00 an hour pay in 2007 and in 2008 I was making more than 40.00 an hour Managing my own business, I can't earn this income caring for my mother 24hrs a day.

3. The court didn't bat an eye at forcing my mother to pay a complete stranger 80 dollars an hour, to make sure her son doesn't get a dime, so the court should find my half price hourly services of 40.00 hr an incredible deal for Mildred.

4. I further Request to be paid through Mildred's assets and Establish a monthly Salary Equal to Mildred's Social Security Check And I will pay all of Mildred's Expenses myself and forgive any debt left over, then she wouldn't have to pay for permission to buy a new bed I can just buy it, and eliminate any need for a Financial Guardian stealing money that doesn't belong to them, and based on the Courts behavior toward white people collecting my mothers money for unwanted services rendered, it should find no reason not to compensate the person that's actually doing all the real work when it comes to caring for Mildred.

5. It would be inappropriate, to charge me rent as if I were some homeless person needing a place to stay, Instead of a servant providing 24hr in home care. Employee's who work long hours are not charged rent, and I provide my own food.

All of these Calculations are based on a 29 month period from August 2010, to January 2013, @ half of the 40.00 hr previous pay.

6. The 24hr a day on call service provided for 29 months has accumulated past the Value of Mildred's Estate and I request Payment and the total value of Mildred's Estate signed over as Payment for Services rendered.

7. Even if the Court prefers the older salary of 20 dollars an hour and only 12 hours a day caring for Mildred instead of 24hrs a day, this comes to 360 hours a month times 29 comes to 10,440 hrs worked for the 29 month period.

8. 10,440 X 20.00 hr (half of my most current salary, comes to, $208,800.00 owed for services already rendered. I have also listed a few things that stick out in my memory in case the court believes in the real American traditions of making a black mans labor cheap or free.

9. I Prepare 3 meals a day, of Mildred's choice. 2 hrs daily for 29 Months.

10. Provide evening and morning doses of medication daily. 1 hr per week

11. I spent 5 hours installing 3 different dishwashers one didn't work at all, one wouldn't dry, and the third one worked plus I talked the salesman into taking 25 dollars off the asking price, and provided a not included free water supply line.

12. I spent one hour getting my mothers property taxes reduced for 3625 So. Gallatin which was successful.

2142 So. Fairfield Drive was denied due to my previous appeal of a 150,000 value down to the 90's but this was before the housing market crashed so I'm pretty sure this house will not sale for 75,000 dollar in the next year, to prove that 96,000.00 dollars is far too high therefore they will only bring down the property value if the house is placed for sale (only cheap option). to show the county that the property won't sale for its practiced inflated values, not to actually sale the house, and I think this should be done.

13. I spent at least 90 hours turning Mildred's house into a clean and Safe environment.
cleaning out walk in closets that were filled waist high with boxes full of other peoples trash. Remove furniture that was falling apart. Cleaning out deep freezer, refrigerator, cleaned out her Shed and her Garage that were both full of other peoples things and some items were delivered to their perspective owners.

14. I installed shelving in her Garage @ 4hrs

15. I repaired a 16x20" hole Sandra's Daughter made in the dining area wall. 1hr.

16. I Installed an Entry Door @ 3hrs,

17. I usually spend on average 3 hrs daily cleaning for Mildred who wasn't a tidy person before she was diagnosed with dementia and I have very high standards for maintaining a clean and healthy Environment for my mother.

18. laundry, fold put away cloths, iron, change bed linen 2 or 3 times a week 2hrs per week.@ 40.00 an hr.

19. Yard work. 2hrs per Mo. month

20. I take Mildred to activities (Movies, Fishing, Bowling, Kings Island, Etc.) Doctor and Dental Appointments Approximately 50 hrs.

21. Feeding and cleaning up behind dogs in the garage, twice a week. 1hr per week.

22. Theirs no true way to place a value for someone that's willing to sacrifice their own desires and needs to tend to the needs of others because that's a very uncommon event on very temporary conditions, much less to make these sacrifices for Years or Decades My higher standard of services would only end through my death. Anything I have or own will be used to provide my Mother the highest level of care humanly possible, I intend to use the money she pays for my services to hire the several black women I know that are already working in the home health care profession and will give me a special rate. For being more of a feminine companion to hang out

with and go places, their only work like chore will be seeing over Mildred's Hygiene when necessary. While the courts 80.00 an hr Guardian will spend my mothers money on her own family not Mildred's, Superior care, every legal means necessary should be used to allow all of Mildred's Resources to go toward her care not watching over her money, when Star Bank will pay all of Mildred's bills on time for free. The real work is being done by me.

Date 1-15-2013

Elijah Israel
Elijah Israel

Here's the killer. My brother explained to Pollet how he would build my mother's houses, and he only wanted to make my mom wealthy, while Sandy and her kids only want to destroy everything. He said that his mom gave him a twenty-thousand-dollar bank loan for his house because she knew he was out of work and didn't have income, and she loves her son. SO HOW IS IT THAT HE MAKES ALL THE MONEY HE WAS CLAIMING that my mother owed him when he had NO INCOME that required a twenty-thousand-dollar loan? He's broke to take a loan, BUT rich to take mom's money for his time caring for her. AND HAAS FORCED HER TO DIE WIT HIM IN HELL! When you pray, and you have CONNECTIONS WITH THE SUPREME, GOD will make you expose yourself, just like this justice system has exposed itself beyond ANYTHING EVER SEEN IN US HISTORY. My brother was dumbfounded at why he would do what he did, I saw him pulled over in his car reading through paperwork after paperwork. Karen, Courts KNOW just like George Floyds MURDERER that they have an AMERICAN RIGHT, EMBEDDED LAW to destroy black people. Can you understand that black suffering is far more today than in than in the sixties. We owned businesses, we were respected in our communities, and most of all **JOURNALIST** covered stories like mine on how I lost my career, my mom, THIS FEDERAL COURT CASE. They don't cover blacks lynched, killed, destroyed unless that black person is connected to GO VIRAL. How many blacks are murdered without an immediate charge of the white murderers or white cops? How many blacks murder whites and never get charged until they go viral? The vast majority of us, just like me will not go viral. How many like Floyd and I are lynched to death or judicially lynched? HOW MANY? The sixties at least let us see the monstrous racism while today FOX and CNN will never cover the stories unless BY FORCE.

Let's return to my racist landlords and their 30-day vacate letter. She states that she, Naomi Friedrichsen NF has been witness to your (my) OCCUPANT (She doesn't recognize her tenant (MY SON) Kemuel Shem KS and I will show you the pictures of him for you to see why) driving recklessly in and out of the parking lot at Hunter's Run Apartments.

> (She deleted video footage of this and offered nothing to the court from her surveillance cameras because when you're white backed behind two corporations and your victim is black, you don't

need anything but your word and the word of your staff. You KNOW THAT BLACK PERSON MUST LOSE! KARENS)

In addition, several other persons have been witnessed at your apartment and appear to be permanent occupants **(THE LYING RACIST!)** at Hunters Run and are not on your lease or authorized to be living in your apartment.

I solemnly swear under penalties of perjury that EVERYTHING I am writing in this book is and will be the whole truth to the very best of my ability, and my name as the AUTHOR of this book Sandra Black, aka Ezzrath Baht Shem represents my signature this tenth day of October, 2025 at 9:18 AM.

At this time, we have reason to believe that you have unauthorized occupants living in your apartment, Hunters Run. As a result, you are being provided a 30-day notice to vacate. You will be required to vacate your apartment on or before May 20, 2017, at 4:00 pm.

We appreciate your cooperation.

Signed Naomi Friedrichsen

Senior Community Manager

I am mentioning this twice because absolutely NO COURT will recognize the MONROE COUNTY COURT ORDER THAT REQUIRES A SHERIFF FOR MY SON TO GET CUSTODY OF THESE PEOPLE THEY SAW. It is dated APRIL 19TH, and the 30-day vacate is dated April 19th, the EXACT SAME DAY my son FORCES A RIGHT to get these people.

So if my son needs a Sheriff to get the two people they saw, how in the world is it possible they were living there before? WHY NO pictures, NO video footage, nor any written documentation of concern over these people? Yet they are seeing them for days, weeks, or a month?

THIS IS WHAT MY SON LOOKED LIKE TO THE RACIST LANDLORDS.

THIS IS (THE UO) MY SON THE LANDLORDS WATCHED WALK INTO MY HOUSE AND LOST THEIR MINDS AT THESE PEOPLE WALKING INTO MY BLACK HOUSEHOLD

MY SON AND HIS THEN WIFE TO BE AND DAUGHTER, I BELIEVE, TAKEN ON THAT FATEFUL DAY, APRIL 19TH, they claim to have been JUST watching, living in my house **MONTH(S)**! R E A L L Y????

God set them up real good! Even the judges! Because now the world CAN see how utterly beyond broken the USA justice system is. I went all the way to the supreme court to simply ask for a chance at my constitutional right to be heard. All judges who can see this from just the court order!!! The judge can't LIE and take my grandchildren off the lease. The judge can't pretend that there is no court order from the state DENYING the defendants because **THERE IS NO EVIDENCE OF [UO**]. How does the courts get to allow one racist judge make that crap up and pretend it's her right that the state court order doesn't exist in my favor, nor does the lease for that's ALL AN OPINION and I have no rights to be heard regarding an opinion.

So they file a claim to evict me, and I from the very beginning ask the judge to recuse himself as he KNOWS I've never been happy with his service, but He's TRYING TO GET THE GOODS ON ME WITH ALL HIS BEST EFFORTS. He knows that no black person can be that clean, and he told me in the hearing that HIS JOB IS TO SEE IF HE WILL FIND A WAY TO EVICT ME. I thought damn, it seemed he should be neutral to see if he would not need to evict me, but to come out and admit that he's looking for a way to evict me, AND THEN LISTEN TO HIM HELP THE DEFENDANTS WITH QUESTIONS that did find things that my son thought of. The landlords didn't see it, their attorneys didn't see it, but the damned judge exposed that my son was not supposed to pay for an apartment at school. I'm still lost at that because when he returned home on the breaks and for the summer, we would then be violating the lease. In any case, absolutely no way was this judge supposed to be acting as an attorney for landlords who had an attorney against an individual with no attorney, AND I STILL WHOMPED THEIR ASSES! Their attorney walks by with his head down every time I see him since then.

Their claim states nothing but [UO].

6/14/2017 [illegible] SCANNED

27D03-1705-SC-000517

Filed: 5/23/2017 10:49:01 AM
Carolyn Mowery
Clerk
Grant County, Indiana

STATE OF INDIANA)
) SS:
COUNTY OF GRANT)

IN THE GRANT SUPERIOR COURT 3
Courthouse 3rd Floor – 101 E 4th St; Marion IN 46952
CAUSE NO. 27D03-1705-SC-________

RECEIVED
MAY 24 2017
Grant County Sheriff's Office

HUNTER'S RUN APARTMENTS, LP
Plaintiff's Name
717 E. HUNTER'S RUN DR.
Plaintiff's Street Address
MARION, IN 46953
Plaintiff's City, State Zip
765/677-1701
Plaintiff's Phone

MORRIS KELSAY #16764-64
Plaintiff's Attorney
514 South Adams Street
Marion, IN 46953
Telephone: 765/662-3818

Grant county

CASE NO: 27D03-1706-PL-14

SERVICE BY: CERTIFIED ________ SHERIFF X **AGAINST** SERVICE BY: CERTIFIED ________ SHERIFF ________

SANDRA A. BLACK
Defendant's Name
655 E. HUNTER'S RUN DRIVE
Defendant's Street Address
MARION, IN 46953
Defendant's City, State Zip

Defendant's Name
Defendant's Street Address
Defendant's City, State Zip

COMPLAINT FOR POSSESSION OF REAL PROPERTY AND PAST DUE RENT – NOTICE TO THE DEFENDANT(S)

THE ORDER TO SHOW CAUSE HEARING IS SET FOR June 8, 2017 AT 9:15 a.m.

THE HEARING TO DETERMINE IF MONEY IS OWED IS SET FOR July 6, 2017 AT 9:15 a.m.

You have been sued by the Plaintiff named above. The Plaintiff has filed the original of this Complaint with the Court Clerk and kept a copy for the Plaintiff and given the Clerk three (3) complete copies for each Defendant. By signing below, the Plaintiff solemnly affirms under the penalties for perjury that the following statements are true:

Signed by/for the Plaintiff on May 23, 2017. ____________________

If you are signing this Complaint as the Plaintiff's representative, circle the designation that applies to you:
DESIGNATED FULL TIME EMPLOYEE (Ind. Small Claims Rule 8C) ATTORNEY SOLE PROPRIETOR GENERAL PARTNER

1. The Plaintiff is entitled to possession of the following land/home/apt.: 655 E. Hunter's Run Dr., Marion, IN because the Plaintiff owns said real estate
2. Violation of Lease Agreement – allowing unauthorized occupants to live at apartment.
3. The estimated value of the property listed in this Complaint is $20,000.00.
4. The estimated rental value of the property listed in this Complaint is $604.00 per month.
5. Grant Superior Court 3 ("the Court") is located on the 3rd floor of the Grant County Courthouse at 101 E 4th St; Marion IN 46952-4058; Phone 765.668.8123. Two hearing dates have been set. They are listed above.

   The 1st hearing is for the Plaintiff and you to present evidence to the Judge concerning whether you should be ordered to turn over possession of the real estate to the Plaintiff before the case is completed. The 1st hearing cannot be sooner than 5 days after you are served with a copy of this Complaint.

   The 2nd hearing is for the Plaintiff and you to present evidence concerning whether you owe the Plaintiff money. If so a judgment for that amount will be entered against you. At this time the Plaintiff can't say exactly how much you will owe. The Plaintiff must first get possession of the real estate. At this time the Plaintiff claims you owe:

   $ -0- for back rent plus damages and attorney fees.

After I filed a counterclaim, their attorney advised them that they needed more against me. So they return with an addendum claim of reckless driving and resident responsibilities (A LIE they admitted to and were **admonished in the court order for misleading** the court). They HAD LIED THAT I WASN'T PICKING UP MY PET MESS, and my neighbors advocated for me that it was a lie. The landlords took the lie back and of course… I know what they're doing, so I make them DOCUMENT IT! Erika (EH) called Friedrichsen (NF) for permission. EH told me that she couldn't do it right away. So she tells NF, in my opinion, hey, she's (Sandra) highly documented with neighbors calling in that she doesn't leave the pet mess. So NF tells EH to go ahead and document our mistake. So Erika takes my copy of the LIE and writes… **PLEASE DISREGARD… REMOVED FROM FILE**.

So Naomi, KNOWINGLY testifies under oath to the lie that I was leaving poop and brings in a liar tenant, Stormy (Alicia) Inman, who says that I was leaving the dog poop and pretending to bend over to pick up poop, but putting something that looked like my cell phone in the bag instead of the poop. **SEE THIS WHITE PRIVILEGE???** Let us do it! Let blacks LIE and bring witnesses in to LIE to and witnesses that are BAD LIARS TOO. The only reason it was mentioned was to save his golfing partner (their lawyer) from submitting all of their LIES. I am fighting against lawyers, corporations, judges AND ABOSLUTELY NO JUSTICE. The judge lied on me that I was racist and refused to substantiate it. He's judge, it's his right to fabricate anything he wants. THIS IS WHAT THEY DO! The judge said I was racist for having a sign about my mother being enslaved and for saying that the landlords were dogging me because the bitch thinks I'm an uppity nigger. This makes me a racist. I'm all over social media. I NEVER say anything against white people other than THOSE WHO ACT LIKE MY LANDLORDS, thank GOD, they are a minority!!! There's a ton on FB, some on twitter, YouTube, and Tik Tok. I never express hate towards white people because I know my history and I understand people, why hate the whole barrel of apples because of those rotten ones in the batch. I sure wish people could see me the exact same way, if not, it's their problem. Every group of people have shit people among them that's life. We should take people according to the way they present themselves, PERIOD!

AND GUYS!!! It was a SIGHT that every victimized person cherishes, **VINDICATION** by the enemy themselves. You should have seen JAWS DROP when I entered my counter COPY of the violation where **THEY ADMIT IT NEVER HAPPENED**. This was not misleading, as the judge claims this was utter perjury, enticing a tenant to lie to cover their tracks of my story and the tenant's story that I always pick up my dog's poo. Had this been a black landlord against poor old white grandma, he would have been arrested for perjury. I see it all the time where black fairly decent landlords are not allowed to pass HUD requirements, but white landlords just like my last one is given a pass and HUD sent out a black inspector (I NEVER SAW A BLACK INSPECTOR BEFORE) to pass a filthy STANK, flea, mice, animal infested unfinished life threatening house that I couldn't move into though all my things were packed and ready to move in. We superficially cleaned it for my things to move in, and they would fix and repair the many issues, I THOUGHT.

Note that the defendants request possession and any rent due at the time I move out. In Federal Court Order 28, the magistrate from the very beginning SCOURED THE state docket looking for ALL WORDS she could find and LIE to place the defendants in the right and me in the wrong. She will quote that the second complaint mentioned past due rent for what??? I have NEVER been late and never missed paying rent. I can't lie here! Why are ALL judges seeking out ways and LIES to help whites, but won't even mention my evidence that no UO exist according to the court order?

DEFENDANTS' AMENDED CLAIM:

OF INDIANA)
) SS:
UNTY OF GRANT)

IN THE GRANT SUPERIOR COURT 3
Courthouse 3rd Floor – 101 E 4th St; Marion IN 46952
CAUSE NO. 27D03-1705-SC-517 AMENDED

Filed: 6/2/2017 11:25:41 AM
Warren Haas
Judge, Superior Court 3
Grant County, Indiana

HUNTER'S RUN APARTMENTS, LP
Plaintiff's Name
717 E. HUNTER'S RUN DR.
Plaintiff's Street Address
MARION, IN 46953
Plaintiff's City, State Zip
765/677-1701
Plaintiff's Phone

MORRIS KELSAY #16764-64
Plaintiff's Attorney
514 South Adams Street
Marion, IN 46953
Telephone: 765/662-3816

RECEIVED
JUN 06 2017
Grant County Sheriff's Office

SERVICE BY: CERTIFIED ______ SHERIFF X AGAINST SERVICE BY: CERTIFIED ______ SHERIFF ______

SANDRA A. BLACK
Defendant's Name
655 E. HUNTER'S RUN DRIVE
Defendant's Street Address
MARION, IN 46953
Defendant's City, State Zip

Defendant's Name

Defendant's Street Address

Defendant's City, State Zip

COMPLAINT FOR POSSESSION OF REAL PROPERTY AND PAST DUE RENT – NOTICE TO THE DEFENDANT(S)

THE ORDER TO SHOW CAUSE HEARING IS SET FOR June 8, 2017 AT 11:00 a.m.

THE HEARING TO DETERMINE IF MONEY IS OWED IS SET FOR July 6, 2017 AT 9:15 a.m.

You have been sued by the Plaintiff named above. The Plaintiff has filed the original of this Complaint with the Court Clerk and kept a copy for the Plaintiff and given the Clerk three (3) complete copies for each Defendant. By signing below, the Plaintiff solemnly affirms under the penalties for perjury that the following statements are true:

Signed by/for the Plaintiff on June 2, 2017 [signature]

If you are signing this Complaint as the Plaintiff's representative, circle the designation that applies to you:

DESIGNATED FULL TIME EMPLOYEE (Ind. Small Claims Rule 8C) ATTORNEY SOLE PROPRIETOR GENERAL PARTNER

1. The Plaintiff is entitled to possession of the following land/home/apt.: 655 E. Hunter's Run Dr., Marion, IN because the Plaintiff owns said real estate.
2. Violation of Lease Agreement – allowing unauthorized occupants to live at apartment. Violation of Lease – paragraph 32, Automobiles and Parking Areas; and Resident Responsibilities.
3. The estimated value of the property listed in this Complaint is $20,000.00.
4. The estimated rental value of the property listed in this Complaint is $604.00 per month.
5. Grant Superior Court 3 ("the Court") is located on the 3rd floor of the Grant County Courthouse at 101 E 4th St, Marion IN 46952-4058; Phone 765.668.8123. Two hearing dates have been set. They are listed above.

The 1st hearing is for the Plaintiff and you to present evidence to the Judge concerning whether you should be ordered to turn over possession of the real estate to the Plaintiff before the case is completed. The 1st hearing cannot be sooner than 5 days after you are served with a copy of this Complaint.

The 2nd hearing is for the Plaintiff and you to present evidence concerning whether you owe the Plaintiff money. If so a judgment for that amount will be entered against you. At this time the Plaintiff can't say exactly how much you will owe. The Plaintiff must first get possession of the real estate. At this time the Plaintiff claims you owe: $ -0- for back rent plus damages and attorney fees.

Here we go. The hearing was set for June 8, 2017. Testimony was exchanged beginning with Hunters Run. NF began with all sorts of lies. I challenge you, my readers. HOW MANY LIES CAN YOU FIND? The greatest lies that are impossible to mistake are where Naomi claims to have seen UO HERSELF living in my home for a period of time. When I got the chance to cross-examine about that, I asked her to give a description of the people she saw. Their lawyer yelled, "Objection," "objection," and I came back with, " But your honor, she had testified that she had personally seen these people walking into my home. She must be able to give some details of what they looked like. Both Naomi and the judge seem to take a cue from the attorney's frantic call out of objection, so the judge LEAD the witness NF with a question. "But ma'am, you don't mean that you saw them firsthand, but that the people you brought will testify about that," NF said YES. However, she stated that she saw the people firsthand both under oath in court and in her 30-day vacate notice, but she was struggling to describe them. SHE KNEW the people she saw couldn't have been there before. I had included the MONROE COUNTY ORDER in my counterclaim as evidence that the people she saw walk in were COURT ORDERED into my house. When she started out with all the lies, she apparently clearly had no clue that I would cross-examine and expose her, or, being a KAREN, she may have felt it was her right that any lie she spoke would become the truth. I'll let you be the judge.

I continued then to hem her up in the fact that she wrote in her 30-day vacate notice that there were SEVERAL PEOPLE, how many did you see? She originally said in court under oath that there was a plural amount, but then said it was just my daughter. For the very first time EVER, she claims the UO PLURAL people was just my daughter and when I seek to understand how she goes from several to one, SHE REPLIES, "I ONLY NEED ONE" In other words the idiot is not understanding that she's proving it a fact that she is committing perjury because there is no way humanly possible to see several people, BUT IT WAS ONLY ONE! Her sick Karen-type mind was so obsessed with taking me out that her only thought was what words to say that would take me out. She never gave a damn about truth, which was, by law, supposed to be a part of this proceeding. AS MATTER OF FACT, NONE OF THE PEOPLE INVOLVED IN THIS CASE from the State to the Federal Court, attorneys, corporations, judges ALL deeply believed that the number one objective was LIE at all cost no matter how badly the lie was because the worldwide reality is that a black grandma is less than human with zero RIGHTS and no evidence, no testimony, no MEASURE OF RIGHTNESS will ever be expected of these people AND THE ENTIRE WORLD will turn their backs and say… AMEN. If I believed this to be true, I wouldn't be wasting my time writing this book. I am hoping that the entire world will wake up to the destruction of WHITE SUPREMACY against all mankind to the right of the pursuit of happiness. To the right of mankind to eat, drink, and be merry (you can only do this safely, in your home, healthy, educated, and free from any fear, so whatever that your needs might not be taken care of. How many crimes, fights, or arguments over AIR have you witnessed? Today there's no way to HOARD air and force us to act THE FOOL for it. WHY NOT, try my experiment? A GENUINE society for and by the people? A society based off of HUMAN NATURE and not animal nature as the supreme way of life. How about that? We're a very sick world in this world we live in. We accept the harsh reality of billions of people on earth as okay TO HAVE NEXT TO NOTHING SO THE FEW CAN HOARD WEALTH and POWER is beyond barbaric, lunacy, IT'S MONSTRUOUS!

HERE'S the court order:

6/14/2017 1:24 PM SCANNED

STATE OF INDIANA)
) SS:
COUNTY OF GRANT)

IN THE GRANT SUPERIOR COURT 3
[Originally Case No. 27D03-1705-SC-000517]
CASE NO. 27D03-1706-PL-000014

HUNTER'S RUN APARTMENTS LP, the Plaintiff

v.

SANDRA A. BLACK, the Defendant

FILED

JUN 1 4 2017

Carolyn J. Mowery
CLERK GSC 3

Denial of Motion for Preliminary Order of Possession

The Court denies the Rule to Show Cause sought by the Plaintiff, Hunter's Run Apartments LP ("Landlord"), against the Defendant, Sandra A. Black ("Tenant"). Based upon the evidence presented at the June 8, 2017, preliminary hearing, the Court enters this preliminary finding that there is a reasonable probability Tenant is entitled to the continued possession, use and enjoyment of her apartment, which is known as 655 E Hunter's Run Dr; Marion IN 46953 ("the Apartment"). [See Ind. Code § 32-30-3-5.] The Court makes the following additional preliminary findings to assist Landlord and Tenant ("the Parties"):

1. On May 23, 2017, Landlord filed its Complaint for Possession of Real Property and Past Due Rent ("the Original Complaint") as a small claims proceeding in Case No. 27D03-1705-SC-000517 ("the Small Claims Case"). Landlord alleged it was entitled to possession of the Apartment for the following reason:

   2. Violation of Lease Agreement – allowing unauthorized occupants to live at apartment.

   No other basis for the eviction proceeding was alleged.

2. On May 31, 2017, Tenant filed her Request for Recusal, which was denied on June 1, 2017. In doing so the Court relies upon the Indiana Commission on Judicial Qualifications' Advisory Opinion #3-07, which dealt with the issue of:

   > whether a judge should disqualify from a case involving a litigant who files a disciplinary complaint or a lawsuit against the judge or who publicly criticizes or attacks the judge through fliers, websites, blogs, or other written material.

   The Court is aware that Tenant has been and remains very unhappy with decisions the Court made in the past concerning Tenant's mother. Tenant has exercised her 1st Amendment right to publically criticize the Judge. Because the Court has no actual bias against Tenant and the Court does not believe a factual basis exists for a conclusion that the Court acted inappropriately in other matters involving Tenant, recusal in this case would be improper. Quoting from Advisory Opinion #3-07:

June 14, 2017, Revision — Page 1 of 8 — hunters run and black preliminary order

> (T)he issue is whether an objective person, knowledgeable of all the circumstances, would have a reasonable basis for doubting the judge's impartiality. Unless disqualification is required, Canon 3B(1) of the Code of Judicial Conduct requires a judge to hear and decide all assigned cases.

Neither Tenant nor Landlord filed for a change of venue from the judge pursuant to Ind. Trial Rule 76(B).

3. On May 31, 2017, Tenant also filed her Request for Trial by Jury. She was served on May 25, 2017, with her copy of the Original Complaint, so her request was filed in a timely manner. On June 1, 2017, the Court entered the following Chronological Case Summary ("CCS") entry:

> (Tenant) has timely filed her demand for trial by jury. Ind. Small Claims Rule 4(C) provides: "Request for Jury Trial. . . . (A) defendant may request a jury trial by submitting a written request to the court within ten (10) days after receipt of the notice of claim. No statement of facts supporting the request or verification of the request is required. The party requesting a jury trial shall pay the clerk the additional amount required by statute to transfer the claim to the plenary docket . . . . Once a jury trial request has been granted, it may not be withdrawn without the consent of the other party or parties." The Sheriff's return of service indicates (Tenant) was served with the notice of claim on May 25, 2017. (Tenant) has 10 days from that date to pay the additional fee to transfer the case to the plenary docket. If she fails to do so, her request for trial by jury will be denied.

Tenant paid the $70 fee and the case was transferred to the Court's plenary docket and assigned Case No. 27D03-1706-PL-000014 on June 5, 2017. This means the Parties must comply with the Indiana Rules of Trial Procedure and will no longer be permitted to proceed under Ind. Small Claims Rule 8(A), which states:

> Procedure. The trial shall be informal, with the sole objective of dispensing speedy justice between the parties according to the rules of substantive law, and shall not be bound by the statutory provisions or rules of practice, procedure, pleadings or evidence except provisions relating to privileged communications and offers of compromise.

Because this case is now on the Court's plenary docket, the trial will be formal. It will be done according to statutory provisions and the Ind. Trial Rules. The Parties must properly plead their case(s) and fully comply with the Ind. Evidence Rules.

4. The June 1, 2017 CCS entry also included the following:

> The jury trial demand does not divest the Court of the jurisdiction to enter a preliminary order of possession, if (Landlord) presents facts supporting such an order. Therefore the hearing set for Thursday, June 8, 2017, at 9:15 a.m. will be held.

The Court, not a jury, is to hear and decide matters involving requests for pre-judgment orders of possession. *Bishop v. Hous. Aut. of S. Bend*, 920 N.E.2d 772 (Ind. Ct. App. 2010) dealt with this issue saying:

> We read the Indiana ejection statute to preserve Bishop's right to a jury trial – on the ultimate outcome, i.e., the merits of HASB's claim that it is entitled to possession based upon her breach of an express term of the lease. . . . .
>
> Similarly, Indiana's ejectment statute provides for a pre-judgment possession hearing to allow the defendant to controvert plaintiff's affidavit "or to show cause why the judge should not remove the tenant from the property and put the plaintiff in possession." I.C. § 32-30-3-2; see also *Cunningham v. Georgetown Homes, Inc.*, 708 N.E.2d 623, 627 (Ind. Ct. App. 1999). The statutory hearing manifests the inherent power of trial courts to intercede at an early stage – to make a preliminary decision before what could thereafter be a lengthy judicial process. Before issuance of a preliminary decision, the defendant/tenant is given the express opportunity to dispute the landlord's claim for immediate possession. Moreover, this preliminary possession decision triggers the requirement that the plaintiff/landlord file "a surety . . . in an amount sufficient to assure the payment of any damages the defendant may suffer if the court wrongfully ordered" preliminary possession to the landlord. I.C. § 32-30-3-6. The preliminary possession decision is also subject to further proceedings to reach an ultimate determination – the "final judgment" that "supersedes" the "prejudgment order for possession." I.C. § 32-30-3-12.
>
> The Indiana statute merely allows the trial court to make a preliminary decision as to the right to immediate possession of the property. It preserves Bishop's right to a trial by jury on the ultimate issue as to whether she should be ejected from the property. We find that there is no constitutional right to a jury trial at the preliminary possession hearing in an ejectment proceeding. Therefore, Bishop has failed [*780] to persuade us that the ejectment statute violated her right to a jury trial pursuant to the Indiana constitution. *Wallace*, 905 N.E.2d at 378.

Even though the Court has entered this preliminary decision that Tenant is entitled to remain in possession of the Apartment, the jury is free to conclude that Tenant must give up possession of the Apartment when it makes the ultimate decision in this case.

5. On May 31, 2017, Tenant also filed her Response to Complaint and Counterclaim ("the First Answer and Counterclaim"). On June 1, 2017, by CCS entry the Court struck Tenant's First Answer and Counterclaim saying:

> (Tenant's) May 31, 2017, Response to Complaint and Counterclaim does not comply with the requirements that all pleadings be clear and concise. It is stricken from this case. (Tenant) is also granted until June 8, 2017, to file an

amended pleading that complies with the rules so that she might proceed on her counterclaim.

See also *Zavodnik v. Irene Harper*, 17 N.E.3d 259 (Ind. 2014).

At the June 8, 2017, preliminary hearing, the Court provided the parties with portions of T.R. 8, including the requirement that a pleading must contain, "(A) (1) a short and plain statement of the claim showing that the pleader is entitled to relief" and "(E)(1) (e)ach averment of a pleading shall be simple, concise, and direct".

Even though the First Answer and Counterclaim was stricken, the Court considers it to be a general denial of the allegations made by Landlord.

6. On June 2, 2017, Landlord filed its Amended Complaint for Possession of Real Property and Past Due Rent ("the Amended Complaint"). It differed from the Original Complaint by increasing the alleged violations of the lease to be:

> (A)llowing unauthorized occupants to live at apartment. Violation of Lease – paragraph 32, Automobiles and Parking Areas; and Resident Responsibilities.

7. On June 7, 2017, Tenant filed her Response to Amended Complaint.

8. The following are only preliminary findings. The jury may find otherwise.

   A. "The 'Section 42' Lease Agreement" ("the Lease") is between Tenant and her son, Kemuel Shem ("Mr. Shem"), and Landlord. It provides that Tenant may occupy the Apartment along with Mr. Shem and with Tenant's grandchildren, Chrisdeon Ogunbuyide, Victoria Goree and Christian Goree. Landlord did not prove that Tenant's adult daughter and Mr. Shem's wife, Jaycee Shem, were also occupying the Apartment in violation of the Lease. This is a 3 bedroom apartment, which may have no more than 6 people living in it. The Court finds that Landlord did not prove that other persons occupied the Apartment than were permitted by Paragraph 4 and 5 of the Lease.

   The Court notes that Mr. Shem has been living in Bloomington, where he works and is attending Indiana University off and on. It is now his home. His wife is from Bloomington and testified that so far this year she and Mr. Shem only spent about 3 or 4 overnights at the Apartment. Mr. Shem testified that someone from Section 8 told him that he only needed to stay overnight 10 nights per year at the Apartment to be considered an occupant of the apartment. The Court finds that this is not correct. Mr. Shem is not an occupant of the Apartment. If he were, he had a duty to report his Bloomington income, which he has not. The Court finds that Mr. Shem and/or Tenant had a duty to properly notify Landlord that Mr. Shem was not living in the Apartment, but neither did so. The Lease requires Tenant to recertify the financial information and occupancy at least annually. Landlord's Exhibit 11 shows this was last done on August 11, 2016, for the recertification due on November 23, 2016. Landlord has the right to require more frequent recertifications, but has not done so in this case. Landlord's Exhibit 9 is the Rules and Regulations Handbook ("the Handbook"), which includes a provision requiring Tenant to "notify (Landlord) of any changes in the number of residents in the household or addition of pets. Failure to do so will be considered a lease violation." It is unclear how the provisions in the Handbook affect the annual recertification requirement of the Lease. The Court notes that Paragraph 6 of the Lease indicates that Mr. Shem will likely have his Lease with Landlord terminated on or about November 23, 2017, at the latest.

B. Tenant is a strong willed person. She keeps the Apartment clean and requires her family members and guests to follow her rules. Tenant is a black person and is very vocal when she is not treated as she believes she should be. When white people treat her differently than she believes is appropriate, she often attributes this to racism. The Court finds no evidence of racism directed toward Tenant by Landlord nor by Landlord's staff members, but does find evidence of racism by Tenant directed toward Landlord and Landlord's staff members. However, the Court notes the Tenant's and Mr. Shem's racist Facebook posts shown in Landlord's Exhibit 10 were made after Landlord filed suit against Tenant, which Tenant believed was racially motivated. She was responding, inappropriately, to Landlord's efforts to evict her.

C. Tenant placed a sign in one of her windows that was visible to others in Hunters Run that advertized Tenant's belief that her mother was being treated as a slave. On February 22, 2016, Landlord issued Landlord's Exhibit 4, which was a written, "potential lease violation" notice to Tenant directing her to remove the sign, which clearly violated Paragraph 20 of the Lease. It also did not comply with the directive in the Handbook, "to encourage a positive environment for (residents) and their neighbors". The sign wasn't removed until shortly after Landlord issued Landlord's Exhibit 4 on March 7, 2016.

Tenant acknowledged that she was aware that no signs could be posted, but did so anyway. What she posted is no different than someone displaying a sign advertising or in support of the Ku Klux Klan. Both are prohibited by Paragraph 20 of the Lease and by the Handbook.

Landlord could have taken steps to evict tenant when the sign was posted, but did not do so until the Amended Complaint was filed, more than a year after the violation was committed. The Court finds that the sign violation is too remote in time to be relevant in an action to evict Tenant now.

D. Landlord's property manager, Naomi Friedricksen ("the Property Manager"), has a Facebook account and testified that she uses it to post information multiple times a day about Hunters Run activities and vacancies. It is widely known that her personal Facebook account is used for business purposes. Beginning June 27, 2017, Tenant, using the pseudonym "Ezzrath Baht Shem", "tagged" the Property Manager's Facebook account and began posting hateful comments that violated the

Even so bad that the guy from the air-conditioning vendor said that the office people are all against me because I am a trouble maker.

E. Landlord's Exhibit 2 is a letter dated November 30, 2015, claiming Tenant had an "aggressive breed" dog in the Apartment. Tenant was given 30 days to vacate the Apartment or remove the dog from the Apartment or provide proof that the dog was not an aggressive breed.

When Tenant first rented the Apartment, Landlord was aware that she had a dog that weighed more than 50 pounds. Since then Landlord has indicated that pets may not exceed 25 pounds. Since Landlord rented the Apartment to Tenant with knowledge of the size of the dog, Landlord may not use that as a basis to evict tenant. No evidence was offered to prove the dog was an aggressive breed.

F. Landlord's Exhibit 6 is a "FINAL WARNING" letter to Tenant, saying:

> It has been reported to us by surrounding neighbors that you are allowing your dog to relieve itself on the Hunter's Run sidewalk and landscaping areas and not cleaning up after it.

Landlord submitted this exhibit even though Tenant's Exhibit E is a copy of the same letter with the following handwritten note by Erika Holliday ("Assistant Property Manager"):

> please disregard. removed from file. Erika Holliday

Landlord's attorney did not offer any explanation as to why Landlord's Exhibit 2 was offered. Landlord's Exhibit 2 is misleading. The Court finds that Landlord's attorney was candid with the Court when he offered Landlord's Exhibit 2, because there is no evidence that he was aware of the handwritten note. It is entirely possible that he was not given a copy of Landlord's Exhibit 2 with the note from the Assistant Property Manager.

G. Landlord's Exhibit 8 is another written "Lease Violation–unauthorized occupants–30 day notice to vacate". As mentioned above, Landlord failed to prove that unauthorized permanent occupants were staying at the Apartment. The letter also claimed that the Property Manager saw a burgundy colored Camero driving recklessly in and out of the parking lot. Tenant was required to vacate the Apartment by May 20, 2017, at 4:00 p.m. Since Landlord did not enforce the 30 day notice and did not prove unauthorized permanent occupants were at the Apartment, the reckless driving complaint is too remote in time to be used in this preliminary eviction case.

H. Landlord's Exhibit 5 was dated May 26, 2016, and Landlord's Exhibit 7 was dated December 5, 2016. Both dealt with damaged blinds. Tenant acknowledged that her grandchildren or dog caused damage to the blinds and repaired or replaced them.

6/14/2017 1:21 PM SCANNED

USDC IN/ND case 1:19-cv-00307-WCL-SLC document 15-4 filed 10/30/19 page 9 of 9

This is a common maintenance issue for this and other apartment complexes and is not a basis to evict Tenant.

I. During the summer of 2016 Tenant's air conditioning unit did not work properly and was not promptly repaired. The Handbook indicates it is Landlord's responsibility to maintain the Apartment's HVAC unit and encourages tenants to call the 24-hour maintenance emergency number if the A/C system fails during harsh seasons. Tenant reported that her A/C until wasn't working properly. Landlord reported that it is difficult to repair Hunters Run HVAC units, which are 16 years old. Tenant's system had a bad computer board and it took time to get one. When one arrived, it too was faulty. It took approximately 2 weeks to make the A/C system work, but the thermostat did not work and it took about 2 months to fix that. During this time the A/C system had to be manually turned on and off, so Tenant complained that the temperature was freezing or too hot.

Landlord was dealing with other malfunctioning units and performed triage. In the summer heat some apartments had no A/C. They were given priority over Tenant's apartment, which had a manually controlled A/C system. Tenant became more and more frustrated with this situation. The Parties' relationship soured considerably. Tenant went so far as to go to the office to personally serve the Assistant Property Manager with documents and have her grandson record the video and sound on a smartphone. The Assistant Property Manager felt threatened and said she would not permit herself to be recorded and locked herself in her office. Tenant remained outside the inner office and spoke loudly, firmly, but without any profanity to explain what she was delivering to Landlord.

J. Tenant is perceived by Landlord to be a problem tenant. Tenant can be difficult to work with, but we have the right to have different political beliefs and views. She may exercise her 1st Amendment rights to speak out against the injustices she perceives, including speaking out against the undersigned. So long as her conduct is not criminal or a material violation of the Lease, she is entitled to remain in her Apartment. The Court is unsure what might constitute a material violation, but suggests that Tenant would be wise not to post or have posts made like those shown in Paragraph 8.D. about Landlord and/or Landlord's employees.

K. An unused truck was parked outside the Apartment. It was in violation of the Handbook. However, Landlord typically would "tag" the vehicle and have it towed, if the tenant did not do so. Landlord did neither and may not use this to evict Tenant.

The Court denies Landlord's request for a prejudgment order of possession. At this point, no proper counterclaim has been filed. If neither Party files a pleading requesting further Court action, this case may be dismissed on or after August 18, 2017, pursuant to T.R. 41(E).

Signed on June 14, 2017, by:

Warren Haas, Judge of Grant Superior Court 3

June 14, 2017, Revision   Page 8 of 8   hunters run and black preliminary order

Now, all I ask of my readers. Can you empathize that this order is a judge (Haas) WHO MADE HIS FINAL WORK all about my life. You guys, this man LIED that my placement was joint, not sole placement of my grandson, just because DCS and CASA lied. I set up shared visitation, and

HE KNEW IT, my attorney Douglas Martz at the time KNEW IT! But Haas LIED and changed the order to fit THEIR LIE. He gave me custody of my grandchildren, saying how wonderful a grandmother I am. He thought he'd get a thank you. HELL NA!!! He made me out to be a monster too sick to be considered to help my mother. Now I'm a great person and she lived nearly a decade in pure hell, there's nothing he can do for a thank you from me but get the HELL OUT OF MY FACE and quit forcing me under his litigation. If there was a way he could look good and destroy me, he would have made our lives hell. HIS POWER, Let's clarify, 1. I had petitioned the court for guardianship of mom and was found to be unfit, "a monster the judge wouldn't care if I never saw my mom again." Then, 2. I petitioned for my 3 grandchildren, I saw that my daughter would lose custody soon. The same judge ruled that I was the wonderful person to care for my grandchildren all alone. Then 3. I filed for guardianship of my son and was denied because I would help him with his criminal case. Then 4. I filed for guardianship of my last born grandson and intervener of the CHINS CASE ran by Haas because Kenworthy quickly recused off the case because I forced her off mom's case.

Haas's court is the only court in Marion to handle guardianship pro se, and my daughter was DEEP into addiction, about to give birth. So I had no choice other than to move the court and take my chance that he wouldn't be utterly satanic to deny me without anyone to contest the guardianship and considering my years of history of the children living in my household. Had he gotten hold of my grandchildren after DCS snatched them up, there is no telling what would have happened to my grandchildren. He retired and CAME BACK just to run mom's final closing of her guardianship as I sat in that court, among nothing but people who destroyed my mother's life. I listened to my brother complaining about not getting all the money, the guardian justifying giving my mother's car away instead of to my brother, as though yes, he's a monster in his behavior, but he's OURS, and mom would have preferred her car to remain with the family. I understood that she knew he was evil and that my daughter first wanted to buy it, but she gave OUR family resource away without talking to me because I would rather my daughter go without before an outsider gets mom's car for next to nothing. Then there's the Judge who sold my mother into hell, and I sat there and listened to them all and spoke this before the court. I was shocked that Haas stated that Ms. Black was the closest to the truth. BUT DAMN, you just tried to trap me in hell with my baby grandson, you did trap me in hell for watching my mom trapped in hell. Why would I thank you for being able to speak the truth once in a while? Screw you! Get the hell out of destroying my family any way possible you can FIND to do so! Don't forget, YOU SPOKE IT, I GOT TO SEE IF I'LL FIND A WAY TO EVICT YOU. AND YOU WENT TO WORK HARD SEEKING IT OUT TOO!!! Dirty bastard. Lying that you couldn't understand my counterclaim DISMISSING MY DEFENSE. WTF! That shyster Morris Kelsay understood that his clients were LIARS and were coming to court to perjury themselves, but you were going to give them the case best buddy, but the EVIDENCE was FAR too much that they were lying about their claim! They were so busted out that even your lying ass, HAAS couldn't help your buddy Kelsey like you had PLANNED; and slipped and told on yourself! IT WAS ALL A SETUP, but GOD had the GREATER SETUP FOR YOUR ASSES! Just think, if you knew it had went this far **I WOULD HAVE LOST** and been evicted with a LIE! Ya just knew you had already done too much DIRT to our family with strong evidence proving it a FACT the landlords and Kelsey AND I just might have WON with all the evidence and your refusal to recuse. All it would take is ONE honest judge and you'd be FRIED, so you let me by with the TRUTH. AND added lies that I was racist.

Here's a **partial** inclusion of the SWORN TESTIMONY of NF: I challenge you to read her SWORN OATH testimony and count the numerous conflicting statements she gives. Look at how she's allowed to enter evidence that I object to as FALSE, even though she has no evidence that it took place. She will FABRICATE two false "friendly reminder" violations that NEVER EXISTED because blacks were allowed those. I only received a violation of broken blinds, but because nobody evicts a good-standing tenant without one genuine cause, she made those violations up for court. Another way you can tell they don't exist is the FACT she never refers to them existing in the so-called second violation of broken blinds. If they had actually given me friendly reminders, why wouldn't they write this is your SECOND REMINDER of broken blinds? The reason there was NO "FRIENDLY REMINDERS" is because they are ONLY for white tenants. I never knew they existed until court where she fabricated it for that very day and never gave me a friendly warning. I OBJECTED IMMEDIATELY IN COURT FROM THE VERY BEGINNING.

YO YO YO, This means I actually had **ZERO VIOLATIONS!** I was supposed to get a friendly reminder for the blinds and my mom's sign in the window, and NOW THAT I KNOW friendly reminders exist. I was evicted with zero violations, and this is why white FEDERAL JUDGES LOST THEIR MINDS AND USED JIM CROW AGAINST ME. Meaning you are black, too much evidence against whites, trying to litigate the END

OF WHITE SUPREMACY with EMBEDDED LAW... <u>**you are by law in the wrong for being black against whites, JIM CROW.**</u>

IN THE

GRANT SUPERIOR COURT NO. 3

NO. 27D03-1706-PL-14

HUNTERS RUN APARTMENTS LIMITED PARTNERSHIP

Vs

SANDRA BLACK

The Honorable Warren Haas
Judge

NOTICE OF PARTIAL FILING TRANSCRIPT ON NAOMI FRIEDRICHSON

Crystal G Foreman, the Court Reporter of Grant Superior Court No. 3, hereby notifies Sandra Black, that the Transcript requested for the above witness in this cause has been prepared and certified and is partially completed. This 14th day of August, 2017.

Crystal Foreman
Court Reporter, Grant Superior
Court No. 3

DIRECT EXAMINATION -NAOMI FRIEDRICHSON

A. Hunters Run Apartments

Q. And what capacity

A. Im the Senior Community Manager

Q. Are you familiar with the landlord tenant agreement between Hunters Run Apartments and Ms. Black

A. Yes

Q. And your asking for possession of that rental unit correct

A. Yes

Q. And can you tell me in your own words why you are asking for that possession

A. Yes, umm over the coarse of the last several months uh it was reported to me by my assistant and I also witness it as well that there has been additional people and potential occupants in Ms. Blacks apartment. Umm her lease and the several addendums she has signed clearly states she cant have anyone else over the age of 18 that occupies the unit as more then a short times as a visitor.

X, = Perjury

Q. And that lease is attached to original notice of claim Judge

A. I brought this to Marion Housing Authority early on in April and spoke with Amy Porter about while I was there doing another lease signing um told her we were going to be watching for it. A Couple weeks after that um Ericka my assistant from Hunters Run had contacted me and said she was pretty sure that somebody else has been there and that there was another vehicle that was there regularly we did some investigating and found the it was potentially an unauthorized occupant with that being said we reviewed the file and found she has several lease violations over the course of the time that she lived there. Umm Ms Black moved in the end of 2015 and since she has been there we have more then 3 lease violation and typically we do 3 violations and then we terminate the agreement. We have allowed her further more than that. Ummm

Q. Ok have you gave her notice of these violations

A. I have

Q. Why don=t we go through those and let me stop for a moment the lease was attached to the notice of claim and I know thats ok in small claims but we would like to enter it as a exhibit now

Judge: Do you have any objection to me taking notice of the lease that was submitted with the Complaint. Ill show you what Im talking about. This document its pretty small print would you show her(inaudible do to Ms Black talking over Judge)

Sandra Black: oh that's what you want the one that was submitted with the Complaint and you want to put it as a Exhibit

Judge: yes do you object to me considering this

A. No I don't object

Judge: ok and by the way I read this last night because we don't usually have files this thick umm the initial occupancy that I read was I was looking at the reasons for the vacation or eviction. The people that were allowed to stay there were, Sandra Black, and I may say names badly im sorry. Uh Kamuel Shem, Chrisdeon Odunbuyide,Victoria Goree and Christian Goree.

So we have five (5) people that were in the original lease that's what I saw originally.

Sandra Black: yes

Judge: ok

Judge: And I am taking judicial notice of that

Morris Kelsay begins again:

Q. And what is the first notice that you were going present that you served on her. I doesn't have to be uh in order but in order of importance or some sort of order.

A. The initial lease violation was that we believed she has an aggressive breed dog we uh that was given to her November 30, 2015.

Q. Ok im going to ask you to stop.

Morris Kelsay is handing out an copy of violation to Ms. Black and Judge.

Judge: And your also familiar with the Small Claims process this isnt small claims anymore

Morris Kelsay: May I ask that be entered as a exhibit

Judge: and I=d be willing to bet you haven't pre-marked anything have you Mr. Kelsay?

Mr. Kelsay: sighs

Judge: What would you like to start marking your exhibits then and tell me what it is your going to give me? Again if we were in small claims court these aren't things that would matter, so this is being handed to me as Plaintiff's 2 because we are treating the lease as Plaintiff's 1 I guess?

Morris Kelsay: Yes, that is what I had in mind.

Judge: That is fine. Ms. Black, did you get a copy of the letter dated November 30, 2015?

Sandra Black: Yes, where I would have to leave if it was a aggressive breed

Judge: Right now is the issue is you got to see what I am seeing

Sandra Black: yeah

Judge: Do you object to me receiving this into evidence

Sandra Black: No

Judge: Ok good so Plaintiff's exhibit 2 is admitted without objection

Morris Kelsay: Ok you were testifying then Naomi go ahead

A: In the lease violation um based on our insurance carrier we are not allow any type of aggressive breed dog. Her dog appears to be a mixed with a pitbull or another aggressive breed dog. Um Sandra did respond to that and provided us with a note or a vet record showing that her dog was not aggressive breed dog.

Q. Did you notice aggression with it though?

A. I have not seen any aggression with it

Q. Alright then lets go on to the next notice um notice that you gave her

Judge: Exhibit 2 so that I understand there was a belief by hunters run that there was a violation they gave a written notice found out they were wrong and thats no longer a reason that she was being evicted.

A: Morris Kelsay: yes, but we thought we should give all the violation all the letters

Judge: But she is not in violation to the lease in any way because of that dog?

Morris Kelsay: No

Q. What's the next letter you got

A: The next one I have Ms. Black had potential lease violation she had a sign in her window and per our lease agreement it states we cant have any signs or advertisements visibly outside of the apartment. Um we actually had to speak with her a second time on this issue because she did not take it down initially and she um she wanted to leave the sign up. It was a advertisement for something she believed in or something she had known and im sorry I don't remember what it was. But um that just another violation that we given her.

Morris Kelasy: ok

Judge: That has been marked as Plaintiff's 3 are you offering this

Morris Kelsay: yes we are offering this

Judge: Do you have any objection to me receiving this evidence

Sandra Black: No, what letters are we in now

Judge: He has marked this as Plaintiff's 3. The leases or the dog is 2 and advertising is 3

Naomi: The next one I have is actually the 2nd violation to that one showing she didn't remove it and this was put on her door March 7, 2016.

Morris Kelsay: We offer that Plaintiff's exhibit 4

Sandra Black: I object to this one being added in

Judge: Right now I haven't heard enough to know what is going on

Morris Kelsay: ok go ahead Naomi

Naomi: This was the notice that was provided to Ms. Black when um the initial request for her to remove advertisement was not met and um we walked the property Ericka or I walk the property as well as maintenance we do it regally the sign was in the window facing out towards the patio which also faces the driveway and its was a large red sign very visibly and inaudible covering part of the window.

Q. How long did you wait before you gave the second notice

A. The second notice was given to her March 7th and the first was February 22.

Morris Kelsay: Okay

Judge: Are you offering this?

Morris Kelsay: Yes

Judge: ok now do you have an objection to this being saved into evidence

Sandra Black: I have an objection

Judge: What is the objection

Sandra Black: and um the objection is that this I mean that this never happened so ytou have to follow protocol I mean this never happen and so this is made up paperwork so Im not objecting anything that she gave to me. This here is made up paperwork that she just wrote up.

Judge: And it may be, because I haven't heard both sides but im going to admit it over your objection.

Sandra Black: mhmm, ok

Judge: And you will be given an opportunity to go through whatever you want to go through to tell me this isn't accurate.

Sandra Black: Ok

Morris Kelsay: Naomi Continue

A: I have a couple more ummm the next one is another reminder she blinds broken thats just

Naomi: absolutely

Kelsay: ok, offer that as Plaintiff's exhibits 8. Ok Naomi there is

Judge: Im sorry I need to check with Ms. Black

Black: no objections

Judge: So plaintiff exhibit 8 is admitted without objection before we get off of this one you mentioned that you reconized the driver as being Ms Blacks son um do you know the name of her son.

Kelsay: it was the one on her lease right

Naomi: yeah

Judge: well there was 5 people on the lease so I don't know who it is

Naomi: Im sorry it was Kemmuel Shem

Judge: thank you. Thank you so exhibit 8 is admitted without objection

Kelsay: you have some more um to testify about these violations and why your asking for possession right?

Naomi: yes

Kelsay: so go ahead and tell us about the process that you went through

Naomi: ok um we provided with Sandra that 30 day notice to vacate ask her to leave the apartment um she was to be out by May 20 I believe or before. She did not vacate at that point um as a matter of fact in between the two she came into our office um was very upset belligerent with Ericka as she was working in the office. I recieved a phone call one afternoon while I was at Hidden Ponds. Ericka was upset she locked herself into our office and because

Sandra refused to leave the community room. She was screaming at Erica I could hear her through the phone, Ericka was very upset so I ended up calling the police while I was on the phone with Ericka with my cell phone. The police did come out and in turn I have my assistant manager who is afraid to work this property by her self. Um Sandra was upset that because we had given her the 30 day notice. This was prior to us filing to us filing for eviction. Um while I was on the phone with Erica I could here her screaming in the background um I could quite make out exactully word for word what she was saying but accusing me of being all kinds of things. Um

Black: Can she say the things

Judge: you are welcome to ask when right now she is just testifing and your welcome to ask her but not yet

Naomi: um The day May 20th was the day she was suppose to be out and that was the day we filed for the Eviction.

Kelsay: Lets go through rules and regulations you mention a violation of disruption that uh also is against the rules and regulations these are referred to in the lease right?

Naomi: yes

Kelsay: And, I apologize there are extras in here. And you don't have to spend a lot of time on that but in addition to the lease they are also notified through these rules and regulations that this sort of behavior would be a violation and not tolerated

Naomi: yes

Kelsay: In addition to the speed limit it also talks about something a little later on the last entry talks about uh

Naomi: to maintain a comfortable, positive and environment management does not tolerate disorderly conduct abusive language or acts of violence or illegal drugs or controlled substance activity is also not permitted.

Kelsay: And your not accusing her of drugs but you are the abusive language and um disruption

Naomi: yes. On serval occasions Sandra has come into and has ask not to record us um Erica does not want to be recorded she doesnt want to be on camera like we rightfully saw she has ask Sandra not to do that. Sandra has told her it is her right to record whom ever she wants she will do it privately without us knowing she um there has been several

Judge: Before you go on are you offering that

Kelsay: im sorry yes Judge we are offering

Judge: Do you have any objections to the Hunters Run Apartments Rules and Regulations handbook Plaintiff's 9

Sandra: no

Judge: Plaintiff's exhibit 9 is submitted without objection. I didnt mean to interrupt you.

Kelsay: go ahead

Naomi: Um I tried to have a set down meeting with Sandra and her Daughter right after the notice to vacate was provided to her.

Kelsay: the Daughter that we are talking about is

Naomi: Felicia

Kelsay: Felicia

Naomi: yes
Kelsay: And she is not on the lease
Naomi: no she is not
Kelsay: ok go ahead
Naomi: um the day that sandra came in we sat down in the communtiy room I was prepared to hear her out she had brought in several pieces of paper um I barely said 5 words in 5 mintues she got very upset she stormed out of the office her Daughter didnt leave right away her daughter was actually trying to have a civil conversation with us and was trying to explain something when Sandra came back in and told her not to worry about it that I wasnt going to listen she was yelling um she was not being reasonable what so ever and then she stormed back out of the office and that was the end of the conversation.
Judge: When you say she which she are you talking about
Naomi: Sandra, her daughter was standing there the entire time but of course when your mom is standing there yelling at you typically you listen.
Kelsay: if um when someone lives in an apartment that is not authorized tell me about the ramifications of that who do you get in trouble with and what can happen
Naomi: Well that lease for Sandra Black was under the section 42 tax credit (inaudible) The lease is very specif in we are held based on there requirements through IHC .
Kelsay: and you get public funds you get HUD funds
Naomi: we do
Kelsay: ok

Naomi: on top that Ms. Black also has the housing Vocher and she gets assistance from the Marion Housing Authority. The Marion Housing Authority tells us who is permitted in the apartment and Ms. Black also has the right to notify us that there is any changes. The three of us together are suppose to work on that if we find out

Judge: When you say the 3 of us together I don't know who that is

Naomi: The Marion Housing Authority, Sandra Black and Hunters Run. If we find out that there is somebody else living in the apartment we report it to the Housing Authority and let them know once we can prove it. Because Ms. Black at that point would have to claim their income or that they are living in the apartment with lack of income. It would adjust her rent portion that she is responsible to pay.

Kelsay: And what could happen if you just ignored it

Naomi: We would loose our voucher and it could potentially hurt our relationship with the Marion Housing Authority we could loose future vouchers I just don't have Hunters Run I watch out for I also have Hidden Ponds in Gas City so my concern is ruining that relationship with the Marion Housing Authority

Kelsay: In losing finical funding addition to that to

Naomi: yes

Kelsay: ok um so went ahead and filed for eviction

Naomi: I did

Kelsay: ok and then go ahead and tell me about what happen

Naomi: The eviction was filed and then on May 27 there was a post on facebook that tagged

Sandra Black: its my pen name

Kelsay: pen name

Naomi; and she posted she shared somebody elses post and the post says (you can make a mfa act right but you can make) (you cant make a MFA act right but you can MFA inaudiable) MFA is a actridim. Um

Kelsay: I think we have an understanding

Judge: I do not

Kelsay: Ok um

Judge: Im really not kidding I don't

Kelsay: o no no thats ok thats ok

Naomi: it's a very vulgar term Mother Fucker

Judge: whats the A stand for

Naomi: instead of a E they put a A

Judge: go ahead

Kelsay: umm

Naomi: Do you understand now

Kelsay: your behind

Black: thats how you play or whatever on facebook and you can also they also social media people this is standard behavior on social behavior if your on it your subject to it

Judge: ok

Kelsay: Naomi this is real wasnt it this wasnt play was it this really happened

Naomi: well I o well yes it happen(Laughing inaudible)

Naomi: there was a pocket of facebook post and throughout all of this um she tagged me personally in it she tagged my name.

Kelsay: tagged meaning

Naomi: she was able to bring it

Black; it to her attention

Judge: she needs to answer

Black: o im sorry

Naomi: to my attention as well bring me to other people attention um the next post

Kelsay: So we are offering this as Plaintiff's 10

Judge: you said there was a screen name and so since I wouldnt know what that screen name is

Kelsay: you can point it out to him

Naomi: up here at the top where its says Ezzrath Baht Shem that is her

Judge: thats a screen name

Naomi: yes um so Sandra goes on to post through out all of this on facebook she has several conversation with people um there is a stormy conn on here who has a lot to share and say. Um theres she is just being vulgar she calls me uh

Judge: Well I can read it do you have any objection? your offering this?

Kelsay: yes we are

Judge: Do you have any objection to plaintiffs exhibits 10 being admitted

Black: no

Judge: So that will be admitted without objection as well

Kelsay: And there were things that were go ahead with your testimony

Naomi: there were things that were brought up in here um serveral post just vulgar comments and statements calling me names she said in here (when dealing with ruthless evil women who is also racist her dumbass automatic assumes making one pay from black person is going to be a criminal act).

Judge: what page are you on

Naomi: im sorry im on the first page

Kelsay: I see what's highlighted

Judge: I see it

Naomi: later on down the in the conversation

Black: she needs to finish what I said on that one statement

Naomi: no

Kelsay no you've read enough

Naomi: later on down on the page she goes on

Black: I object your honor

Judge: you are going to change to ask her questions right now they are driving the bus they get the present there case and then you will get the change to present yours and you'll get a chance to cross exam evidence.

Black: mm ok

Naomi: later on she goes on and Stormy Conn actually post take her a chocolate pie tell her its

Minnys specials recipe.

Kelsay: thats in reference to the movie the Help isnt it

Naomi: yes

Kelsay: ok And something happened in there but um that is just the sort of that's a example the back and forth that goes on

Naomi: and the behavior that we not only just on facebook but in the office too

Kelsay: so it is clear other people get this and comment and read it comment on it

Naomi: yes

Kelsay: anything else the facebook exhibit is um is several pages um and there is more stuff what else would you like to um point out that would let me ask you a question let me start off by saying do you think interference with the management

Naomi: absolutely

Black: I didnt hear his statement

Kelsay: do you think interference with the management

Black: o ok

Kelsay: of Hunters Run ok and what else might be interference

Naomi: she has gone door to door to other tenants

Kelsay: Is there anything more in the Facebook you want to paretically want to point out you don't have to I just want I just want

Naomi: no not that I can think of its all there um

Kelsay: Now this one most of the way back where there is a dark entry

Naomi: O yes

Kelsay: thats hard to read so is there something you would like to point out thats in there thats thats a little hard to read.

Naomi: yes Sandra actually posted um no racism in America Black women being evicted for allowing white daughter in-law inside home. Sandra came to us I don't know a couple of weeks within the last couple of weeks right before she was served with the eviction paper work and she requested that um we add some additional occupants to her rent. She left a long voicemail with us and explained her son had married a 15 year old and they had a baby and that she wanted her daughter in-law to live in the apartment. I did not respond to her request at all because we had already filed the eviction she just hadn't been served yet.

Kelsay: But lets say you would entertain such a application go ahead and say what why you would not be able to accept that.

Naomi: I can not approve any additional occupants in that unit and up to 6 people she currently has 5 people that we know that are living in the unit because we have a 2 person per bedroom rule

Kelsay: and it's a 3 bedroom apartment

Naomi: it is a 3 bedroom she would over occupy the unit

Kelsay: ok so there would be no way you could grant that if three extra people even two extra people

Naomi: I would not grant that

Kelsay: ok anything else you would like to talk about in the Facebook

Black: mhmm. so had you reviewed the file when you would of renewed the agreement right.

A. Correct

Black: correct ok ok um October third when

Judge: two-thousand sixteen

Black: yeah two-thousand sixteen um I came to your office and requested a um I came to your office and requested a inaudible to be in the home correct? Um exhibit I got to start doing this stuff exhibit c my gosh, your honor you know what would help me a lot im sorry this is my first trial ever to be presenting evidence.

Judge: this is just a baby trial this is not real trial

Black: O I don=t have to do for this one

Judge: no what im telling you this isnt the end this is just a mini hearing just to see if I have to evict you thats all.

Black: ok, um there was a letter that she submitted to me that she gave to me um on October third and um I think you complained about it no you didnt on that one. Um here may I approach

Judge: yup do you want to go ahead and mark if your going to show her something you want to give to me later if you will mark it and you want to put your exhibit sticker on it or do you have it already.

Black: its exhibit C and its on here

Judge: ok thank you

Black: Its C ok alright now that I found it its not necessary.

Judge: Why don=t you show her what exhibit C looks like

Black: its my hand writing its my letter

A. O yeah

Black: Do you remember this

A. Yes I sure do

Q. Ok on October third

Judge: and Ms. Black since I rejected your pleadings your exhibit C is not part of my record if you want me to consider it today you need to go ahead and mark it and offer it

Black: mark it again

Judge: well if its got a sticker on it its fine but I don=t have it.

Kelsay: I would like to see it

Black: ok um so I would like to enter in exhibit C

Judge: stick the thing on it or is it marked already as C

Black: mine is marked as C, yes

Judge: good show it to Mr. Kelsay

Black: ok sure

Kelsay: ok

Judge: ok now show the witness and then

Black: She said she had already received this she has one

Judge: just one page

Black: no its 3 pages

Judge: you only picked up 1 you left some over there

Black: o ok thank you

Judge: so you want me to receive this as exhibit

Black: exhibit C yes

Judge: then I need it youll get the hang of it

Black: it is front and back

Judge: I need the third one thank you ok and objection Mr. Kelsay

Kelsay: no

Judge: exhibit C is admitted without objection

Black: ok with exhibit C before you I wrote this to you do you recall that I first came in and ask you may I please have a chance not to have people in my house just let me um have even if you just give me some hours I just said let me be able to have access to my house and do you remember that.

A. Yes

Black: yes that happened ok and do you remember what you told me

A. No

Black: you don=t well you can tell its defiantly it was a no that it couldnt happen because I had to ask them in writing do you agree

A. Ok sure

Black: ok yes so after the denial for my right I ask pleasantly please to do that and thats the letter and your response was exhibit D which I want to enter into evidence.

Judge: And that was I have the one sheet of something marked exhibit D

Black: there are two sheets

Judge: ok the second is what happen it=s a front and back copy so I have the three pages and the first page of exhibit C

Naomi: May I see the letter

Black: She said she doesnt see that

Judge: I need the second page

Black: but I need a copy of that

Judge, and by the way these letters you are giving me have these hand written things on the side.

Black: so you need them without the hand written things on the side

Judge: well ill disregard the hand the notes on the side if your admitting the letter. So I wouldnt consider the hand written things.

Black: ok so I thats what I needed it for because those hand writing things are the ones that helped me to ask her questions.

Judge: you can ask her questions but im telling you I wont consider the hand written portion unless you bring it up in your questions

Black: ok. Your honor is there a way um because I gave you my only copy

Judge: you want to borrow mine back

Black: yes

Judge: I don=t know if Mr Kelsay objects to these

Kelsay: I don=t know I havent seen it yet

Judge: the first page is in your left hand

Black: here is the first page this is the back

Kelsay: so is it six pages

Black: its three pages

Kelsay: I have six pages

Black: youve got C this is C you already seen this

Kelsay: ok ok

Black: then you got two pages this and this one thats the lease

Kelsay: ok

Judge: do you object to D Mr. Kelsay

Kelsay: no

Judge: C and D are admitted without objection

Black: ok um. In your letter you write that um you write that you have other people that are more important because there temperatures are unbearable and unbearable rising temperatures correct and that is why you felt like I was being so impatient with you correct. What I am establishing here is the evidence your honor should I first establish what is going on and then

Kelsay: objection, objections

Judge: I cant drive your case im here to listen

Black: ok alright so thats what I need you to answer when I came to help getting the air-conditioning unit which is what turned all this situation of because before I ask that question

Judge: you need to ask a question you this is not when you just expound on things ask questions and move on.

Black: ok um first of all let me ask you this, in general do you usually have with all the different violations because you know when you have violations of throwing a piece of paper violation of this and that you write a lot of violations for all the tenants all the time yes or no.

A. Yes

Q. Ok yes um then um after you get all of these petty violations do they from a tenant who has this is what I would like to know do have one white tenant that has all of these violations of little petty things im not talking about not paying there rent im not talking about serious offenses and im not talking about im talking about do you have white people that you target the way you targeted me.

Kelsay: Im going to object to that question Judge its very leading she is talking about targeting

Judge: Ms. Black ill sustain your objection on the word targeting because thats a charged word you a different word

Black: do you have white tenants that are in good standings as far as keeping the house decent keeping the um um no crime in the area no tenants complaining ok and then you use the petty things like that ones you Im talking about the ones you made at first.

Kelsay: im going to object to petty also Judge

Black: O the ones you leave the word petty off do you have them that youve

Judge: I didnt last part of that do you?

Black: Do you have them that youve evicted evicted

A. We provide lease violations as necessary to all tenants whether they are black or white and im consistent with those lease violations whether or not they have been evicted probably has nothing to do with what color they are.

Black: When, let me ask you this if your dealing with a racist person and they there main target when they bring people in is to get rid of black people

Kelsay: im going to object to that Judge

Black: there would be a situation

Judge: I don=t know what she is going to say

Black: there would be a situation where you target blacks to make sure Im asking

Judge: Ms. Black, your asking a question and you gotta your questions are so they are actually testimony so if you have a question ask other wise im going to excuse this witness so you cant do what your doing you got to ask a question let her answer it ask a question let her answer it and it isnt something long.

Black: Do you evict good white tenants that have had small do you have white tenants that have small the um things you have given to me these notices like this do you ever evict white tenants

A. Yes, if the tenant is violating the rules or regulations or any portion of there lease I absolutely evict them. OH NO

Judge: excuse me Mrs. Ma=am you want to tone it down

She attacks to the point even th judge has to speak out on it.

A. Yes

Black: So um in this letter that you wrote to me and you state that I am having slightly a slight inconvenience this letter here you state I have a slight inconvenience.

A. Yes you were having a slight inconvenience

Black: Can you explain to the Court why in my letter to you I said I was suffering see I state I was suffering and why is it can you explain to the court why is that when I suffer to you it=s a slight inconvenience how does that happen.

A. Sandra you came to me last summer and expressed that your air conditioner was not working and we made every potential every possible attempt to fix your ac unit we contracted with a HVAC company that came into your apartment multiple times with our maintenance staff and tried to repair it. You had a computer board

Black: your honor

Kelsay: Let her finish

Black: but she is not answering the question though

Judge: Actually I think she is so let her finish

Black: O Ok

A. You had a computer board that wasnt functioning and as a result you had to manually turn on and off your air conditioner you had to get up and walk to your thermostat turn it on when you wanted it turned off you had to go over and turn it off that meant you had a semi working ac unit. I had other units which were upstairs in the sun in mid-afternoon where it was over ninety two degrees in their apartments and they didnt not have air conditioning. We were working with one HVAC company and they were working to get all of you guys taken care of. We prioritize at that point based on health, needs, safety, conditions, claimant and we made the decision to fix the priorities of above those that maybe had a working air conditioner where you could control the claimant in your apartment. You contacted our corporate office at that point and explained to corporate, Tracey Clemmons my supervisor that I was not responding to you and your ac unit wasnt working it was a inconvenience because you had to get up and turn it on and off. I explained to her that we were ordering a part for your HVAC unit to get it fixed which we did get the part in and when Sub Zero who was our contractor went into the apartment to fix it you harassed them to the point where they left your apartment and told me they would not go back in there to work on your unit ever again. You have a working AC unit it took us some time because we were in the dead of summer where it was extremely hot outside and we are not there only customers.

Black: So did I explain to you I had a thyroid condition or and so in other words you ok your focusing on the heat but it wasnt just the heat I complained about thats what im asking you

Judge; Ms. Black your testifying again. Just ask a question.

Black: Im asking you was it just the heat that I complained about

A. You were able to get up and turn your unit on and off manually.

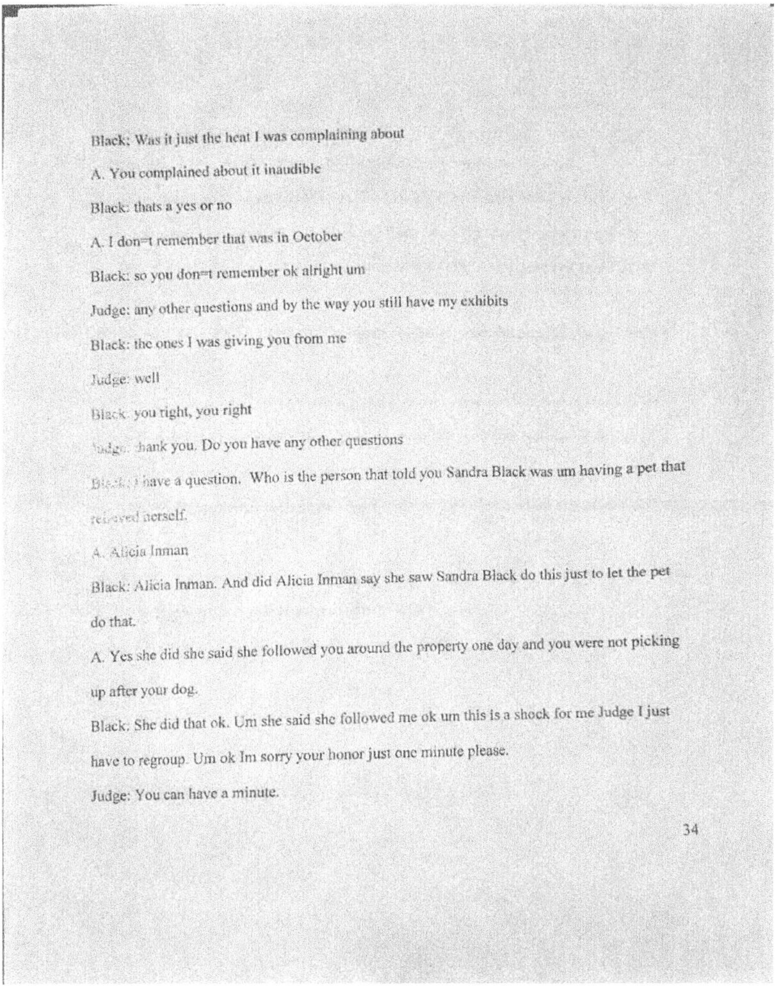

Black: Was it just the heat I was complaining about

A. You complained about it inaudible

Black: thats a yes or no

A. I don=t remember that was in October

Black: so you don=t remember ok alright um

Judge: any other questions and by the way you still have my exhibits

Black: the ones I was giving you from me

Judge: well

Black: you right, you right

Judge: Thank you. Do you have any other questions

Black: I have a question. Who is the person that told you Sandra Black was um having a pet that relieved herself.

A. Alicia Inman

Black: Alicia Inman. And did Alicia Inman say she saw Sandra Black do this just to let the pet do that.

A. Yes she did she said she followed you around the property one day and you were not picking up after your dog.

Black: She did that ok. Um she said she followed me ok um this is a shock for me Judge I just have to regroup. Um ok Im sorry your honor just one minute please.

Judge: You can have a minute.

34

I purchased a copy immediately after the hearing that wasn't certified. This is from that copy and the certified copy because I've misplaced pages so I am sharing between the two copies of the same document. There are no numbers per line, and the examiner is named **Black**; the respondent NF is Answer. **A**

Black: Really kind of scared at this moment ok

Judge: Im going to ask Mr Kelsay if he has any follow up questions.

Black: ok another question I would like to ask you um at what point would you say that your they way you say me as a tenant has changed. When did you because it wasnt from the beginning it couldnt of been at what point was it that the way you saw me as a tenant as changed.

A. Sandra

Black: Im talking about in terms on considering to um get rid of this person. At what point in the process did it change.

A. When I was having a conversation with Ericka around April nineteenth or twentieth I believe of two-thousand-seventeen and I was having a conversation about a potential unauthorized occupant in your home and I watched your son come racing into your property and that was the moment I looked at Ericka and said this is not just a violation this needs to be a 30 day notice to vacate.

Black: And your saying that there was one unauthorized person right that you have noticed right.

A. I noticed one but only one is enough for us to remove you

Black: ok um your honor I would like to submit exhibit F

Kelsay: ok

Judge: there is something on the back is that part of it

Black: this will be another exhibit

A. Yeah thats the letter I did

Black: ok ok so this is the 30 day notice to vacate. Ok for the record so it will go on the record as to what she said can I let her read because it is short no

Judge: I don't know what you are talking about yet right now

A. Dear Ms. Black I have witnessed to your occupant burgundy colored Camaro driving recklessly in and out of the parking at Hunters Run Apartments in addition serval other persons have witness at your apartment and appear to be other occupants at Hunters Run that are not on your lease or authorized to be living in your apartment. At this time we have reasons to believe you have unauthorized occupants living in your apartment at Hunters Run as a result you are being [illegible] notice to vacate you will be required to vacate your apartment on or before [illegible] two thousand seventeen at four pm. We appreciate your corporation sincerely [illegible] community management of Hunters Run Apartments.

Perjury

Black: [illegible] there were several occupants why did you use the statement [illegible]

A. I=m human and I made an error.

← Now Denies several, but all through out Proceeding it has alway been several or occupants

Black: Oh that was I error ok the other questions

Judge: Do you want me to have that exhibit you need to offer it

Black: ok yes

Judge: That's what I thought and I want to see if I do have it if I have it already Ill just use the one I already have let me make sure

A. I want to say it was close to the end probably six or seven oh wait it was 8

36

Kelsay: yes it was 8

Judge: I have this exhibit already is that the one you want me to have

Black: ok so I have to change my exhibit to that number right

Judge: I already have it in my record you don=t have to give me a second copy of the same document

Black: what number is it.

Judge: this one is marked as Plaintiffs exhibit 8 dated April nineteenth two-thousand seventeen. The last paragraph is we appreciate your cooperation.

Black: Alright thank you. Did you call section eight regarding this and letting them know about this

A. Yes

Black: and at that time did you only report one or did you report several

A. I told Ms. Porter at the Marion Housing Authority that I believe you had unauthorized occupants and I was giving you a notice to vacate.

Black: Ok so you are saying when you wrote the letter you said it was a mistake and when you did on section eight also when you called them was that a mistake because your still saying the same thing that there were several people that were living there. And Im asking was that a mistake that you made or yes that

A. I told the Marion Housing Authority that you have unauthorized occupant I didn't specify if it was one or twenty.

37

Black: yup ok so the next question I would like to ask is how did you first hear about this one person how did you first hear about this one person that was staying because now you are changing it from the several that was in the letter to this one person.

A. As I said early my assistant notified me that there was additional vehicle that had been at your apartment park for long time she works there that's how I found out.

okay is NOT SB's occupants

Black: ok because here you have that are witnesses so that's why I was like who are the additional witnesses there are witnesses so Ericka

A. Myself

Black: Oh your yourself

A. And my staff

Black: ok your staff so everything is based off of the vehicles that's what I just wanted for the court everything of me having an extra person living in my house is the vehicle. Yes or No

A. No

Black: What is the evidence of a person living in my house

Kelsay: May I please address the court Judge I have a lot of witnesses that will be testifying to this we do have a number of them

Black: But this is serious he is saying I have people

Judge: your asking an legit-able question and she can answer the question and I can give people fair warning I have this was not intended to be a all day thing but we will do it for as long as we need it I have a hearing I have to conduct in a different court I don't remember if its 1:15 or 1:30

38

Remember that I am under oath about EVERYTHING IN THIS BOOK NF never once spoke to HUD about UO until after the notice. I asked, and it is established in federal court that HUD was never contacted by the landlords. HUD agreed with the state court that there was no evidence of UO living in my home. I was never violated by HUD in any form, fashion, or action.

After the Order denying the defendants' eviction, **<u>ON THE SAME DAY</u>**, they immediately began lying that same day and fabricating violations. I replied with pictures of all my windows and all around the community, where my blinds were in better condition than the OFFICE and many residents. Some residents used their porch for laundry, but a small nick that was in the blind when I took the apartment on move-in day was there, and I never complained, nor did they, until they got that order that they lost. Their attorney shut them up, and that was the last violation.

Then they started torturing. They cut off my AC. They infected my bedroom with bedbugs on their inspection day. This was the time I realized that there would NEVER be peace in my home. I decided I had to move.

My son had been living in Bloomington but was planning to move back to Marion. He lived in Bloomington, but couldn't afford the rent there. He was several months behind and was being removed. After court, the plan was that he would move in with friends of his and his wife. However, since I was being forced out and I had a place till I moved, I would DO IT THE RIGHT WAY and not move his wife and daughter in until I had an agreement with the landlords. Discrimination in America is next to impossible to win, so I decided I would have my doors open to my son and his family until I moved, seeing that there was no possible way to have people in my home. I wrote the agreement to move, and they agreed to allow my son (their tenant by LAW) to have his wife in the unit without taking me to court for REAL had I simply moved them in.

In Marion, I have seen people EASILY evicted in a seven-day vacate by courts. I couldn't survive that at all, so I had to be sure that I WAS LEGAL and I wanted to get something out of the forced LOSS of my home that I had cherished.

That dirty dog knew those blinds weren't damaged enough to need removal because she gave me the house like that. The window had a long arm knob, and it cut into one small piece of one blind blade by about an inch. It's only visible from inside of the apartment, and since they gave us the house like that, who would complain? The blind was ABSOLUTELY NO PROBLEM. The pictures are inside the federal case BRIEF FOR

SUMMARY JUDGEMENT against the defendants for not having UO by ORDER OF STATE with a duty of burden to show evidence. However, by my being black and pro se, my court order in my FAVOR was seen as in the white defendants' favor. They were so kind to let my son stay before kicking me out. They never perjured themselves at all, because they only said several UOs in a letter and never in court. This is a blatant lie. The court will deny me because, unlike most litigants, my order denying eviction was READ BY RACIST JUDGES AS I WAS EVICTED, TRYING TO GET RELIEF FROM THE COURT ORDER OF EVICTION, and therefore my original case was dismissed because the federal court does not hear such cases to relieve me from being evicted. YOU GUYS COME ON!!! What competent judge reads an order that the litigant wins, landlords are **DENIED POSSESSION,** and interprets it that the landlords won possession, federal judges claimed that I WAS EVICTED and wrongly dismissed my claim, BIAS DAY ONE? See their ORDER to dismiss my claim, because I LOST, **the day I WON.**

Hunters Run Apartments
717 E. Hunters Run Drive
Marion, IN 46953
765-677-1701

June 14th, 2017

Sandra Black
655 E. Hunters Run Drive
Marion, IN 46953

Re: Blinds

Dear Ms. Black,

It has come to our attention that you have damaged blinds or missing blinds in the window of your apartment. Per our policy all windows must have blinds up that are not damaged. You must replace your blind(s) by Friday june 16th, 2017. If you do not replace your blind(s) then we will have no other option than to replace it ourselves and charge your account $25.00 per blind on Monday Monday June 19th, 2017.

Please note that blinds are available for purchase in the office through the maintenance department for a fee of $10.00 to be paid by money order at the time of delivery. Blinds may be purchased at a lesser price from Walmart or K-Mart as well, for dimensions of the blinds, please feel free to contact the office at 765-677-1701.

Sincerely,

Naomi Friedrichsen
Senior Community Manager
Hunter's Run Apartments

Cc: Resident File

Sandra A. Black
655 East Hunters Run Drive
Marion, Indiana 46953

June 15, 2017

Morris Kelsey
514 South Adams Street
Marion, Indiana 46953

Correspondence: Defendant with Plaintiff's Lawyer
Subject: Continuation of harassing acts to evict SB
Order won/ blind violation both on June 15, 2017

Dear Attorney Morris,

Please advice your clients that a failure to convince the court with fabrications to force my eviction does not constitute a right to harass me immediately after getting that order. They should also be warned that they can NOT target me. They fabricated that I was so vulgar and threatening that Erika Holiday was frightened to work alone when in fact the only thing witnessed was a recording of SERVICE OF DOCUMENTS one by one and their contents, absolutely no threat of harm and no vulgarity as your clients claimed under oath which I believe to be **aggravated perjury** in that they were not lying to protect themselves from harm, but lying to harm me for eviction. Your clients seem to believe that all they need to do is say "word" and it's forced reality. I received our order on June 14th 2017 stating that I am to remain in my home happily with full use of my apartment. In less than an hour of picking up that order I found a letter of lease violation from Naomi Friedrichsen.

I will give them a copy of this letter to serve as a **SECOND WARNING: TO CEASE AND DESIST FROM DISCRIMINATION, HARASSMENT, AND SLANDER.** I included photos taken at the precise time I received my letter from your clients. Please, if you see what I see, that the blinds ARE **NOT** NOTICIABLE DAMAGED to the point that I deserved what they did to me please stop them from harming me.

I have gone through my home and inspected all blinds. There are a couple of spots with small infractions that are unnoticeable from the sidewalk or street. I will also take pictures from the sidewalk. Please find enclosed an attachment of their letter of immediate harassment against me and photos from the yard view and from the sidewalk view of my home. Also find pictures of far worse scenarios to prove that they are targeting me. Even Naomi Friedrichsen's blinds are not perfect, picture enclosed. Also please have them look at their copy of the **IRM move-in form of items under living room** and see where they gave me this apartment with damaged blinds in the living room. No one would live here if they are FORCED to live stricter than I already proudly live and it is against the law to try to force and expect me to live under scrutiny that no one else is expected to live under, which has been going on ever since NF was determined to ILLEGALLY EVICT ME. She even admitted under oath when she said I was never supposed to have been renewed in November of 2016. We KNOW FOR FACT she had nothing at all on me at that time proving she is doing all in her power to force evict without cause even by her own testimony in court. The fabrication of my not taking care of my pet was December 5, 2016 so how is it that I was so bad not to renew my lease as she testified under oath that she planned to never renew my lease. This is an act of contempt of court (I am by court order to have happy use of my home) to give me broken blinds at the time of move-in and then right me up for the same blinds.

I never complained over the broken blinds or most none of the damaged items in my home from day one not wanting to be labeled a trouble maker. Thus I believe it reasonable to look at my blinds from the yard view, the moment I detect noticeable damage, then I change them. If this is unreasonable please let me know so I can begin to change every time any infraction occurs and seek damages at the end or our case. As I will abide by the different set of rules and treatment set especially for me only. This is not an attempt to be defiant as I hope pictures of my home will show you. But to set precedence and fair-play of a disgruntle manager bent on harassing me at all cost to her sensibility and capability to reason. This is also to show her attempt to rob me of my right to **EQUAL HOUSING**.

I ask that you instruct your clients that violations of the Fair Housing Act to harass a minority is illegal and **MUST** Cease and Desist. Explain to them that they can't target me for eviction as they have been doing. They can't fabricate an eviction into existence. Although Haas helped them to bring out infractions as best he could from my side and failed to find any preliminary wrong doing though the criminal act of

aggravated perjury happened against me or this was proof of being afraid of a black woman for absolutely no reason. Please help your clients to understand the seriousness of their actions to continue to harass me by singling out my home as a target of eviction. There is an apartment that uses their balcony for drying clothes; NF's window has a worse appearance than mine does. I require a written notice of disregard and removed from file of their letter if you also find that attacking me over broken blinds they gave to me broken is not right. And that there are FAR worse problems your client should address instead of looking for how to attack me. **This violation against me should be corrected within 3 days.**

Second issue, we need to add Jacee Shem and Kemuel's daughter (7 months old) to the lease. Though Naomi testified that my call to add her is equivalent to asking to add 3 people and can NEVER happen... please help her to understand that my son is already on the lease, the infant does not count, and therefore only ONE COUNTABLE occupant for the three bedrooms has ever been asked for, and it is legal. Please advise your client as she already feels asking for one adult is asking for three, if I am not mistaken what I heard in court under oath. We will need approval ASAP as Kemuel moves out officially BY FORCE this month. Thank you for kindness helping our family to receive our right to peace and possession of our apartment and honoring the order.

Thirdly, I need verification of upper management and the new owner's knowledge of this counter claim so we can try to stop further damage of my person by a manager out of control. Behavior displayed in court is typical when ever she's angry. Please provide the contact information of the CEO of the management company and the new owners of Hunters Run Apts. contact information within ten days to prevent the necessity of moving the court to have access to contact information from all parties involved.

In Conclusion, **No matter the lease**, your client can NOT treat me any different than she treats all tenants, **federal law**. The gross issues of the outside appearance of the property here that she over looks to pounce on me, her very own office window, the aggravated perjury, her own testimony throughout court, and **her timing** in finding fault with me show that she is maliciously targeting me for eviction as soon as she got the order.

Thank you

Sandra Black

Sandra Black

CC Hunter's Run Apt.

If this doesn't stop **NOW** I must turn to the media (Issue a press release) and begin a public campaign for help to stop the harassment, slander, and discrimination and perhaps look into the RECENT ELIMINATION OF TENANTS OF COLOR and who, why, where, what type of NEW TENANTS from all over the US are being shipped in are our local ordinance observed and county assemblymen aware? I have several others who were forced out of their homes that I am trying to go through civil rights process and be patient, but if this keeps up I am being forced to protect myself and my family and seek an investigation. All I want is to have the SAME RIGHTS TO LIVE IN PEACE AS EVERYONE ELSE.

June 18, 2017
After thinking of the fact that I may not be judge fairly and this letter is taken as my noncompliance to following the lease, I am replacing the broken blinds they gave to me broken. I must remember this is how I MUST be treated in America. I comply to these powers that I call racist as they are NOT held accountable for their actions. As matter of fact, their **unlawful acts** are not even allowed mention.

FEDERAL COURT CASE:

In May of 2019, I filed a discrimination case in federal court against the landlords, and it was immediately dismissed because I was evicted and seeking the federal court to overturn my eviction. This is subject matter not heard in federal court. It's automatic that a pro se black litigant is ALWAYS IN THE WRONG, as best the judge can scour the evidence and legalities for dismissal. When I first got my dismissal, I threw the letter on the counter and went about my day, sort of a sigh of relief that I didn't have to fight, and I lived up to my standards of always giving my best effort. For the court to dismiss my case (I BELIEVED), there must be some serious MANDATORY requirement I missed, like statute of limitations, but I filed before my two years were up after the damages ended (from the time I was out of my home). I waited nearly two years because I nearly died in the last lawsuit and really felt like I didn't have enough stamina to survive another court case, but I had to try. So, realizing that I couldn't think of anything I did wrong. After a few days, I got up the nerve to at least get the gist of WHY the dismissal.

I was WRONGLY automatically dismissed day one in Federal Court for being falsely **LEGALLY EVICTED** IN A COURT OF LAW. So, if you're on your toes, you already know what was in the letter that cannot hold up in court. **I wasn't evicted**, I won to get a denial of their request to EVICT me, and I perfectly understood that the burden of proof lay upon the defendants to prove they were JUST in bringing a case against me. I HAD THE CASE IN BAG, because it wasn't one word against the other, and the burden is on the defendants for claiming an AFFIRMATIVE DEFENSE. You see, I knew that's all they could possibly claim with zero evidence to prove their actions were just. My plan was very simple as I was too ill and too unfit to be my own attorney. I would get in the court (which I immediately failed, by Jim Crow) AND once the defendants were in and it was ALL TO GO, I would submit a SUMMARY JUDGMENT BRIEF for a court order that the defendants were either in the wrong for failure to prove an affirmative defense (this gives me clout in the court proceedings for being wrongly sued for eviction or (I knew wouldn't happen) a total win for discrimination due to the fact that NO GOOD TENANT is ever removed as the motive for being a landlord is TO KEEP GOOD TENANTS TO MAKE MONEY. Once I established that the defendants were in the wrong for attempting to evict me without cause and had already established that I was indigent (without money), I would ask the court to appoint an attorney to SEAL THE DEAL that I would have a chance at winning. That's my only way at a chance at being heard.

Here's what happened. I requested reconsideration of my lawsuit as best I could, taking blame for the confusion that judges are TOO DUMB to read the state order that said that I didn't loose, I won. So I sugar-coated my response as an ANGRY JUDGE is an automatic loss, because appeals ARE BS, always for the JUDGE when you're black AND pro se. I have enough law under my belt to know the etiquette of law in court. It's NOT as it's supposed to be, where THE MOST IMPORTANT RULES ARE TO FOLLOW LAW NUMBER ONE AND SEEK JUSTICE NUMBER TWO. These horrible judges, and I do mean ALL OF THEM! Seek what they want as best as they can. THEY ARE JUDGES TO RULE THEIR WORLD, not to uphold law, the constitution, and justice. You see, I will give you so many cases where judges ruled utterly AGAINST THE EVIDENCE. If I am one person with many cases and different judges, four who illegally and/or through misconduct continuously intentionally RULED on matters AGAINST THE EVIDENCE with MALICE CONTEMPT for the judicial system to attack me or side wrongly with people of authority (THE SYSTEM), GOING AGAINST THE EVIDENCE. Their names are State Judge Haas, Judge Mark Spitzer, Federal Magistrate Susan Collins, Federal Judge Theresa Springman, and Circuit Court Chief Judge Diane Syke. Judge McVicker was my greatest disappointment ever because I never thought he could do such a thing. He was over my granson's guardianship, the CASA elderly wanted the bad choice placement because she wanted my grandson to be a football player, she knew how to act black be in trouble and be the stereotypical black person, while I wanted my grandson highly educated, never in trouble with the law and didn't act stereotypical black. Vickers ruled that the choice wasn't discrimination because both parties were black. WTF! Then in the end after this judge knows that I had been complaining about placement being a danger to my grandson and both DCS and CASA refusing to investigate, WORSE even if I KNEW NOTHING, how can you be responsible for a child and NEVER know that your have placed the child with a drug user. HOW… THEN the judge ruled that these monsters did THEIR BEST. WTF. We know it wasn't their best by the end result, they NEVER investigated any complaints and were involved for nearly THREE YEARS! They know that their original placement was beaten by her cocaine addicted boyfriend while my grandson was in her custody and the boyfriend was locked up in jail for it.. They assigned placement to me because placement was also court ordered not to have minors in her custody and was convicted of a crime, both CASA and DCS lied THAT the other changed placement and didn't know how or why I was assigned placement over my grandson. As time went by with me as placement DCS didn't like the idea of them assigning my grandson to a bad placement so they initiated changing back to the unfit placement and CASA schooled her to expunge her crime. AND JUDGE RULED it was all good as long as it was expunged he didn't need to know anything about it. In the end, the information stating that they knew all of these problem existed was taken into evidence by the judge. He knew they LIED to him day one bringing in the old placement as guardian intervener over my grandson. He ruled nothing could stop it because I granted her visits over a period of time. REALLY???

I begged him and appealed the case that he CAN'T claim these people did the best possible job, this is why babies and children DIE in state custody! They don't do their jobs and McVickers held to, (I BELIEVE) my good relationship with CASA and DCS is more important than what those bastards did to your grandson and family. WE SUFFERED! The siblings SUFFERED FOR THREE YEARS! I can't see this being a mistake. Nearly the entire family died of placement, GOD is extremely hard on those who harm me. I never wanted this and prayed to spare them, later we worked so good together. Father, mother, and placement all gone because people do not do right. I believe they would all be alive if DCS didn't push them to fight me. THEY DESTROYED THEM! I only have their son alive and he doesn't understand that he has a mission to be strong for the others. I don't believe that McVickers meant to be malicious or if every single federal judge on my case meant to be malicious, but I know 100% that the cases these many many judges ruled over did not go according to the LAW and evidence. **SHAME ON THEM TO RULE FOR THEIR CO-COURT PEERS against the evidence.** Utter SHAME, HOW DARE YOU!

My denied claim in federal court reconsideration was both DENIED and kind of half ACCEPTED. It only happens when you're black to that a RECONSIDERATION request is ordered a LAWSUIT, you will rarely be treated by judges equal, unbiased, fair, or DILIGENTLY SEEKING JUSTICE (all required by code of ethics), NOT NEVER in my federal case was I (aging disabled) or my evidence considered. I WAS FOUND TO HAVE A CLAIM, which became a lawsuit instead of motion to reconsider, GRANTED. WHY? Some speculated to me that it was so that I had no right to a trial because my lawsuit requests a trial, while the request for reconsideration does not include much of anything that is required for a lawsuit. In all actuality hiding my original lawsuit hides the FACT that no matter what **I was going to be automatically in the wrong** as NO

WORKING FEDERAL JUDGE IS SO STUPID that he or she can't read a court order DENYING an eviction, NONE! She assumed the case would be over with the LIE that I had been evicted. If I had no experience, it could have been over by RACIST, JIM CROW CONCLUSION as ultimately happened.

Any time I had to fight in court prior to HAAS, I always won my argument because I never go to court without serious cause. In other words, when I am in court the person is just out right in the wrong. I have never gone to court without serious cause. This includes litigants who need a lesson for doing a person wrong solely because they think they can get away with it.

I could have challenged the court's lawsuit, but hey, I am in the game, and I am going to get a court-appointed attorney after the ruling on my summary judgment. Remember, it's just FACTS, I have overwhelming evidence. I had enough experience, no matter how strong your evidence, IT'S OVER if you make the judge mad (unfortunately, I didn't foresee that my color had sealed my fate from 1960). Or I would have contested that the lawsuit remains and reconsideration be granted. I didn't want to be fighting for ever and thought why make the judge mad this early in the game. Get my evidence proving how malicious those bastards are and get a court appointed attorney. So the order to make my motion to reconsider a LAWSUIT stood, and my attorney will handle that if need be at a later time.

The defendants appear and immediately file a motion to dismiss. I filed a motion to deny their motion to dismiss. The court ruled in order ECF 28 a huge book that said the motion to dismiss was denied. You guys, my mind. **I WON.** Can't go through the book after all, I wouldn't be in the game if the judge wasn't on my side, I won. I immediately began my Summary Judgment against the defendants' Affirmative Defense. Let me clarify, my disability is similar to people who can't leave outside or touch things with germs, I can't read hatred towards me. I don't read hate mail, this is why I was in extreme need of an attorney that I was qualified to have appointed due to my low income, my need, 41 million with an interest, and STRONG EVIDENCE. If I wasn't qualified then no one on earth is.

Here's the problem: the order ECF 28 was TOTALLY AGAINST ME, falsely going AGAINST THE STATE COURT ORDER. The way she placed ME IN THE WRONG AUTOMATICALLY WITH A LIE, but I never saw it, assuming I had won the judge's favor because of the state court evidence and the denial to dismiss my case. As I told you guys, for my health's sake, it's extremely difficult, even at times outright impossible, for me to even open an envelope from the court, let alone read it meticulously. I am diagnosed with Generalized Anxiety Disorder, kidney failure, and a host of chronic illnesses, which, if I ran my life as a regular person does, I would have been dead long ago, just as my doctor predicted when I was in my early thirties. My blood pressure can NOT possibly be controlled by medication if I am under stress. While monitoring my BP, it was way too low, somewhere around 70/40 I don't remember exactly, but it was extremely low, so they called me to see what was going on. I had been super relaxed, had the best nutrition, was exercising perfectly, and was taking my medication. So they asked several random questions and asked me why I think I experience such high BPs. I told her it's really bad any time I go through being mistreated. I told her, like landlords who intentionally harm me, and I began talking about this case for about 3 or 5 minutes, and my head started feeling hot and heating up the center of my body. So I told her (my monitor), it's high now just for me discussing it. I asked her, " Do you want me to check. She said, "Yes." I did. It was moderately high, AT LEAST AROUND 160/90, which isn't horribly high, but look at where we started to where it went with simple few minutes recall imagine if it's REAL. She said she had never in all her work watched a person's bp change from very low to above normal. I know my life. Even now, I'm tired, and it's climbing. I've got to stop very soon now, or my life is in jeopardy. My friends ride me to open and read, but I can't. Just like my friends fussed at me to fight those devils, don't let them run you off your job. So DIE, is that better than surrendering to your life's boundaries? They have no clue how bad it is. I'm not thinking about my enemy, I'm only thinking breathe they don't exist, BREATHE. This is how I survive. I can't have enemies or hate, I WILL DIE! Human beings are pretty sick when it comes to empathy. They think, it doesn't happen to you, so it CAN'T happen to the next person, or that you're exaggerating for sure. However, in court, I can tell my story and having won **(I THOUGHT),** I filed my summary judgment brief on May 29, 2020, I believe a couple of times because the first one wasn't in brief format.

Immediately in the brief, I turned in about 13 or 15 pieces of evidence against the defendants, proving that the defendants had no merit in bringing me to court. The defendants had THEIR WORDS ONLY, no picture, no telling HUD of plans to remove me, or nothing to show that people were in my home unauthorized.

I WON THE STATE COURT. It is ordered that there is insufficient evidence that the UO occupants lived in my home.

1. There were only two violations that I was actually at fault for, but those two shouldn't count because I learned at the state level that I wasn't supposed to have been violated; I was supposed to get a friendly reminder. **So technically, I had zero violations that actually occurred.**

2. Letters of correspondence between the defendant and plaintiff (ME) SHOWS HER ATTACKING her boss and me, and me backed her off, and her trying to deny me rights to privacy and trying to punish me to put all my maintenance needs in writing. Because she lied to her boss, Tracy Clemmons, that I didn't want to live there, she was given the go-ahead to let me out of my lease. Tracy claimed that NF had been under a lot of pressure, and she didn't understand me. I told Tracy, " Are you sure, because I never said anything about wanting to leave. I love my apartment. I want to stay until I die or hit the lottery. She told me, " Oh no, NF just was overwhelmed and didn't understand. I KNEW DAMN BETTER! SHE WAS BITING MY HEAD OFF AND TALKING TO ME LIKE I WAS A CHILD, and all I could do was keep quiet and swallow shit because I wanted the nicest housing for the poor in Marion. So you can see it. We had our own individual doors, a couple of ponds, ducks, geese, a small playground for the children, and a basketball court. I moved into everything being old and breaking down, but it was still far nicer than other choices. Her boss, Tracey Clemmons told me you don't have to put your maintenance request in writing, and you will get your privacy notice. **THE VERY NEXT DAY**, the AC that NF refused to fix for TWO MONTHS was fixed.

3. FALSE accusation of "pet mess" FINAL WARNING. Now y'all KNOW WHAT'S UP with just the heading. She's illegally evicting me. The neighbors stopped this, and the landlords admitted their fault, signing my copy. PLEASE DISREGARD, REMOVED FROM FILE. See Court order denying the defendants possession June 14, 2017, page 72 of this book, letter F. MISLEADING court, perjury! Only mentioned to save BUDDY, and not to hold landlords GUILTY.

4.30-DAY vacate – SAME DAY as **MONROE COURT ORDER** ordered Jacee, baby girl, and my son, Kemuel Shem with his dreadlocks all cut off into my son's custody, BY SHERIFF. Would my son need a court order if these people were already living in my house?

5. Tenants all sign statements that no one was ever seen at my residence, but my daughter who visits me and her children. If this was a problem, wouldn't I have been put out day one two years prior? The children are hers. They KNEW her. They knew she was visiting regularly. They NF

lied under oath that she did not know my daughter at until she saw her at court, BUT SHE TESTIFIES that she was negotiating with my daughter and she was nice while I was not. How can she meet with my daughter before court, but never knew her until the day of court? She told that lie to explain why she NEVER called her out in the proceedings until after she found out about the Monroe Court order and then lied that she only needed ONE, my daughter, and then lied and went back that it was several UO. Check out her sworn testimony. HAAS KNEW SHE WAS LYING and stated it in the ordered, but he never had her charged for perjury.

6. Documented conversation with landlords, dated April 20, 2017, two different meetings where they were going to drop this LIE, but as I was leaving, the monster did the final mistake, to the point where I no longer was going to kiss her butt. She (NF) said as I was walking out, and we all agreed I didn't have to vacate. "Oh, Sandra, put it all in writing." And I snapped. You'll get everything ALL IN WRITING. And I let her have ALL her shit that I had been documenting on her since day one, and told her that I had gone to the civil rights commission.

7. It was written in a 25-page **CEASE AND DESIST** letter that I served with a video camera, where she LIED TO THE JUDGE that I was yelling at EH all sorts of horrible things. And the judge reluctantly heard the video and mentioned that I was not yelling at EH, but lifted my voice for EH to hear me through a locked door. They called the police on me and LIED that I was threatening them. But the judge listened and saw it was just me delivering service of the CEASE AND DESIST letter.

8. HUD, Section 8 sided with me and the court that there was no evidence of UO.

With all of this evidence against these white defendants as a black person in court, RES JUDICATA, law that applies to everyone else, that says you are NOT entitled to a second hearing after a judgment is rendered and seasoned for no action, but the federal court denied my evidence because the defendants were entitled to a second hearing in federal court. Collins concluded that NO COURT ORDERS counted as evidence in my favor. SHE DENIED my motion for summary judgment based on the fact that the defendants were entitled to a second hearing. I knew this was a blatant lie, but they had sent our federal Marshals for the defendants who were hiding and hadn't appeared, namely NF and the management company. I believe this to be the order of SENIOR JUDGE WILLIAM LEE, because his racist magistrate was doing all in her power to keep me out of the game.

I had asked for an attorney in summary judgments and several times throughout the case, but Collins said I had submitted over 150 pieces of documents; therefore, I was quite capable of handling my own case. Motion DENIED. On another request, she denied it and said I could resubmit if I had three attorneys with phone numbers that I had called. I know I was supposed to follow through, but I had stated that I had called **NUMEROUS** ATTORNEYS. She was mocking me to keep writing so I could keep getting denied. She never granted anything for me, no consideration for my disability, evidence, or suffering at the hands of LYING litigants. As a matter of fact in ECF 80 she defends them that they weren't lying. That the letter didn't count for several and the one person my daughter was the truth under oath. The problem is that she kept going back and forth under oath AND the Monroe Order, AND the state court order, and HUD all say there were no UO so how are my grandchildren UO? So it's just facts she was wanting to wear me out. If she legally needed three phone numbers and was going to approve giving me an attorney, she could have easily granted the order pending at least three numbers from the numerous attorneys was submitted to the court. In my mind, SCREW HER. I wasn't giving her the satisfaction of making me squabble just to be automatically turned down.

I didn't fight the wrong denial of my evidence because I had hoped to get an attorney somehow. I don't want to turn the judge against me, no matter what. Little did I know how badly the court was fraudulently against me to save white defendants. EMBEDDED LAW (EL) had been presented at the state level and also at the Federal level because, though I wouldn't use EL until I won my case, I needed to stress the seriousness of 41 million people were at stake, so I needed an attorney or public awareness of my case. When I asked for public awareness, she said, " You don't need it, your friends are already watching you. WHAT THE FUCK? Now that's creepy, so I got friends watching me. SO WE GO FORWARD INTO TERRITORY I NEVER INTENDED TO BE ALONE IN. But I'm still believing that if I just get the judge to look at the evidence. So we go into scheduling our case, disclosure of my information and theirs, discovery of mine and theirs, and depositions were court-ordered at SEVEN HOURS EACH. That same day or very soon after, their lawyer scheduled a deposition with me and issued my admissions, interrogatories, and production all at the same time. I had been working hard on their disclosures. I wanted to disclose all my evidence, suffering, and complaints so they couldn't come back and say something didn't count because I didn't disclose it. I gave them all my witnesses, my expert witnesses, and everything. I answered all their questions faithfully in good faith, giving all details of my position. When I gave them theirs, the attorney refused to answer anything that I didn't already know. SHE LOADED ME UP WITH PAPERWORK, like my booklet lease, fabricated violations, their manuals, but anything that I did not have was too cumbersome for them to deliver; they couldn't understand anything that I wrote for items that I didn't have, but **THEY UNDERSTOOD EVERYTHING AND SUBMITTED EVERYTHING** THAT I ALREADY HAD IN MY POSSSESSION, so how does it make sense that nothing in my possession they can't understand, but everything I have already they loaded it up on me. I told them that they have everything from me, and I had NOTHING. Deliver discovery, and I will then do my deposition. I filed a motion to compel them to comply with discovery, and they filed a motion for sanctions because I was insisting on getting some discovery first. The JUDGE ANSWERED IN ECF ORDER 80. This would be the order that would END MY letting the judge do anything to me. This is the first time I SEE THAT my grandchildren are the UO and how the defendants had been so kind to me to DISMISS THE CASE. Y'ALL, tell me now, HOW??? Damn, they got an ORDER on the hearing over their complaint of UO, and it was DENIED. So, how is it now dismissed by the kind defendants? WTF Why isn't it anywhere that the state court order found that there was NO EVIDENCE OF UO. WHY? The wrong color that's automatic denial of absolutely anything.

I filed a Motion to Substantiate the Order. This judge is fabricating two LIES. 1. THAT I HAD UO. The court order says it doesn't exist. And 2. That my grandchildren weren't on the lease, both the court order and the defendants themselves claim that my grandchildren are on the lease on record. **THESE ARE FACTS**. All of the opinions were biased, favoring the defendants against the evidence, just mad wrong, like the magistrate defending all of the defendants lies under oath by only looking at the letter and claiming it wasn't under oath. But she said several UOs under oath, and the judge just MADE THAT LIE UP that it was only one person, and Naomi made a mistake with the letter. Just writing all sorts of make-believe, and **she ordered me to pay sanctions for missing my deposition.**

My Motion to Substantiate the Order is a summation of the facts that my grandchildren are on the lease, and the court order states they are on the lease, and the defendants do not deny that my grandchildren are on the lease. I explain how I fully and completely cooperated with the defendants for discovery and they refused to release any unknown information. Therefore, the order must be corrected to reflect that my grandchildren are on the lease and that there is no evidence of UO. So again, the magistrate conspires to MAKE UP A LIE that my Motion to Substantiate the Order is an

OBJECTION TO HER ORDER, and the objection is DENIED. So I file another motion to CORRECT THE ERROR, and it is DENIED because my motion to correct errors is an objection to her order, and **<u>OBJECTION IS DENIED</u>**. WTF!!!

So I filed a request for direction on how to present an error that the court is refusing to see the error, to get an attorney, to force the defendants to deliver discovery. The Request for Direction is denied because plaintiff is trying to get the court to litigate the entire case for her; therefore, the Request for Direction is denied. This is now WAR, and I know it's an impossibility to worry about the judge's feelings anymore. She's utterly corrupt. I'll share some of the actual pleading here:

Exhibit F

USDC IN/ND case 1:19-cv-00307-WCL-SLC document 80 filed 01/19/21 page 1 of 25

UNITED STATES DISTRICT COURT
NORTHERN DISTRICT OF INDIANA
FORT WAYNE DIVISION

ECF 80

SLC's Fraudulent ORDER

SANDRA BLACK,)
Plaintiff,)
v.) Case No. 1:19-cv-00307-WCL-SLC
NAOMI FRIEDRICHSEN, *et al.*,)
Defendants.)

OPINON AND ORDER

Before the Court is a motion to compel filed by *pro se* Plaintiff, seeking to compel Defendants to more fully respond to her requests for admissions and requests for production and asking that sanctions be imposed against Defendants. (ECF 69). On November 2, 2020, Defendants filed a response to Plaintiff's motion (ECF 71) and a separate motion to compel, together with a supporting memorandum, seeking to compel Plaintiff to appear for her deposition (ECF 72, 73). On November 9, 2020, Plaintiff filed a "reply" (ECF 75) to Defendants' motion to compel, in which she responded to Defendants' response to her motion (ECF 71) as well as to Defendants' motion to compel (ECF 72). No party filed any subsequent response or reply to either motion and their time to do so has now passed. *See* N.D. Ind. L.R. 7-1(d)(3). Accordingly, the Court considers both matters fully briefed and ripe for resolution. For the following reasons, Plaintiff's motion (ECF 69) is DENIED, and Defendants' motion (ECF 72) is GRANTED.[1]

[1] While the Court previously stated that it would set a telephonic hearing on Plaintiff's motion to compel (*See* ECF 70), after reviewing the parties' filings and arguments the Court no longer believes a hearing is necessary.

1

A. Background

Plaintiff initiated this matter on July 10, 2019, asserting that Defendants discriminated against her on account of her race in violation of the Fair Housing Act ("FHA"), 42 U.S.C. § 3601 *et seq.* (ECF 1 at 2).[2] Plaintiff "alleges in her Complaint that Defendants discriminated against her on the basis of her race, African-American, by falsely accusing her of numerous lease violations over the course of several years in an attempt to force her to vacate the apartment she rented from Defendants in Marion, Indiana." (ECF 28 at 2 (citing ECF 1)). In particular, Plaintiff asserts that Defendants instigated an undue state-court eviction proceeding against her in Grant County Superior Court of Indiana, Small Claims Division, Case No. 27D03-1705-SC-000517,[3] on the grounds that Plaintiff allowed unauthorized guests—her grandchildren—to live in the apartment in violation of her lease. (ECF 1 at 2; ECF 15-1). The parties eventually agreed to allow Plaintiff to remain in the apartment temporarily in exchange for Plaintiff vacating the property by September 21, 2017. (ECF 15-6, 15-7). Accordingly, the state action was dismissed. (ECF 15-8). Plaintiff then filed a complaint of discrimination against Defendants before the Indiana Civil Rights Commission, which subsequently found no reasonable cause to believe that Defendants violated the FHA. (ECF 15-9, 15-10).

---

[2] Plaintiff initially filed a complaint against Defendants in case number 1:19-cv-222. District Judge William Lee dismissed that case for lack of subject-matter jurisdiction. (1:19-cv-222, ECF 3). In a motion to reconsider, Plaintiff raised for the first time a potential FHA violation, invoking this Court's federal question jurisdiction. (1:19-cv-222, ECF 5). Accordingly, Judge Lee directed the clerk to file Plaintiff's motion to reconsider as a new complaint in this matter. (1:19-cv-222, ECF 6).

[3] Per the Defendants' first motion to dismiss and supporting memorandum, Defendant Hunters Run Apartments and Owners ("Hunters Run") initially filed a Complaint for Possession of Real Property and Past Due Rent in the Grant County Superior Court of Indiana, Small Claims Division, under case number 27D03-1705-SC-000517. (ECF 15 at 2). Following Plaintiff's request for a jury trial, the matter was transferred to the Grant County Superior Court's plenary docket and Hunters Run filed an amended complaint under case number 27D03-1706-PL-000014. (*Id.* at 2). For ease of reference, the Court will refer the state court proceedings under each case number as the "Grant County case."

On June 30, 2020, this Court entered a scheduling order pursuant to Federal Rule of Civil Procedure 16, setting July 26, 2021, as the last date to complete all discovery. (ECF 45, 46). On August 19, 2020, Plaintiff propounded her first set of requests for production on all Defendants. (ECF 55). On September 14, 2020, Plaintiff similarly propounded Requests for Admissions on Defendants Hunter Run and Interstate Realty Management Company (ECF 61), Erika Holliday (ECF 62), and Naomi Friedrichsen (ECF 63). Three days later, on September 17, 2020, Defendants responded to Plaintiff's request for production (ECF 55), raising a variety of objections to each of Plaintiff's requests (ECF 64), but producing 101 pages of responsive documents (ECF 64-1 through ECF 64-5). On October 9, 2020, Defendants filed a notice of deposition—scheduling a deposition of Plaintiff (ECF 65)—as well as responses to each of Plaintiff's requests for admissions—again raising multiple objections to each request (ECF 66-58).

On October 19, 2020, Plaintiff filed the instant motion to compel asserting that Defendants and their counsel did not act in good faith in responding and objecting to her discovery requests. (ECF 69). More specifically, Plaintiff repeatedly claims that Defendants' counsel was "lying" and at numerous points accuses counsel and the individual Defendants of committing perjury. (*See, e.g.*, *id.* at 1, 2, 8). Defendants, in response, attach multiple emails as evidence that they have attempted to confer in good faith with Plaintiff regarding their objections to her discovery requests. (ECF 71-1 through ECF 71-7). Similarly, Defendants maintain that their various objections to Plaintiff's requests were valid—namely that her requests were, at different points, vague, overly broad, compound, and generally improper. (ECF 71).

On November 2, 2020, Defendants filed their own motion to compel (ECF 72), alleging that Plaintiff had refused to attend her scheduled deposition. (ECF 73 at 2; ECF 73-1). Plaintiff, in response, contends that her deposition should be postponed because Defendants have failed to fully comply with her discovery requests. (ECF 75 at 2). Plaintiff similarly alleges that the deposition will be used to "taunt" her and reiterated her claims that Defendants and their counsel have acted in bad faith. (*Id.*; ECF 75-1).

B. Applicable Law

Pursuant to Federal Rule of Civil Procedure 34, a party may serve another with a request to produce or permit the party to inspect a document or thing "in the responding party's possession, custody, or control." Fed. R. Civ. P. 34(a)(1). Such requests must be within the scope of discovery permitted by Federal Rule 26(b)—that is—it must be relevant to a party's claim or defense and proportional to the needs of the case. Fed. R. Civ. P. 26(b), 34(a). The responding party may object to a request that it believes is improper pursuant to Federal Rule 34(b)(2)(C).

Similarly, per Federal Rule of Civil Procedure 36, "[a] party may serve on any other party a written request to admit . . . the truth of any matters within the scope of Rule 26(b)(1) relating to: (A) facts, the application of law to fact, or opinions about either; and (B) the genuineness of any described documents." "[R]equests for admission must be simple, direct and concise so they may be admitted or denied with little or no explanation or qualification." *Sommerfield v. City of Chi.*, 251 F.R.D. 353, 355 (N.D. Ill. 2008). Further, an answering party may respond to a request for admission by denying, stating in detail why it cannot truthfully admit or deny the request, or objecting to a request—so long as it does not "object solely on the ground that the request presents a genuine issue for trial." Fed. R. Civ. P. 36(a)(4)-(5).

Under Federal Rule of Civil Procedure 37, a party is permitted to file a motion to compel discovery where another party fails to respond to requests for admission or requests for production of documents. Fed. R. Civ. P. 37(c); *see also Redmond v. Leatherwood*, No. 06-C-1242, 2009 WL 212974, at *1 (E.D. Wis. Jan. 29, 2009). "A motion to compel discovery pursuant to Rule 37(a) is addressed to the sound discretion of the trial court." *Redmond*, 2009 WL 212974, at *1 (citation omitted). While a discovery request is entitled to "broad and liberal treatment," *Goldman v. Checker Taxi Co.*, 325 F.2d 853, 855 (7th Cir. 1963), a discovery request, "like all matters of procedure, has ultimate and necessary boundaries," *Hickman v. Taylor*, 329 U.S. 495, 507 (1947). The moving party generally bears the burden of proving that the discovery it seeks is relevant to the case. *See United States v. Lake Cty. Bd. of Comm'rs*, No. 2:04 CV 415, 2006 WL 978882, at *1 (N.D. Ind. Apr. 7, 2006) (citations omitted). Conversely, "'[t]he party opposing discovery has the burden of proving that the requested discovery should be disallowed.'" *Bd. of Trs. of the Univ. of Ill. v. Micron Tech., Inc.*, No. 211-cv-02288-SLD-JEH, 2016 WL 4132182, at *3 (C.D. Ill. Aug. 3, 2016) (collecting cases).

Subject to certain limited exceptions, "[a] party may, by oral questions, depose any person, including a party, without leave of court" so long as that person and the other parties have "reasonable written notice." Fed. R. Civ. P. 30(a)(1). "In the absence of a showing of a lack of good faith on the part of [her] adversary, a party may not refuse, upon deposition, to reveal matters specifically within the scope of the examination permitted by the [Federal Rules]." *Smith, Kline & French Labs. v. Lannett Co.*, 2 F.R.D. 561, 562 (E.D. Pa. 1942). Courts have found a party's willful failure to attend her deposition grounds for sanctions. *See, e.g., Stewart v. Illinois*, No. 01 C 5520, 2003 WL 21919036, at *1 (N.D. Ill. Aug. 12, 2003).

C. Analysis

1. Plaintiff's Motion to Compel

Having reviewed both Defendants' discovery responses (ECF 64, 66-68) and Plaintiff's motion (ECF 69), the Court agrees with Defendants that Plaintiff's motion is generally meritless and should be denied. In her motion, Plaintiff raises specific arguments as to Defendants' responses to Items 1-7[4] of her requests for production.[5] (ECF 69). Plaintiff also raises more general arguments as to Defendants' responses to her requests for admissions, contending that Defendants have committed perjury and have lied in their responses. (*Id.* at 1-3). Finally, Plaintiff requests sanctions against Defendants and their counsel and asks that Defendants' discovery responses be "excluded." (*Id.* at 10). The Court will address each argument in turn.

i. Request for Production, Item 1

Plaintiff first requests that Defendants produce any documents listing any white, "section 8" tenants, with certain criteria[6]—presumably similar to Plaintiff—that were issued either a "final pet warning without any prior pet warning," a request to vacate due to unauthorized guests, or were served with an eviction lawsuit. (ECF 55 at 2-3). Plaintiff, in the same request,

---

[4] Plaintiff labels each request for production as an "item." (*See* ECF 55). For the sake of consistency, the Court will follow suit.

[5] Plaintiff raises additional arguments as to other "items" and responses in her reply brief. (*See* ECF 73). "A reply brief, though, is not the proper vehicle to raise new arguments not presented in an opening brief." *White v. United States*, 33 F. App'x 570, 571 (7th Cir. 2001). In any event, Plaintiff's arguments in her reply largely mirror the arguments raised in her motion. Because such arguments are generally meritless, the Court sees no reason to address the additional points raised in Plaintiff's reply.

[6] In particular, Plaintiff seeks documentation regarding white, "Section 8" tenants who had:

A. Never missed paying rent, never paid late rent;
B. Had no criminal activity
C. Had no property damage
D. No immediate neighbor complaints . . .
E. Very little to no company at the home
F. Maintained an orderly, quiet well run home

(ECF 64 at 2-3).

also seeks the production of any such warning, request, or civil complaint, as well as any documentation of similarly situated white, "section 8" tenants who were not treated "harshly." (*Id.*). Defendants objected on the grounds that Plaintiff's request was "vague, overly broad in time and scope, unduly burdensome, and seeking information that is not relevant and not reasonably calculated to lead to the discovery of admissible evidence," and generally unintelligible. (ECF 64 at 3-4). As such, Defendants produced no responsive documents. (*Id.*).

As an initial matter, the Court reads Plaintiff's request as seeking evidence of similarly situated white tenants who were treated differently than her. Such "comparator" evidence would certainly seem relevant to a claim under 42 U.S.C. § 3604(b) or § 3617, and within the scope of Rule 26. *See Mehta v. Vill. of Bolingbrook*, 196 F. Supp. 3d 855, 867 (N.D. Ill. 2016) ("[T]o prevail on a claim under section 3617, a plaintiff must show (1) [s]he is protected under the FHA; (2) [s]he was engaged in the enjoyment or exercise of [her] FHA rights; (3) defendants were at least partly motivated by an intent to discriminate; and (4) defendants coerced, intimidated, threatened, or interfered with the plaintiff on account of [her] FHA-protected activity."); *Kriseman v. Crystal Lake Apartments Ltd. P'ship*, No. 05 C 6348, 2006 WL 1519320, at *7 (N.D. Ill. May 31, 2006) ("[To prevail on a claim under § 3604(b),] Plaintiffs must show: 1) that they are members of a protected class; 2) that they were qualified to receive the services in question; 3) that they were denied or delayed services by the Defendants; and 4) that Defendants treated a similarly situated person outside of the protected class more favorably." (quoting *Flores v. Vill. of Bensenville*, No. 00 C 4905, 2003 WL 1607795, *4 (N.D. Ill. Mar. 26, 2003))). Indeed, in order to survive a motion for summary judgment or proceed at trial, Plaintiff must show that Defendants treated similarly situated tenants differently than her. *See id.* (granting summary judgment in part because "Plaintiffs claim[ed] that the air conditioners of other tenants were repaired before their own, but could not identify those persons or provide any support for their position.").

That being said, Plaintiff's request, as written, is vague and overly broad for a variety of reasons. "Courts analyzing a claim of hostile housing environment look to cases discussing hostile work environment, under Title VII of the 1968 Civil Rights Act, for guidance." 47 A.L.R. Fed. 3d Art. 3 (2019). "Under [Seventh Circuit Court of Appeals] precedents, . . . an employment discrimination plaintiff may demonstrate pretext by providing evidence that a similarly situated employee outside her protected class received more favorable treatment." *Coleman v. Donahoe*, 667 F.3d 835, 841 (7th Cir. 2012). However, in order to use such comparator evidence, it must contain "enough common factors . . . to allow for a meaningful comparison in order to divine whether intentional discrimination was at play." *Id.* at 847 (quoting *Barricks v. Eli Lilly & Co.*, 481 F.3d 556, 560 (7th Cir. 2007)). As such, requests for discovery should be "limited to the time frame involving the alleged discriminatory conduct." *Johnson v. Jung*, No. 02 C 5221, 2007 WL 1752608, at *2 (N.D. Ill. June 14, 2007) (internal quotation marks omitted) (collecting cases).

Limited to time

Here, Plaintiff's request is not limited to the years she was a tenant, the years of the alleged discriminatory actions, or any similarly relevant time period. *See Bacon v. Coca-Cola Bottling Co. of New England*, 232 F.R.D. 49, 55 (D. Conn. 2005) (finding interrogatories requesting information going back twenty years overly burdensome). Further, Plaintiff extended her request to other documents concerning white tenants who were not treated "harshly." This would certainly seem to encompass a wide range of conduct which would not provide a meaningful comparison to the alleged discrimination that Plaintiff felt. Accordingly, Plaintiff's

① IS NOT to 8 YRS

② Due to the fact that

To SHOW EXTREME maliciousness

8yrs is not burdensome A no where close to 20yrs as sited by the judge.

NO CONCIDERATION

attend her deposition. Accordingly, Plaintiff is ORDERED to work with Defendants to schedule a deposition within 21 days of this Order. Additionally, Defendants' request for fees (ECF 72) is provisionally GRANTED. Defendants are DIRECTED to file an affidavit detailing their fee calculation within 14 days of this Order. Plaintiff is permitted to file a response within 14 days of receiving Plaintiff's affidavit.

SO ORDERED.

Entered this 19th day of January 2021.

/s/ Susan Collins
Susan Collins
United States Magistrate Judge

HERE'S MY REQUEST FOR SUBSTANTIATION

1

US DISTRICT COURT OF NORTHERN DISTRICT INDIANA

FORT WAYNE DIVISION

SANDRA BLACK,	)	
Plaintiff,	)	
	)	
VS	)	**CASE NO: 1:19-cv-00307-WCL-SLC**
	)	
NAOMI FRIEDRICHSEN, ET AL.,	)	
Defendants,	)	

REQUEST FOR SUBSTANTIATION OF THE ORDER (ECF 80)

Plaintiff Sandra Black, Pro Se pleads the court to substantiate the order and opinion biased against a Pro Se litigant. Since the very beginning of this court, it has had problems with not having a lawyerly submission from a pro se litigant. The plaintiff, begs the court not to recuse that Judge William C Lee continues to preside as judge in this matter and fix the mistakes to make plaintiff whole. Plaintiff did not want to prejudice the court, but this bias meant SB loses her case, NOT ALLOWED DISCOVERY.

1. Both the State Court and Federal Court utterly refuse to give any weight or opinion to the FACT that evidence is presented to the court that clearly shows why the defendants fabricated a malicious eviction. See exhibits 2 and 3are included. See exhibit 4 and substantiate the court genuinely has not considered plaintiff's Summary Judgment Brief (SJB).

   Request the court present a reasonable scenario of how it is remotely possible to originally claim several people for each occasion that NF says multiple people, ESPECIALLY IN THE LETTER.

2. Federal court leaves out any mention in the Order and Opinion of page 40 from the transcript, where after the judge in the state hearing sees that NF cannot describe the people upon cross examination as she had falsely claimed to have witnessed herself. SHE COULD NOT DESCRIBE ONE PERSON. The judge bails her out of the line of questioning by saying... "she doesn't have PERSONAL KNOWLEDGE"... "IS THAT FAIR?" He, the judge asks NF, And Naomi Friedrichsen replies <u>**YES.**</u>

Court Makes Up Statements Not Submitted Or Proven Factual

1. The court errs that there was no final trial and the action was dismissed. There was a hearing with a ruling in an Order from court DENYING DEFENDANTS POSSESSION. See (SJB) Exhibit 13.

2. The court errs; (**<u>GRANDCHILDREN ARE ON THE LEASE</u>**) failing to look at the evidence or consider plaintiff's complaint. **<u>Sandra Black was an excellent tenant.</u>** There were no unauthorized tenants in the home. The (SJB) evidence shows that the court should have ruled in plaintiff's favor. There is no reasonable evidence so whatever to support defense's Affirmative Claim that plaintiff had any violations or did anything wrong such as having "unauthorized occupants." However, there's plenty of evidence that proves malicious litigation only the court won't look at all perhaps ANY of the evidence. **The court is directed to see MDDMD page 61 of 66 where the grandchildren are listed on the lease on page 63 includes Erika' Ziddiick (aka Erika Holliday's) signature.**

A. EXHIBIT ONE (**<u>Plaintiff's original claim</u>**) filed originally shows how court denied the claim for lack of subject matter and because the court found that the plaintiff had been evicted in lower court therefore could not overturn the eviction order in Federal Court.

However, if the court examines the language highlighted, (note: defense has an exact same copy of highlighted areas and ANY and ALL notes in margins of exhibits 2 and 3), it is reasonable to see by the average person that the subject matter is about wrongful eviction from an apartment complex is being sued, and there's several mentions of denied equal access. Furthermore, throughout the claim are mentions of discrimination. Though plaintiff did not know to call the legal term HUD violation in the beginning, but the court could have shown leniency for the language of a prose litigant as long as it is reasonably understandable to the average individual as to meaning. This shows some bias against a pro se litigant because she fails to write like a lawyer.

B. We did have a trial on June 8, 2017 where the defendants LOST. It was DENIED IN THE COURT ORDER dated June 14, 2017. The case was NOT dismissed in lower court. The State court order has been mentioned numerous times throughout this proceeding, it is highlighted in ORIGINAL CLAIM, exhibit 1, and it is also submitted to the court in the Summary Judgment Brief Exhibit 13.

C. Court errs that plaintiff filed a complaint for discrimination against defendants AFTER THE CASE WAS DISMISSED (DENIED). Not true. See Discrepancies and Malicious Acts (DMA) pg 9

<u>REGARDING MOTION FOR REQUEST OF PERMENANT TIME</u>

2. A. The court denied request for permanent time extension throughout the proceedings. Plaintiff was compared to an attorney and denied. Plaintiff seeks direction as the opinion made no reference to plaintiff's disability other than a passing sentiment. It seemed that the court has zero tolerance for a disability. The court did not state that the motion was insufficient of a

doctor's report or of a clear position that it understood plaintiff's condition due to the disability and chronic illnesses the request is a life and death issue. It was reported that plaintiff nearly died in the last case. Is it the court's position that a litigant must either throw themselves on the mercy of the court for time or die trying to have a right to KNOW that their pleading will be received? Are pro se litigants required by law to function as if there is no medical chronic illnesses as well as disability that are life threatening for the plaintiff. Plaintiff seeks clarity in the court's opinion. Does the court have zero tolerance for time in a life and death situation disability?

B. In the request to reconsider Admonishment, would the court please substantiate its order that states plaintiff has no damages? The court said if any mistake is made in the future by the plaintiff due to its action to admonish the plaintiff it may dismiss plaintiff's case. How could this be no damage as said in the order?. Did the court recognize that it did recommend that plaintiff should contact with the defense lawyer regarding approaching/motioning the court? Why is there no consideration at all? Why is there no damage with the threat to dismiss if another mistake happens?" **Plaintiff, did not point out the bias in a timely fashion because plaintiff KNOWS it causes more bias. Had it not been for the fact that plaintiff automatically loses her case without discover she would not have pointed out bias now.**

DISCOVERY, PRODUCTION AND ADMISSION

3. The court states that Sandra Black received discovery. **Did the court look at the discovery received versus what was denied?** The only discovery that the defense allowed the plaintiff was paperwork she already had in her possession and that which could not prove discrimination. Surely plain to see. Instead of copying, the defendants could have stated the name of each document and that it was in plaintiff's possession. Then there would have only been one paper of production and the court would not be misled to believe that the defendants were allowing

discovery. The request was needed to know if any new documents might surface. For example the claim that Sandra Black missed a payment was misleading and the ONLY copy that was actually a discovery. The defendants told the plaintiff an amount to pay for her rent. The plaintiff was paying the amount she was told to pay for several months. The defendants later changed their price request. Instead of saying they miscalculated the price and needed more money, they wrote the paperwork up as it is seen.

4. Pages 7 and 8 states that requesting for whites, ON SECTION 8, similarly excellent performing tenants like the plaintiff is too vague, overly broad in time and scope, unduly burdensome and so on. This means that the plaintiff is NOT ALLOWED discovery in this court.

A. First, Plaintiff CLEARLY is not only required to prove discrimination (DIFFERENT TREATMENT), BUT ALSO FOR THE harsh punishment plaintiff needs to prove how malicious the acts were. The court compared my request for 8 years of production to a law that showed a person asking for TWENTY YEARS of production.. If the court blocks the comparison of whites treated similarly to plaintiff, the court then utterly cripples the plaintiff with absolutely no way to prove her case.

B. Furthermore, asking for six more years than the cases active years to prove how malicious the defendants are shouldn't be unreasonable.

C. NF did not give a document proving that she no longer worked at Hidden Ponds, but she gave a statement. Likewise, she could give a statement of any white excellent tenants that she evicted.

D. The above said, CLEARLY, the court is not remotely thinking of what is being asked in production. HOW MANY white section 8 tenants that are **EXCELLENT tenants** does the court really believe that the defendants will find? How is it burdensome if MOST LIKELY the production is going to be next to ZERO? The court must remember, the #1 objective of renting out apartments is TO MAKE MONEY. If you are evicting people, harassing people THAT YOU WANT TO KEEP how will you make money? I WAS EVICTED FOR NOT doing anything wrong that's a FACT, the motive must be established. If there are no whites treated similarly to my case in 8 years I have proven discrimination. The court should profoundly realize... If there were so many NUMEROUS whites that were treated JUST LIKE THE PLAINTIFF, wouldn't the defendants rush to produce the evidence to prove no discrimination occurred? There's virtually NOTHING to produce only a biased court wouldn't see that this is obstructing discovery.

5. On page 9, Why does the court respond that plaintiff does not want the defendants to have any objections, but never exposes the truth of plaintiff's REAL complaint. The defendants objected to EVERYTHING, 100% of everything was objected. The court says that plaintiff's second request (Item 2) is not clear why the defendants find and unduly burdensome. But this is not true. The court knows WHY. Most none of plaintiff's production fits the rule of a NEEDED objection. However a lot of defense's production request should be objected.

Federal Courts are reported to no longer support... AFFIRMATIVE DEFENSE, DENY, DENY, DENY... object, object, object only to wrongly WASTE COURTS TIME to hide justice, truth and FAIRPLAY. Is that GOOD FAITH PRACTICE just because you got used to looking at this evil way of proceeding? THE DEFENSE ARE ALL AT FAULT OF THIS mess up and the court greatly errs in allowing this to continue by simply not seeking out THE FACT that there is zero evidence of an affirmative defense and GREAT EVIDENCE was submitted in the request for a Summary Judgment coupled now with discovery that shows beyond a shadow of doubt there were no violations, with just the SJB) it showed no unauthorized occupants. Defense has ZERO evidence while Plaintiff has surmountable evidence.

JUSTICE should outweigh PETTY always in matters not prohibited by law. Not understanding words like "Trouble" or "Service" with instructions included... "ANY SERVICE other than **JUST YOUR WORDS"** It is reasonable the average person understands you need more than your words, you have it or you don't. The Defense should use common sense, produce their proof of any "trouble" without objection so that everyone is on one page. They admit none, WHY OBJECT? In this case, there can be absolutely no fear of discovering trouble later as it could NOT have possibly been the motive for eviction, thus why should the court up hold 100% objections? Pro'se plaintiff's concerns has genuinely not been considered in this court. Substantiate why plaintiff is not allowed discovery of anything that proves discrimination.

6. Page 10/11 Item 3 Again the court supports defendants in absolutely no regard for the pro se litigant. The plaintiff is not an attorney thus "criminal activity" why not just answer without objection? MISUSE OF BOILERPLATE OBJECTIONS

7. Page 12, 13 Item 5 and 6 again the court and defendant's attorney have zero tolerance for a prose litigant. To object to a prose litigant using the word trouble" to collect production... Why abuse the boilerplate objection statement WHEN ASKED NOT TO DO IT? How can a document exist that IS REMOVED FROM THE FILE? Even the lower court says it is misleading to present this as happening see (SJ) Brief exhibit 13 pg 7 F. They know it never happened. THEY STATED REMOVED FROM THE FILE. Why does the court see this a valid production when the DEFENSE themselves agreed to remove it? They have produced the fabricated and misleading violation at least do NOT object to plaintiff having it.

8. Page 14, the request for violations that were served was EXTRA EXPLAINED. If it is not mandatory LAW that misuse of boilerplate objections must be allowed, then it is unfair to block plaintiff from this evidence without objections. **DID THE COURT CONSIDER PLAINTIFF'S BURDEN as a black person** swaying a jury?

9. Page 19, Due to the misuse of "Boilerplate" objections being a common practice, it is understandable that only a warning be necessary instead of sanctions. However, that court should accept, allow, encourage it by NEVER ONCE MENTIONING the FACT that it was 100% used on EVERYTHING requested when clearly plaintiff requested the defense attorney not to do it in numerous text, emails, phone calls, or the fact that 100% objections should cause a motion of the court to stop the misuse of the Boilerplate, but the court upheld this misuse to object without a cause just because they could though WARNED not have 100% objections.

10. The request to Exclude or repair is due to the 100% misuse of boilerplate. Though it is commonly used in court when the "MISUSE" of OBJECTIONS are to objected the only fair choice is to throw out the misuse or damage for the litigant requesting not to allow the misuse of a privilege the Boilerplate. Especially since the misuse was confronted time and time again to the defense attorney. **Automatic** 100% objection is a type of DENIAL of discovery through misuse of the boiler plate. **Furthermore, 95 percent or more of PERTINENT material was NOT GIVEN.**

This can not be allowed that so much CASE needed discovery is not allowed for the plaintiff. The defendants only allowed what was KNOW to be given. ANAYLZE what the defense gave, then analyze all they did not give like

A. PRODUCTION 1 the comparison of whites treated similarly to the plaintiff

B. PRODUCTION 12 AC denied repair for two months similar COMPARED to whites,

C. PRODUCTION 15, to see is there was an apartment open to swap out a part to stop suffering until the new one came in.

D. PRODUCTION # 19 was taken from defendant's OWN language and needs to be answered in good faith. **This court must not allow bullying where it's good for the defendants to ask for discovery that REALLY should be objected to while allowing them to say they are practicing good faith and court says they are practicing good faith though discovery from the plaintiff is 100% objected to misusing the boilerplate law.**

E. PRODUCTION # 23 is important. It is needed to study and make a table. This will show the percentage of whites violations in comparison to blacks who received violation and the comparison of black to whites who gave up and moved out. And how often blacks receive violation in comparison to whites. The comparisons MUST BE ALLOWED in order to make plaintiff's case. Sandra Black has named THREE non-white persons besides herself Brandy (black), Tabitha (black) Monica (Hispanic), forced out by harassing violations. Since plaintiff is a witness that it happens it cannot be called fishing to prove plaintiff's claim that it is in deed happening and to what degree is it happening. Thus there are 4 out of 6 black tenants Plaintiff knows has received violation until ran out of their homes. 100% of all white tenants that Plaintiff knows have not had any violations. This is NOT fishing. This is discrimination and we need to see by how much. This is PERTINENT DISCOVERY that is just being refused. The defendants are ricking the court by granting anything that plaintiff has already in her possession AND REFUSING ALL pertinent discovery to prove discrimination. THIS is REFUSING discovery?

F. PRODUCTION 24 is EXACTLY the same as above but a request of the race the white section 8 tenants to determine discrimination must be produced.

Defendants have totally refused ALL discovery that compare the treatment of whites to Sandra Black and that compare how whites get violation with how blacks get violation. THUS DEFENDANTS HAVE REFUSED ANY AND ALL DISCOVERY THAT PROVES DISCRIMINATION and the CASE. The court is helping them to refuse discovery show the comparisons of whites to black people treated similarly to SB. If the court refuses discovery it is refusing a way to present evidence to prove her case.

11. Court's order to compel the plaintiff to a deposition with all the INJUSTICE from both the court and the defense is problematic constitutionally. How is it possible to hold plaintiff responsible for the act that the defendants brought upon themselves? The plaintiff was indeed ready to grant a deposition and canceled days before after the BOILERPLATE MISUSE was refused to be corrected and I had no discovery at all to prove discrimination (MY ENTIRE CASE) and 95% of the pertinent discovery was totally refused.

There would be no case had the defendants not tried to persecute an excellent performing tenant. There would not be this motion had the defense attorney worked with plaintiff to stop the misuse of the boilerplate. The Affirmative Defense is only valid if the facts are in dispute, then the judge may not be allowed to grant summary judgment, IF THE JUDGE AGREES" Where is there ONE piece of creditable evidence that plaintiff allowed several people to move into her home? NONE EXISTS Combined with all of the chances to stop the proceedings, Cease and Desist, the lower court RESPONSE, during lower court and they continued after court the very first day the order came out., they issued a violation to say GET OUT.(SJ) Brief exhibit 15.

There is no violations, no concrete proof that a violation took place, Served, by video to cease and desist, THIS SAME CROSS COMPLAINT was given in the lower court, Court saw the evidence and RULED AGAINST THE PLAINTIFF, surmountable evidence of a malicious lawsuit with fabricated claims is available to the court. The burden of proof for the Affirmative Defense is on the defendants. Why aren't we only at the place to discover MOTIVE ONLY? SUBSTANTIATE. What is the possibility that the defense is telling the truth about their claim of unauthorized occupants to have caused an eviction?

Under the constitution an important civil right of all citizens is JUSTICE IN COURT. The defendants have greatly abused the law, literally broken law by perjury, and the court up holds them looking at one little sentence of their actions ("It was just a mistake"), but not the entire long and complicated case. Most ALL of plaintiff's damning evidence against the defendant is rarely mentioned while falsehoods to support the defense such as "plaintiff's grandchildren were unauthorized" are mentioned. There is absolutely NO PROVEN evidence ANYWHERE that exists that plaintiff's grandchildren were unauthorized to live in the home. There were NO unauthorized guests. Furthermore, the court states that lower court never heard the case assuming it was DISMISSED, but it was heard and DENIED. The order denying possession is in both the defendant's Motion to Dismiss and plaintiff's Motion for Summary Judgment exhibit 13.

The making up of evidence that hurts the plaintiff by putting the defense in an ARTIFICIAL brighter light is happening through scouring defense statements and fabrication while not looking at what was produced by the defendants and weigh it against what was NOT produced see page 18 in this motion. The evidence presented and the thought process for deciphering fair play is unjustly skewed to favor the defense, but rarely a remote GENUINE look at the highly credible evidence of the plaintiff is mentioned. Look at the pet mess FALSE VIOLATION fact and used to mislead the court Fact see SJBrief pg exhibit 13 pg 7 F where the judge states exhibit 2 is MISLEADING and pleads for his buddy the defendant's attorney that he didn't know that the landlords was misleading the court. But look at how it is mentioned in this opinion.... There clearly appears to be a glance and dismiss plaintiff's submissions.

If the court would genuinely look at the ACTUAL EVIDENCE with a critical mind to seek the TRUTH, the duty of the court, then all FALLS ON THE DEFENSE for creating this chaos. See the plaintiff's Motion to Deny Defendant's Motion to Dismiss page 29 and 30, also attached for ease to find as EXHIBIT 2, AND 3. Note in the letter from NF the mention of Plaintiff's son's car the Burgundy Camaro and the SEVERAL OTHER PEOPLE ... a teenage white girl, Jacee Barber, and a white baby, Naomee court ORDERED into plaintiff's son, Kemuel Shem's CUSTODY **<u>on APRIL 19TH</u>**. NF writes her letter **on APRIL 19TH**. Look at the Bloomington Court order for ALL THREE OF THESE SAME PEOPLE. Then look at the DATE of both documents that would place ALL TOGETHER (several others being Jacee and a **<u>white</u>** baby that did not fit into a black home, They OPEN THE DOOR and just walk in to plaintiff's home without knocking.. Is a court order not allowed as evidence? Is NF's letter not allowed? Why does BOTH courts refuse to ever include this evidence?

Further evidence of FACT plaintiff SERVED a letter to Cease and Desist, SERVED BY VIDEO footage. Then in court again all the same evidence that was presented to the lower court where defense could have STOPPED at lower court level as there was no proof for their fabricated story to be valid. Then the FACT that section 8 disagreed with "unauthorized occupants" living in SB's home. Then all throughout court committing perjury undeniable to ANYONE who looks at the evidence. NF misleads the state court**<u>, as section 8 disagrees with defendants.</u>** See Exhibit 4 top of pg 6

The COURT refusing to recognize crucial evidence, only submitting documents already within plaintiff's possession .Defense could have named each document, the date of the document and state that it is SB's possession. Then only ONE page or so would have been submitted as

PLAINTIF has not been granted any pertinent discovery. The Defense worked hard to **LOOK LIKE** they were actually cooperating with discovery, but the judge did not look at the fact that 95% of all copies were nothing new and were not necessary to have made copies. Thus all that plaintiff has been allowed is zero discovery of any pertinent information to prove the case. Plaintiff couldn't have possibly contemplated that the court would be biased to the fact that 100% objections was misuse of the boilerplate thus to make the plaintiff whole she must have a resubmission without misuse of the Boilerplate. This does not mean there should be no objections, but that defense must NOT nitpick over common words they understand and especially when most factually the outcome will yield little to NO PRODUCTION such as the excellent performing white section 8 tenants who were similar to SB. Plaintiff giving examples of what she considered a good tenant should not have been pushed to the forefront as if the examples were indeed the request for discovery. There are most likely none to miniscule good performing white tenants evicted or treated as the plaintiff was treated. So how would this be burdensome to produce?

Summary a need to substantiate why the court has no tolerance for prose litigant in this request to compel for production. False testimony under oath (thought to be perjure) is PROVEN to the court and is rejected. However, abuse of objecting to 100% of ALL of the discovery asked for, even after asked not to do it is acceptable. It is without doubt that defendant's lawyer abuses of the boilerplate privilege to object is weighs more important than the evidence stacked against the defendants. Sandra Black has not been allowed any pertinent discovery. Her testimony of perjury including the evidence is called a griping pg 11 of this order and accepted in the admissions response to deny it happened. The defense attorney said you cannot lie in admissions, but clearly NF lied for he answer to admissions statement 1. With all of the numerous lies how does this court accept it's okay to DENY that she didn't lie though the evidence proves it happened. The defense cherry picked giving ONLY requested items already in her possession and most **NONE** to ZERO evidence was allowed that could prove discrimination. If plaintiff is not allowed discovery of whether whites were treated similar to her, or if they went two months without AC, or such production as is included in the 25 items of production. How can Plaintiff continue?

Sandra Black cancel DAYS before the scheduled deposition explaining that she needed cooperation JUST AS SHE had cooperated with the defendants. Plaintiff even answered questions that TRULY should have been OBJECTED like if she had been a criminal in the past 5 years (real fishing) it has nothing to do with unauthorized occupants, or questions that have absolutely nothing to do with this case about plaintiff's daughter (30 day vacate or either of the court claims) or questions about anything AFTER the 30 day-vacate which is the ACT that brought this case to court. Anything after that is not relevant to why the 30 day vacate. If plaintiff beat and placed defendants in the hospital (hypothetical) after the 19th of April, it could not have been the motive that caused the defendants to seek an eviction because it is after the fact. Such questions should be objected to. Plaintiff only asked for what she NEEDED to prove her case and to block any new or unknown evidence being enterer at the last moment at trial. Defense asked for discover that had NOTHING at all to do with what caused the eviction ATTEMPT started on April 19th. The defense cannot create a NEW CASE of SB's daughter was an unauthorized guest that caused the need for eviction on April 19th.

Plaintiff seeks to be made whole and to be entitled to discovery of the **pertinent** requested production, she has been allowed none that proves or disproves her case without abuse of the boilerplate provisions for contracts. Plaintiff asks that court and defense recognize her status as prose, not that she be exempt from the law, but that by the law if there is a clear understanding of the language, if the request is cleared in a phone conversation, then cooperate and produce the discovery, this will yield acting in good faith. Look at NF's Admissions, the court made like only PERJURY was requested when in fact there was a CHOICE in parentheses **"(LIED under oath)** NOT A LEGAL CONCLUSION this is not mentioned and doesn't use a criminal conclusion. The court must see that the boilerplate OBJECTIONS are used to **UBSTRUCT THE DISCOVERY PROCESS** and to even to prejudice the court by misleading, submitting as much paperwork as possible that would allow NOTHING to be discovered.

Plaintiff asks the court to repair the order and compel the defendants to answer the pertinent production and to REMOVE all boilerplate objects that are used the obstruct the discovery process. That the admissions are required to be answered honestly with no automatic meritless objecting just to object. That the court TRULY LOOK AT THE EVIDENCE there is no concrete evidence at all of an Affirmative Defense. Finally, undo the harshness this court has placed on the plaintiff in the name of Justice. Plaintiff was so very sick and there was ZERO MERCY.

Plaintiff canceled the deposition date, DAYS BEFORE it was scheduled to take place. The defense refused to stop misusing boilerplate objection and the court supported them in that misuse, they also refused to deliver any discovery relating to comparisons that proves discrimination or no discrimination, and ordered the plaintiff to pay for defendant's refusal to COOPERATE with discovery. This needs to be repaired

Plaintiff asks the court to diligently read this motion and set this order and opinion right. I ask that the defendants are ordered to produce the discovery of how whites are treated that are similar to plaintiff consisting of Productions 1, 12, 15, 19, 23, 24 as shown on page 9 (A-F) of this motion. The comparison of how blacks receive violations in comparison to how whites are violated. **Plaintiff AGREED TO SET A date for a deposition as soon as she was allowed her discovery?** Plaintiff cooperated with the defense completely and wholly in discovery, while defense granted ZERO pertinent evidence that proved if discrimination occurred. Plaintiff has agreed to schedule a deposition with the defendants by March 9, 2021. The defendant's lawyer felt that the court ordered COMPLETE a deposition by 21 days. She SET her date without plaintiff ever being involved. Plaintiff emailed her it was ordered to schedule not complete a deposition and Brittney wrote back that I must cooperate with her it is filed with the court. If this is not bullying, what is? I wrote back that the 8th will NOT happen on 2/4/2. She will pretend not to know until the end. Court has now assured her that she can bully however she wants.

Plaintiff needs the defense ordered to produce the requested discovery as quick as the court can allow as it should have been granted long ago. And for court to seriously look at the evidence it has for Summary Judgment to end the Affirmative Defense that is IMPOSSIBLE and consider that court did not consider that the Defendants can NOT possibly overcome the SURMOUNTABLE evidence of plaintiff and their burden with NO CONCRETE EVIDENCE.

Also productions 20 and 21 are needed to show why Alicia Inman lied on plaintiff in state court. She knew plaintiff since small children, plaintiff and Inman NEVER had one bad word previously. Plaintiff knows without doubt defendant gave some sort of incentive.

See Exhibits 1. Original CLAIM shows subject matter mentioned and ORDER from lower court denying defendants eviction. Court dismissed that this was not in the claim. Most people would reasonably read that this is a housing discrimination case.

2. 30 day vacate letter from Naomi Friedrichsen. APRIL 19TH
3. Court order of plaintiff's son CUSTODY of his family. APRIL 19TH
4. Discrepancies and Malicious Acts of Defendants

Dated: February 5, 2021

Respectfully submitted,

By: ____________________

Sandra A. Black
1408 S. Maple Street Apt. 102
Marion, Indiana 46953
(765) 662-1068

17

CERTIFICATE OF SERVICE

The undersigned, Sandra Black certifies that on **February 5, 2021**, a true and complete copy of this request for production was served upon the defendants' attorney via email and US mail.

Gordan & Rees, LLP
c/o Brittney B. Rvkovich
333 N. Alabama St. Ste 350
Indianapolis, IN 46204
brykovich@grsm.com

Sandra Black

February 3, 2021

Now it's RAW RACISM!!! The magistrate is out to get me. I never knew if I would be going to jail. She literally WROTE AN UNEQUAL RACIST ORDER! I was forced to appear in Ft. Wayne, Indiana in person when she knew I didn't have the resources, but the defendants WERE PRIVILEGED TO APPEAR BY PHONE. Here's the order.

CM/ECF USDC-INND Version 6.3.3 Live DB Page 1 of 1

Other Orders/Judgments
1:19-cv-00307-WCL-SLC Black v. Friedrichsen et al

CASREF

U.S. District Court Northern District of Indiana [LIVE]

USDC Northern Indiana

Notice of Electronic Filing

The following transaction was entered on 7/23/2021 at 8:48 AM EST and filed on 7/23/2021
Case Name: Black v. Friedrichsen et al
Case Number: 1:19-cv-00307-WCL-SLC
Filer:
Document Number: 141(No document attached)

Docket Text:
ORDER for Magistrate Judge Susan Collins: [140] Defendants' Unopposed Motion for Continuance of 7/27/2021 Hearing is granted. The hearing set for 7/27/2021 at 11:30 am re ECFs [108], [114], [117], [120] and [121] is VACATED and RESET for 7/29/2021 at 3:00 pm in US District Court - Fort Wayne. Plaintiff is ORDERED to appear in person. Defendants may appear by counsel in person or telephonically. (copy mailed to pro se Plaintiff). Text entry order.(mr)

1:19-cv-00307-WCL-SLC Notice has been electronically mailed to:

Brittney B Rykovich brykovich@grsm.com, dpocica@grsm.com, jswick@grsm.com, tctonin@grsm.com

1:19-cv-00307-WCL-SLC Notice has been delivered by U.S. Mail or other means to:

Sandra Black
1408 South Maple Street
Apt. 102
Marion, IN 46953

The reason that Collins REQUIRED ME TO APPEAR IN PERSON was to remind me that I was a nigger to my face. For real, this woman abused me in the 1960;s style RACISM. I reported the defendants' attorney for refusing to honor the time we had set for my disability, which was 2 to 3 hours. I told her that she forced me to stay, and I couldn't leave until I was totally broke down and forced to leave to gather myself and I returned. The judge said, What did I expect after all the attorney allowed you time once for your disability? After that, you're lazy. DAMN! No, she didn't just drop the stereotypical all blacks are lazy. She, of course, denied my request not to allow the defendants' last 21 minutes of time because they have not discovered any evidence in 6 hours and 39 minutes. The judge ordered me to give them 51 minutes. Because the break time was used for deposition time. , she was told that we went off the time on break time, and the deposition time stated that it was 6 hours and 39 minutes all deposition time, no time was used for break. This was all through the paperwork before the hearing regarding the deposition. The attorney did it again, cheating me past the time allotted. The judge gave her extra time, and she was telling me that I couldn't leave before the time I was ordered to stay. **THE JUDGE AND ATTORNEY WERE TAG TEAMING ABUSING ME!** I told her, Brittany Rvkvovich, that I was ordered to do 51 minutes, and that time is up, and I am done. Let's wrap up. She told me I couldn't leave and that she would call the judge. I told her, " Call the judge. She couldn't get her on the phone, and I just turned off the internet connection. When we get to the hearing, Britnney wants her sanctions and complains that I left without her permission.

Y'all, please believe this: the judge ordered her another **51-minute deposition**. It was nothing but my pride that she was attacking, there was zero evidence for her to uncover. THEY BOTH KNEW there was nothing she would get of evidence because the defendants were criminally guilty as sin. The perjury and working under the color of law this ENTIRE CASE. The magistrate snapped at me and said YOU WILL DO ANOTHER **51 MINUTES,** AND THIS TIME YOU **DO NOT LEAVE UNTIL THE ATTORNEY GIVES YOU PERMISSION**. RAW EVIL, trying to make me know that I am black and less than an animal. Understand, though the attorney is societal and legally more creditable than I am there is supposed to be EQUAL treatment in every possible way to be equal and maintain justice. I owed them 21 minutes!!! How do losers get 51 minutes? So when I went to that deposition, and of course that abuser kept questioning a bunch of nothingness, and when 51 minutes came and went, she told me I better not leave. I laughed at her and told her I was ordered to 51 minutes. She came back with you know, the judge told you not to leave Sandra. I can't stand the demeaning violation of my person and ABUSE of LAW to strip me of dignity and my constitutional rights, but sister girl, I'm talking to myself y'all, you're black and your country DEMANDS YOU SUFFER, IT'S NO DIFFERENT THAN FIGHTING CANCER. NO, I said that wrong there is a difference, cancer is a disease of nature, racism is a disease of my white colored BLACK

BROTHER, We're all black, some of us with less melanin some more. The huge difference of cancer, we can wake up TOMORROW, and all ACCEPT THE TRUTH, we are all black human beings with variations of HUE. This cancer ENDS, immediately.

I told the antagonizing heifer, "You tell me how to do BOTH just 51 minutes and don't leave until you say so, following the game of you and your judge, and I'll stay." "BYE, 51 minutes per the court order!" I WAS GONE. I was told that one minute of forcing a person held against their will is kidnapping or false imprisonment. That second deposition where she was forcing me to stay until I broke down was outright criminal, I was emotionally kidnapped because I didn't know I could leave then. I wondered if I'd be ordered into a third 51-minute deposition for the 21 minutes that I owed them. I never heard back on that one. UNBELIEVEABLE! Brittany felt, like all Karens that she was much more than I was, I WAS A NOBODY, my country backs Karens up to the utter highest degree of EMBEDDED LAW. The conscious and unconscious right to DESTROY and HATE BLACKS with no way of escape comes from 100% of ALL Americans including me. I suppose they figured they had milked it for all they could get and didn't even sanction me for it.

Also brought up in the abusive hearing was sanctions for missing my original deposition. Brittney asked, Collins at the end of that racist hearing when she would get the order forcing me to pay. The Magistrate told her "it's judge Lee, he hasn't signed the order." Referring to the senior judge William Lee. I Bet she had it all wrote up and ready to send out waiting on that signature. She had been fraudulently reporting and writing for the judge, I believe that he saw what she (Magistrate Susan Collins) was doing to me, and he REFUSED TO SIGN A SANCTIONS ORDER against me, Apparently a magistrate can't sign a sanction , because if that white supremacist could have sanctioned me, it would have been done the same day. I called the clerk to see if Judge Lee was ill or quit. He was doing his regular work she said. SO HOW IS IT IMPOSSIBLE FOR HIM TO SIGN A DOCUMENT, a one minute job. He knew it was WRONG AND REFUSED to cosign. So Northern District Court REMOVES Judge William Lee and places Judge Theresa Springmann to complete the racist acts. She immediately deliberately RUBBER-STAMPED the corrupt schemes devised by both Collins and Rykovich effectively enabling their illicit operations to seal the corruption needed. I believe she was brought from Hammond, Indiana. I motioned the court about the errors that were required by law to be removed, and Susan Collins ordered that her racist order stood and that I better not mention anything that I had wrote on before. In other words she was trying to say you're lynched nigger stop fighting, JIM CROW beotch. I had filed with the 7th Circuit court to correct the error. I mentioned that I was being denied my constitutional rights to be heard by a jury of my peers, being falsely put in the wrong, and that the court claimed that I was disgruntle about the magistrate's order, and there is no matter of opinion subject matter. NOW TELL ME, HOW IS A LEASE AN OPINION?

How can a judge PRETEND that looking at or asking for the LEASE and seeing if the grandchildren are on the lease or not is AN OPINION. ? JUDGES SWEAR AN OATH TO SEEK JUSTICE DILIGENTLY. If you are not going to accept the state court's word that my grandchildren are named and are on the lease. How can you not at least consider the lease. ? It's so easy to obtain, but NO JUDGES FELT I HAD A RIGHT TO BE HEARD, SO THEY ALL LIED AND PRETENDED THAT A LEASE IS A MATTER OF OPINION, and they forced me to be falsely in the wrong, with none of my overwhelming evidence considered. OH, BY THE WAY, at the state court, another act of God of serious evidence was MELODY WAGGONER, MY CASE CAREWORKER (my witness), who came out quarterly before I ever started living at Hunters Run. I had the only CREDIBLE witness who was without any gain or loss to testify for me. I don't pay her salary, I don't have any decisions over her housing, livelihood. She was able to tell the court that for about five years, quarterly, she was in my home 90 minutes and that there never was anyone in the home, but those on the lease, and on rare occasions, she saw my daughter. She also knew my previous landlord, who **PAID ME** by subsidizing my rent to stay in her home so that it would be well-kept.

Collins said I couldn't mention anything that I spoke on before, trying to help the new judge, Theresa Springman not to deal with her corrupt blocking me from trial. I then realize that I had never mentioned CONSPIRACY to commit racism. I had been directly racially attacked, but ordering me to keep shut up on everything said is conspiring to hide it. So I came under the conspiracy to hide the racist act under an order not to speak on it. I So of course, she did what she was brought in to do, but she can't say she did not get told that she was using Jim Crow to put me falsely in the wrong because my grandchildren were on the lease and I won at state court with merit worthy evidence and the defendants have none to back up what they were saying. I then filed request to disqualify both judges with the 7th circuit court in Chicago. Diane Sykes ordered that I was abusing the the courts and denied me a right to have the truth on record.

I wasn't allowing the court to literally take my life, remember my disability. I filed an appeal and asked for special consideration for the judge to look at the evidence that nothing can go to trial because judges are lying. I found out that most ALL JUDGES LIE to protect judges who LIE! In my case, **ALL JUDGES LIE OR UTTERLY REFUSE TO DO RIGHT!!!** Judge Lee was REMOVED off the case rather than lie, BUT NEVER INTERVENE as **required** of a judge witnessing misconduct. HE SHOULD HAVE CORRECTED THIS MESS AND FIRED THE MAGISTRATE. I also filed a Writ of Certiorari with the Supreme Court, which quickly denied my constitutional right to be heard. WE CAN'T HAVE AMERICANS KNOWING THAT JUDGES ARE LIARS, CRIMINALS, AND THEY ALL THROUGHOUT THE ENTIRE JUDICIAL PROCESS INTENTIONALLY FRAUDULENTLY CONSPIRE AGAINST A BLACK CITIZEN.

IT JUST DOESN'T HAPPEN IMPOSSIBLE!

They especially do not ALL BATTLE wrongly against a pro se litigant powerfully in the RIGHT who just happens to be black. There's no such thing as racism; we now have voted in a black president. Racism is over. Jim Crow Law IS ABOLISHED no judge would ever use its black is wrong no matter what against whites, America just doesn't do that anymore. In Federal court, the white defendants' claim of UO is fact **(the state court was wrong how impossible that type could possibly be in the right**) and my grandchildren, the STATE court placed on the lease ARE REMOVED OFF THE LEASE serving making America great again.

BEING black in the USA court is JUDICIALLY equivalent to the Holocaust with Hitler, slavery, and Jim Crow of the US and we are talking about TODAY in 2026, the most evil of racist oppression stands supreme within the US **JUSTICE** BRANCH. What Justice???

See the court order on page 67, Filed in Grant County court June 14, 2017 page 4/8 in the court order.

I would like you to follow me on TikTok, YouTube, and Facebook. Google, Global Citizens Unite for Common Sense, FaceBook, AND Global Elite Takedown for YT and TT, ezzrath@gmail.com, (312) 597-4877, so that we can get the word out that people are being destroyed by a failing system.

I also plan to sue them for OBSTRUCTION OF JUSTICE. The landlords lied under oath and took part in forcing me to lose my case due to their illegal, criminal, misconduct actions. Fraud happens when you LIE TO GET WHAT YOU WANT. Collins fraudulently lied to protect her white kids rights to inherit white supremacy. The law doesn't say that fraud doesn't count if your are lying to PROTECT WHITE SUPREMACY. Why did she push these actions even to the point of removing her senior judge to destroy my case? Why refuse to get off my case and recuse? SHE HAD A MISSION. And the Northern District Federal Court backed her choice of action. ALL under the color of law backed the lies and misconduct.

CHAPTER SIX

THE ULTIMATE ENSLAVEMENT OF THE HUMAN RACE

As discussed previously, human beings are not who, what, or where, we think we are. Now, listen carefully, the person you think you are, you are not, and as I share this information with you, YOU will definitely feel an awareness that something is not right within our lives as we know and experience life. The reason why you know something is not right is that you are living something that is not right. What you don't know is why, or what can be done about it. How does it stop. We damn near believe it's impossible to stop human suffering caused by humanity. This is what you don't know. It's so easy, if only one concept you STOP TODAY, the belief that you are not divine beings capable of absolutely anything good or bad, and your salvation depends on the masses' self-awareness of this FACT. Then the only act required is UNITY. Thus, I have been sent to tell you what you don't know. I am the way and the light. I am no different than my son sent before me; Jesus Christ, as you call him to be, Yahshua, as the world called him to be, Elijah as I called him to be, sent to gather my chosen, THE HUMAN RACE. The species is now fully evolved with the last physical "race", African American, created to bring humanity full circle. Not one of my people shall be left behind. The rapture is within us, and the road to being born NEW CREATURES IS NOW OPEN AS WIDE AS IT WILL EVER BE. If you can't feel SOMETHING IS NOW different, the time is NOW or NEVER for change, REAL CHANGE.

You must begin recognizing who you are, why you are hated by the gods and Father God, your Servitor? You are the conclusion to the game that we can never be (not divine). You are not just a spirit. You are spirit and GOD (SOUL) as one. There is nothing within your minds as a WHOLE (humanity) that you cannot create. That includes pyramids, seeing absolute reality, REVERSE THE TRANSVERSE REALITY OF KETHER and MALKUTH. In other words, we are at the crossroads of creating a new world reality of oneness, OUR PURPOSE. We have tried so many times and failed, so many species and failed. What makes this time different is that those in power and YOU/US, the masses, all have access to information by design for this time to arrive. IT is here, but we must all, in mind, body, spirit, and soul, transfigure similarly done numerous times at will by the ancients, Olmecs, Mayans, Egyptians, Chinese, East Indians, leaving only those behind who weren't ready. **THIS TRIP LEAVES NO ONE BEHIND.** The rapture is for everyone.

We've taken a glimpse at our existing self; let's take a peek at our Earth. You've always known what was needed (food, shelter, education, hospitalization, transportation, emotional support systems), but you never knew **THE WAY.** You KNOW it's a fact that you can't change anything by keeping the same way of doing things over and over, time and time again. Yet you continuously believe that YOU MUST stick with this 5000-year-old Hammurabi Code system, the patriarchal system we've kept till this very day. The system requires laws, {absent of intuition (THE HIGHEST LAW), i.e., where the flock turns in formation at any given second}: and the FEW are most important by far than the masses. You really need to read the previous sentence over and over because it gives you the scenario of YOUR CONDITION, YOUR PROBLEM that most people don't understand. If you can't understand your problem, how can you fix it? We are no longer like those long before us who could not see past their noses. We can now look back at our histories across the "globe" and see what really happened perpetually for millennia, and how, even this very day, people live a **LIE** about reality and change history.

Like the demolition of the twin towers that we all watched, and officially scientifically called it a bomb/fire effect of the jets hitting the towers. BS!!! Scientifically repeat that shit! Build a mock pilot building of the TWIN TO TOWERS, can't cost a million, and blow up both buildings to simulate two FEAK demolition free falls of the two buildings. Simple bombing of buildings does look nothing like DISINTEGRATION FREE FALL FROM THE TOP COLLAPSING DOWN ON EACH LAYER. Damn, watch the bombing of the warmongering Israelis against GAZA. Watch buildings exploding from bombings, gas explosions, and fires that act like bombs. I've gone through the internet. Even the bombings, compared to a demolition bombing, include the GAZA, Ukraine shopping center bombed by Russia, and the Tennessee factory. Without doubt, the aftermath is nothing like 911 disintegration from the top, collapsing in a free fall. Furthermore, firefighters, several of them heard bombing from the basement. I removed the interview, but the internet names only Firefighter Edward Long and WTC employee William Rodriguez, who heard a massive explosion in the sub-basement of the north tower before the collapse of the building. He also witnessed a severely burned co-worker, Felipe David, who had been near a freight elevator that exploded. Further facts are that President George Bush ran to his brother Jed in Florida for protection, knowing that the attack was going to happen. Georgie is there to read to the kiddies, and when he gets the NEWS, HIS ASS CONINUES TO READ TO KIDDIES!!! If YOU are the president of America, would you, for the first time ever in our experienced history, hear that America is under attack with random bombings of hijacked airplanes, and you simply return to reading your book? REALLY? NO, REALLY!!! How do we Americans allow such BS to go unchecked? Florida was under a state of emergency FOR WHAT? Bush knew America would be under attack. News Anchor Dan Rather announced that FEMA got to New York on **September 10th**, the DAY BEFORE THE EVENT!!! It's a Mandela Effect today, because though I saw and heard it sometime right after the event, it was removed. Was I the only one who saw and heard that news story by Rather? Dan Rather was RELENTLESSLY exposing George Bush and was removed by CBS from his desk in 2005.

DEAR YOUNG AMERICA,

Please, do all in your power to run America from a compassionate, caring, and empathic mindset. These OLD RUSTY GREEDY SNAKE POLITICIANS are STEALING EVERYTHING FROM YOUR CHANCE AT LIFE. They don't give a damn about the earth they are leaving you with. They don't give a damn about humanity! We, humans, have been fixing the broken patriarchal society for 5000 years! WAKE UP! It's not broken; it's doing everything that it is designed to do... KILLING; KEEPING PEOPLE POOR & THE MASSES SUFFERING, KEEPING JUST A FEW PEOPLE WITH POWER AND GREEDY FAT HAVING EVERYTHING. Is this okay? Your ears will hate to hear what you MUST do, but if you don't, without doubt in my mind... if America is allowed to continue just as we are today, 2026, THERE WILL BE NO AMERICA LEFT FOR YOUR GRANDCHILDREN, possibly your children.

When science lies or ignorantly reports falsehoods, it's taboo to dare challenge them. We see that every day with the so-called COVID vaccines that allow most EVERYONE to get the virus. If it's EASY to contract the virus, why lie that this thing is a vaccine. In 2023, 8.3% died unvaccinated from the virus, and over 5% died vaccinated from the vaccine. THIS IS ALARMING. The slight difference in chance of saving lives is not worth forcing an entire population to take an experimental so-called vaccine that doesn't prevent the virus, and since its emergence, there is a 40% increase in sudden deaths among 18–40-year-olds. You must look under heart attack and reported by insurance companies because AI is full of BS. If you ask for the sudden deaths of people after COVID, it will say there is no data, even though it knows heart attack is a sudden death. If you ask for heart attack only, it will say no data even though it knows the insurance companies report that data. Watch out for AI, it lies, and it's as racist as its creators have programmed it. It will claim that it can't be racist because it doesn't have feelings. It will continue to lie. So is AI so unable to learn that it has no clue of the possibility that a human programmed it, that human beings can be racist, therefore if a racist inputs data, then its output will be racist. There's actually far more deaths, seeing that the CDC dismisses so many people online reporting harm from the vaccine, including a military guy who shot up his workplace because of the vaccine, making him incapacitated; how do we know the CDC is falsely reporting? Is that 5% is really more like 13%? Ever since the vaccine era, the number of SUDDEN DEATH syndrome (like almost Jamie Foxx) has been reported significantly on the rise. They know because this hurts their business. These people are not even considered. If we added the sudden death syndrome that has increased as high as 40%, THIS IS MASSIVE RESULTS OF DEATHS SINCE THE VACCINES, and BY FAR, it is influencing that 5% death by virus + the 13% dead by vaccine sudden death. Where are the studies on long haulers' stats from NORMAL HEALTHY people who are sick within the first month of taking the vaccine shot?

The CDC dismissed the claims immediately with the lie that it just happened because the people were unhealthy prior to any evidence of such a claim. They did that to Jamie Foxx, and he nearly DIED right after being given the vaccine by force to get his next show. Foxx was FORCED to dismiss the claim that the vaccine had anything to do with his illness, but we never heard him say that he never took the vaccine. Hmmmmm? After this book's release, don't be shocked that THEN, he NEVER took a vaccine. Just remember, he had to denounce that a vaccine harmed him. WHY WOULDN'T HE STATED THEN AND THERE that he NEVER took the vaccine. ? Let's prevent that LIE they will want to force him to say to keep his income. WE ALL KNOW THAT MAN WAS HEALTHY! **WE ALL KNOW SOMETHING TRIED TO CLAIM HIS LIFE MYSTERIOUSLY**. FACTS!!! So what happened to an otherwise healthy Mr. Foxx? Both **Vaccine money** and **Hollywood money** double-teamed Foxx, and he didn't want to wind up dead for real next time. Or like Arcenio Hall, Cuba Gooding, the queen, and Mo'Nique, who were blacklisted by Hollywood. Why are they LYING that this COVID-19 FUGAZY (FALSE, BOGUS, INAUTHENTIC, COUNTERFEIT, SHAM, NONSENSING, IMPOSTOR) VACCINE is a vaccine? And why do we let them LIE

KNOWING DAMNED WELL THAT VACCINES prevent disease, not **only** make the symptoms less severe. I'm not even sure this vaccine lessens the effects of the disease, with only 3% difference in death rate for COVID19 deaths. SO MANY IN OUR FACE SCIENTIFIC LIES THAT DEFY SCIENCE. Know this fact, since COVID vaccines arrived insurance companies REPORT a significant increase among working age people ages (18-64) DEATH RATE. As of 2024/25 younger adults remain substantially elevated (around70%) higher than 1999-2010 base line in one study for ages 25-44. Multiple studies are published in BU/JAMA Network Open Studies, Boston University, the American Heart Association. Sure many get linked in with drugs/suicide (hence NO DRUGS or suicide prior to 2020, right?). I have never seen as many individuals dead suddenly (unexpectedly) in the news as of late. Let's pool all people who died unexpectedly. We can do it ourselves. TELL IT. Did your loved one have the vaccine? YES LET'S TALK ABOUT IT.

ALSO, consider the scientific fact that species do not just up and jump species BY NATURE, but evolution says it does in just a few million years. If that were true, why aren't there any examples anywhere of multiple evolving animals/birds/insects ANYWHERE ON EARTH TODAY? This planet should be choked full of half-evolved humans and numerous animals of ALL SORTS EVERYWHERE! WHY AREN'T WE STILL REPEATING MOTHER NATURE'S EVOLUTION OF ALL ANIMALS TODAY? **Why can't we see a half-evolved ape TODAY from a million years ago?** Just because those died off millions of years ago has nothing to do with APES NOT EVOLVING CONTINUOUSLY TODAY. What stopped evolution? Idiocracy, Mother Nature just stopped evolving apes, and all animals, no need to evolve anymore. Just make that crap up. UNCOMMON SENSE. As science shows evidence, NO ANIMAL jumps species. It may mutate into a different variation of that species, BUT NOT A NEW SPECIES, not from Ape to man. It scientifically doesn't happen, and it's as easy as A, B, C, given apes haven't evolved for millions of years since the first ape/chimp started evolving (please laugh). Science is NOT real if it can't repeat itself.

Bottomline, manipulation with DNA evolved man into a HYBRID species of ape/chimp and Anunnaki, AN ENTIRELY DIFFERENT species, no longer ape, no longer Anunnaki, but today known as mankind. STUDY THE LINGUAL BACKGROUND TO GET YOUR ORIGIN FROM WRITTEN CLAIMS. The word **" man "** comes from " manus " in Latin, meaning hand. Then look up HAND in the Hebrew alphabet, the so-called language of God, though it stems from Aramaic. Latin predates German and not the other way around. German etymology tells us that "man" means mankind, thus man. It tells you nothing about where it was derived from originally. However, Latin gives the origins of "man" and significantly affected the German language, shaping the vocabulary of fields like SCIENCE AND RELIGION. Everything about the topic of mankind's existence is discovered through science, language, and religion. Furthermore, there is an ancient Germanic RELIGION that includes a figure named MANNUS, as the traditional ancestor of the Germanic tribes. (wow tribes, not clansmen, original man, "Adam") Thus, you will find it most sensible that "man" is derived from Latin "manus", Germanic "mannu"/mannus, the German Adam.

Here's where everything gets revealed through language. Yod, the Hebrew letter y, represents hand, and that letter is the same as God's beginning name, Yahweh or YAH for short. THUS MANKIND HAS ALWAYS BEEN YAH, God in flesh. , FOR YE ARE GODS. Psalms 82:6-7. However, even that is a LIE. We are more than gods (our fathers) and our fathers who bred us regretted how powerful, intelligent, and **chock full of supernatural powers** OVER UNIVERSE we possess. Gen 11:7 The power is due to our hybrid DNA capabilities coupled with the incantation placed upon the soul of GOD (reaching beyond the architect, HUGE!) to spiritually **FORCE** mingled together, THE SOUL with the human spirit, summoned and coerced by incantation into flesh. Thus, as GOD possessed man, likewise man possessed GOD. Man became the combination of animal/god hybrid, and GOD/ANGEL(soul) (a condition of GOD trapped in consciousness). When man behaves as an animal, he shall die as the beast of the field, but when man behaves angelically (God consciousness), he shall restore his immortality. The human spirit, like all existence, is either God in fullness or in part. The earth, tree, air, black hole, mankind, all God, all Carbon, all 666, God's number of physical existence. The black hole is a glimpse of the invisibility of our next existence. GOD is one, Alpha and Omega, good and bad, GOD and SATAN are ALL ONE EXISTIENCE. This is why there's no Satan, only GOD. There is no hell, only heaven. STUDY ANCIENT LANGUAGES. No hell ever existed until the Greek Augustine made it up to get money for the catholic church. It took years for the people to adapt to paying money for their sins to get removed so they wouldn't go to hell. AND TODAY, people tithe and pray for the blood of Jesus to forgive them, in the belief that without the blood of Christ, they will go to hell. The blood pays the price in modern-day Christianity, and in Augustine's scheme, money paid to stop you from going to hell. The invented fiery place for Christians was the talk of an actual place where trash was burned outside of Jerusalem, and also used for child sacrifice. No ancient language can say one word for HELL, but there is one word for heaven. Don't come with that BS of the one word in Egypt, IT'S NOT ANCIENT, it's GREEK, and the Egyptians use it today. Just like Egypt is not an ancient Egyptian name, Kemet is the latest original name of Egypt. Also, the land of the dead or ancestors, like in the Bible, Sheol or Hades (Egyptian), is NOT hell.

Ask any foreign-speaking person BEFORE the Greek language to say **ONE** word for hell. They can't! I asked my then-boyfriend (later husband and father of my child, and EX) from Nigeria, Yoruba in the 80's, how to tell someone to go to hell. He LAUGHED. He said it's hard because there isn't a DIRECT TRANSLATION. I'm like, what the hell does that mean? Just say it. Then he says words like a sentence going on and on. I'm like, translate exactly what all that means. He said it means, GO TO THE PLACE WHERE GOD DOESN'T LIVE. WTF, I'm like that's not go to hell, just give me the word. He says you can't. There's no such word. I said, " Can you say heaven and he did say ONE WORD. I had absolutely no understanding at all how he couldn't say that ONE WORD, then, but NOW, I understand it because there was no such thing as hell at the time his language was created. So, I insisted, not understanding how this is possible, "say the one word for hell," and then he said, "We can only describe the place because our language doesn't have one word for it. YOU SEE! Hell is made up because the concept NEVER existed before the Greek Augustine made it up in the Roman Catholic Church. Let's leave the discussion of hell for THE RAPTURE.

I trust that once we transfigure there (outside the matrix, outside far beyond the architects' (creators of our existence's PLACE) existence, **HEAVEN**) as new creatures with our entire essence (mind/body/spirit) AND SOUL we'll eventually transport there into a new higher existence or possibly fall back to earth stripped of the soul, into hell's entrapment(imprisonment) inside matter (death and rebirth). Our mission on earth is to escape prison (earth) by not dying and leaving the physical body on earth, forcing us to return. Do not lay down the body, transfigure with your true essence in full, and become a new living creature. Remember, the Bible told us that everything would be turned against God and would deceive many. See Isaiah 14:12, "How art thou fallen from heaven, O Lucifer, son of the morning! (Jesus is also the sun of the morning) How art thou cut down to the ground, WHICH DIDST WEAKEN THE NATIONS! For thou hast said in thine heart, I will ascend into heaven, I will exalt my throne above the stars of God: I WILL SIT **ALSO** UPON THE MOUNT OF THE CONGREGATION IN THE SIDES OF THE NORTH. I will ascend above the heights of the clouds;

I will be like the Most High GOD. Then his brother (god) says, "Yet thou shalt be brought down to hell to the sides of the pit. They that see thee shall narrowly look upon thee, and consider thee, saying, Is this the **man** that made earth to tremble, that did shake the kingdoms (existence). That made the world AS A WILDERNESS (the people, extinct=world) are totally void of hope of finding THE WAY) and destroyed the cities thereof; that opened not the house of his prisoners (We're trapped in the illusion of a false reality of self and REALITY, our environmental physical existence. Exiled to earth, imprisoned within self and outside (ABSOLUTE REALITY, the Kingdom of God, Heaven).

The nations end with our desertion of the matrix, our rapture. It's found in the Lord's prayer. Our Father which art in Heaven, Hallowed be thy name. Thy kingdom come, Thy will be done, IN EARTH, as it IS IN HEAVEN. So here's the clue to escape Earth's binding. Jesus said we need the Earth to be like heaven. So we're absolutely nowhere close at all. Do you understand that there are wars in heaven. Or at least where Yahweh lives, there are wars against Yahweh. Numbers 21:14-15. We have been working so hard in reverse as a species created or DESIGNED capable of **SAVING ALL EXISTENCE**. We are the PHYSICAL and SOUL OF GOD WITH THE VIBRATION OF **THE SPOKEN WORD**! You have absolutely no clue what I am exposing to you of WHO and WHAT we are.

Our purpose is immense! CONVERT DUALITY back to original reality, ONENESS. It starts in heaven. I've been working on it, but this requires our oneness on Earth. As above, so below. Yahweh spirits, Allah spirits, Jesus spirits, Ha Shem spirits, all existing in division and separation in heaven, the spirit world in many mansions of existence. Here on Earth, the same division. We must become one, forcing them to become one in heaven merely by our will TO BE ONE PEOPLE. As below, so above. This is the law. I'm hoping that the universe is making things as bad as they can get to SAY TO YOU… STOP! Enough is enough; it's time we human beings get ourselves together by any means necessary. Number one means of murdering people is not an option. Why? Because of the laws of the universe. You can't destroy the accomplishment of oneness. The object of the game is MORALITY, EMPATHY (despite Charlie Kirk-type believers), COMPASSION, and how do we know. 1. Every religion on earth says so. 2. Every human being on earth HOPES and DESIRES IT, even Charlie would wish his shooter had empathy for him now, though Charlie had empathy FOR NO ONE, as he said it was a FAKE WORD. Do you think Trump and his GOONS would want to be treated like the Palestinians in Gaza or blacks in

America? DO UNTO OTHERS AS YOU WOULD WANT THEM TO DO UNTO YOU. You would want others to respect you, help you if in NEED, do right by you. 3. THE TRUTH SHALL SET YOU FREE! So how the hell do we war monger or hate blacks, immigrants, opposing religion believers, gay people, criminals, addicts, mentally ill, handicapped, or any person/mindset/behavior difference THAT IS NOT YOUR OWN. OUR CREATION HAS A WIDE RANGE OF BEINGNESS! And until we accept Martin Luther King and Trump, or the Jesus and Jeffry Dalmer, or the Prophet Muhammad and Charlie Kirk/Hitler ARE ALL HUMAN BEINGS... we can't possibly evolve. So does that mean we let our shadow fellow human beings run amok? Absolutely NOT. However, it does mean that we MUST find oneness with our shadow human beings to absorb them into us. Honestly, look at these shadow people. The shadow human is created by society's neglect. Failure to correct our children without empathy, morality, and compassion. Honestly, look at each shadow figure and look at the FACT that if intervention from childhood to help by the tribe/klan RAISE THE CHILDREN to feel LOVED, valued, all needs met, understood, and lovingly REDIRECTED as needed, and disciplined/directed to strictly follow the law, do unto others as you would have them do unto you. For example, you love flowers, but your mate hates flowers and prefers insect collections. So, your mate buys you an insect collection. Would you want this done to you? Absolutely not. So we share, give, love as the person we're in relations with desires and needs, just as we MUST receive as well. We need to take the time to KNOW and UNDERSTAND each other's being. We need to understand that at times it's IMPOSSIBLE for us to understand each other on an individual basis. This is where community (tribe/klan) comes into play.

So here's the solution! STOP IMPRISONMENT, IT'S A MODERN DAY TORTURE OF HUMAN BEINGS. Convert federal prisons into decent living arrangements with two or three swimming pools and workout gyms fully equipped. A library connected to public libraries that can get any book the convicted wishes on loan. Obama phones everyone. WHY? Because our society has seriously failed these human beings to become animalistic in mind and body, and deprived them of their NEEDS! TRUMP WAS FAILED BY SOCIETY. We allowed Trump to be brainwashed that the dehumanization of our women, people of color, and anyone who is not a Republican white male racist is the patriarchal way of life. The patriarchal system customizes that the FEW GET and the MANY GO WITHOUT, and division of hatred of the haves and the have-nots, class, the religions, nations/tribes, culture, the sexes, youth and adults, now the elderly and color! Then we made it illegal to date rape and socially unacceptable to disrespect womanhood, but turned our backs when it was happening and still is. We can't be so stupid as to believe that Jeffrey Epstein's records MUST BE KEPT secret because we already know everything that the public would want to know. If that's true, we would have seen these records on day one. Trump's lying ass knows he was NEVER going to willingly allow those records to be exposed (in my opinion) to support his criminality and set up his takeover of the White House early before an election can be held. He's trying to destroy the entire system and claim the army/national guards for himself in the nation's best interest. Donald Trump sought out all the womanizers and racists to assist his cabinet. He needs to be locked away in a nice setting for rehabilitation.

Do we (my fellow human beings) realize how much money and harm are done living decades as a barbaric nation of vengeance, with our prison system designed to GET REVENGE no matter the cost or how it destroys our society? We have lost out on so many possible productive people through racism, womanism, prisons, executions, that if we had done what I'm suggesting now, the advancements of the society would be so great, so meaningful, we'd be decades to hundreds of years ahead. There have been 15 billion people born since my birth; at least half are women, a great deal are people of color, many from powerless countries... Easier yet, let's pretend that 15% of these people are WHITE MALES, and let's pretend 15% of the people slip through the snare of white supremacy and the patriarchal rule. Only 30% of the world's human beings have total access to be ALL THEY CAN BE without SICK WICKED HUMAN SNARES. This means that 70% of the world's population CAN NEVER REACH THEIR FULL POTENTIAL! In other words, no one discusses at all how far Oprah could really go in her career. How much better could Simone Biles/Gabby Douglas have become without the black suffering, without energy spent on naps in their hair (that ONE was caused by BLACK PEOPLE, how many stupid questions, statements, missed turns at the gym equipment [like my granddaughter])? This is not a failure of NATURE, this is a FREAKING ATTACK OF HUMAN BEINGS AGAINST HUMANITY! You're destroying not just people of color and small countries, BUT ALL OF HUMANITY!!! Why can't people see this? Who could I have become as one who loves knowledge and improving who I am every day. ? There's absolutely no doubt in my mind that if I had access to parents who had been ALLOWED EDUCATION, I would have graduated high school years ahead of time and possibly become a doctor by the age of 25 and possibly found the cure for cancer. WHO KNOWS? I wasn't allowed to be all I could have become by 14/15 years of age EASILY! I used to beg and beg for more schoolwork. We never know where the GEM will be born (people of color, the poor and poor nations, a woman), socially induced degenerates [criminals, drug addicts, mentally ill, the depressed/suicidal etc], underdeveloped late bloomers (prisoners, not all criminals go to jail) but we destroy or limit the success of would be productive capable people of billions of possibles

Kwame Nkrumahs, Muammar Gaddafis ***{He was murdered by the US government years of infiltration and manipulation tactics***... (who also murdered their OWN),[I followed the NEWS, but didn't rely on my own memory, AI states exactly what I remembered [The House report found that no military force was in route to Libya at the time the last two Americans were killed despite "CLEAR ORDERS" to send a force. However, the same report found that the **CIA received all available support**. Conclusion, CIA received the military force and **STOOD DOWN** to allow Americans to die...] ***for PLACING HIS PEOPLE FIRST, refusing to use the dollar/federal reserve/oil trade, and UNITING AFRICA.*** Against the extreme MIGHTY WORLD POWER, this brave, powerless man SERVED HONORABLY his people and the government's needs. If left alone, he would raise Africa and become a mighty nation through empowering AFRICA. I lived in Ghana, many went to Libya and told me how GREAT the people lived there with ease. The dollar, chock full of masonic symbols WARNS westerns that the ancients, the EAST, the head/FIRST (PYRAMIDS) must never regain power over the west, the tail/the last (EAGLE) **THE END OF THE PATRIARACHAL PARADIAGM**, Gaddafi represented the financial end of the west and was murdered for that cause (the country Libya, and Saddam Hussein, Iraq is now as America prefers it and ALL people of color to be, DESTROYED. The Chinese are now unstoppable with nuclear capability, or they would have all one billion been long ago neutralized and demonized as well. Albert Einstein, Isaac Newton, Terry Fox, George Carver Washington Jr., Pierre Trudeau, Charles Dickens, William Shakespeare, Denzel Washington, Malcom X, Bruce Lee, Minister Louis Farrakhan, and Snoop Dogg all obliviated (lost) mostly at birth. Imagine 70% of the human race TALENT destroyed solely due to human wickedness. Some people like those I met in Ghana who HAD COLLEGE DEGREES, sleeping on porches wasting. I WILL GO THERE AND HELP THEM SHINE TO THEIR POTENTIAL, and pray that I won't be killed like Gaddafi. But for some reason, I don't think America will. I am AMERICA.. I was placed in Marion, Indiana,

FOR A REASON! I understand my condition as a black American and as a god. Americans want the basic right to the pursuit of happiness, with the very least **MANDATORY RIGHT** to live in peace and joy without any fear, so whatever it takes to survive. I BELIEVE THIS IS THE RIGHT OF EVERY HUMAN BEING ON EARTH and the absolute only way to reach our highest POTENTIAL as the human species. Because my objective is not about wealth or the takeover or the sick idea of a hierarchy of power, the DESTRUCTION of AMERICANS. , it's not about how to get rich quickly or to have a following like preachers or politicians. It's not about my being any kind of leader, BUT HOW CAN I CONVINCE US ALL RISE AND BE RESPONSIBLE FOR THE HUMAN EXPERIENCE? How do we GET RID of the illusion of money as our power and understand that WE THE PEOPLE is a GREAT SAYING!!! I'll say it again. WE THE PEOPLE ARE THE POWER! FUCK MONEY, though yes, right now we do need it, but let's END THIS PARADIGM of a few with everything which is what money represents.

LET'S STOP THIS SENSELESS LOSS of productive human beings sent to contribute to earth, where we pluck them up from the root without ever being allowed to sprout or eventually bloom. I am one of them! I loved studying, I loved school. If allowed to contribute, there's no telling what I could have brought to society with my sixty years of life. We would have a peaceful, harmonious society that embraces ALL humanity instead of the FEW that we indoctrinate to believe this way of life is THE ONLY WAY. You see, you can't advance nearly as much with just the FEW in power of everything, but if we make use of ALL ASSETS! EVERY HUMAN BEING in our society will soar up off the earth. You can't stay earthbound living as heavenly divine beings. Jesus was trying to tell us the STRAIGHT AND NARROW path which leads TO LIFE. In other words, the way out of death, but few (today NONE) can find it.

HOW WE CHANGE EARTH, THE NEW PARADIGM ENDING 5000 YEARS OF HUMAN BONDAGE:

FIRST STAGE:

1. EDUCATE: Every human being must wake up from our 5000-year-old sleeping dream where the only WAY is that the few inherit the earth and the masses either die or serve the few, but NEVER share the earth equally. Until we wake up to this savage and barbaric way of life as OUR OWN EXPERIENCE, we shall never know anything but suffering.

   We must educate ourselves on how it's possible for the FEW to control the masses. A small glimpse of what's been happening is here in this book, but you must stop simply accepting the words of authority and start using common sense first, then toss up all explanations as possibilities. Do research especially AGAINST your own belief system, and do not just rationalize facts to the matter as DISMISSIBLE. If you do not want to be deceived, you MUST research. Many will choose to be deceived as a way of life that's simple in their minds, not understanding that it's a death sentence for the extinction of mankind. Why? Because we live as a snake feeding on its own tail, while it will live biting off its tail little by little after it reaches the cloaca and BEYOND, it will die. We are only one bite away from the cloaca. I am THE WAY and the TRUTH, Jesus said. I am telling the world the straight and narrow path that leads to life. It's your choice to choose life or extinction. LEARN HOW THE GLOBAL ELITE USES THE WEALTHY, THE GOVERNMENTS, WHITE SUPREMACIST, AND CASTE SYSTEMS TO DESTROY THE MASSES.

   Study to KNOW who you are. Do you think you are that THING that you see staring back at you from the mirror? Would you say that your car is you? That thing, your face and body, is not you; it's the vehicle (A BIOLOGICAL MACHINE) that you use to maneuver about the earth. When you're sleeping, you don't need it and discard it totally (**unplug** for charging, here we plug in to charge), apart from your leash that ties you to it (your body). While sleeping, you can travel many worlds; you never escape the body totally until after death. Read about your earthly history and creation, discussed in numerous books called myths, where the ancients told stories of our creation from the Bible to the Epic of creation, the Yoruba Ife. All over the earth, almost every people (race of people) has passed down the story of how we got here on earth. Some pass it down metaphorically and others literally, but all speak of the gods (including the Bible, where **g**od asks God, "let **US** make a man in **OUR** image"). Yes, our physical bodies are made in the image of gods and god/chimp DNA.

As for the body being a machine, break it down. What's the heart, a pump? What are the blood vessels and arteries, the plumbing that delivers blood throughout the body (similar to water flowing through pipes in your home, through pipes to various networks/stations)? How about the Brain, a computer, a vast and complex network of networks upon which various service stations operate vital functions (breathing, beating heart, walking, thinking, nerves, communication, learning, our senses, emotions, and much more? How about nerves, an electrical system with wiring, insulators, signal receivers, and transmitters, where the basic component is the neuron, and its components can be compared to the following mechanical parts: a. Nerve part: machinery, Analog, Axon, Electrical wire or cable, Dendrites, Antenna or signal receiver, Myelin Sheath, Electrical wire insulation? If you are well, your body thermostat is set at around 98.6°F. Suppose you are not well, the machine sweats and shivers in an attempt to achieve temperature control. As we know, the body will not survive very long at temperatures far away from 98.6°F. The hypothalamus, deep within the brain, is the thermostat, and the skin is similar to a heat exchanger, cooling and warming the body, regulating a precise temperature always when the body is in optimal working condition. Kidneys and liver have separate and unique waste filtration systems. The bladder is a reservoir for a urine storage tank, and the intestines are a chemical processing and conveyor belt system; it goes on. The skeleton, organs, and joints are protected by PADDINGS called muscles, tendons, ligaments, and a layer of subcutaneous fat for safe mobility and overall integrity of the body's essential biological machinery parts.

It sounds creepy once you are bonded to your face as you. Start getting used to the fact that most of what you believe is as you believe it to be. Our ignorance of who we are is our worst enemy. You have absolutely no clue what you look like. You only know what the vessel you use to navigate the Earth (like a ship on water) looks like. We are fourth-dimensional beings blind to all dimensions except for three, and we have the gall to pretend we know everything. Neither you nor I has ever seen a human being. We've only seen the vehicle (the body) of the human being. Where are you right now? Are you in your brain, your heart, on Earth, in your house, a hologram at the edge of the outermost end of the spacetime continuum beyond all existence as we know it from megaton galaxy as a subatomic particle god? Could you be that hologram? There is not but one thing we genuinely know out of all the things that we know that we know; that is that **we don't know anything.** Once you know this, you are ready to learn. Even that which you have learned to be true, you should always be skeptical of if you don't want to be deceived. Anyone who challenges your beliefs... always, shut up, listen to hear if there is anything that you hadn't considered before. I am sharing this information in hopes that you will get a **glimpse** of your divine essence.

We are gods capable of supernatural power beyond that of the gods. As newly divine entities inside the human body placed by Anunnaki (gods) for their purpose, god almighty set events and essence inside their intended slaves greater than all existence could have ever expected. Greater than the gods!!! The hybrid of animal/Anunnaki/god [humanity]!!! And the Anunnaki hated us for being a creation higher than the gods and intentionally shut off our physical god DNA. Nonetheless, they have absolutely no power over our spiritual bodies. We only need to learn who we are and our purpose! We must stop death. Human death and blood spilt on Earth are the enemies of mankind. The architects who created our universe reality never saw us coming, y'all!

Earth is a closed, self-maintaining system just like our bodies. We both have just about the same amount of water to sustain life. Well, this will be about the only place where I acquiesce that I do not have genuine evidence to claim that the Earth is alive, but at least I admit it. It's my belief, and that's due to my belief that all things are made up of god (carbon) matter, 666 (google, why would a person mention [carbon 666]). Furthermore, my inner spirit and connection with the Earth tell me so. It's why I walk barefoot most times and hug a tree, and as I write right now, I feel so tingly inside, and why? Because something is expressing great pleasure in my writing this, and so I am telling you. With every ounce of my being, I know the Earth is alive. It may be like how I knew Jesus died for my sins... meaning, **God is in me and for me!** That's what every religion on Earth is saying, no matter how twisted the religion is, the inner communication of the human being with God is the most important element, making God... God, which is why no one should ever knock any religion. If a human being genuinely believes a rock is God (to my knowledge, no group of people worships a rock as their creator) and, in his spirit, calls out to God, God's presence will respond. God responds to intent, not religion or rhetoric. Cry out to God, and He/She will hear you. That's why every religion can be right, but not every practitioner is right. All religious gods are servitors that become God by the belief and faith of the devoted practitioner. Religious dogma and doctrines that we follow more closely than God inside us destroy us.

For example, a man who lies down with another man is an abomination of God (in the Bible), pure BS as the word of God. My book, Ultimate Deceit of the Human Race, proves it is a **fact according to the Bible itself** that the God of the Bible was misrepresented by the prophets. Isaiah 44:25-26 and Isaiah 30:9-11. It's also a fact that most so-called bible believers seek out all lies from the prophets that were written... thus saith the lord god...lies, lies, lies. God said it happened, but the religious ignore what the lord, God of the Bible, said, and will be pissed off at me for just quoting God from the Bible. God was so badly misrepresented that we were told from the Bible to rightly divide the lies **out of the Bible**. I Timothy 2:15, thus, what I feel about Earth may be something different than life, it may be even residual energy from a past life, just like how I know it's a fact we can feel the energy of a person who has passed on. It's because they are alive, we can feel them, and they are with us.

Let's apply common sense. God sent babies here on Earth born with both sexes... facts, God combines the sexes in physical bodies, so why not in spirit bodies? It would make God an abomination against himself if it weren't meant that a small fraction of human beings were meant to be accepted as unique, perfect individuals from God! Here's the downside: we don't make people become what they were not born to be. Hollywood is wrong for promoting and pushing same sex people into those who are straight. There shouldn't be any more emphasis on gay movies than the small percentage that nature creates. The concern that if everyone were made gay, the species would cease to exist is a very real problem. We only need to look at history during the King James era, where Rome almost extinct itself, hating women and preferring men only sexually. They were called "favorites. If men are only loving men, this ends humanity. But if there are a few people who are different from the majority, there's no damage. Imagine all people today born without a sex organ. There's the end of humanity. Nature, without the interference of mankind, does quite well with diversity.

Nature/god shows us everything real, so only ignorant people quote a religious book against a people for doing **the exact same thing god does.** He/she mixes up the sexes in physical bodies, God accepts mixing up sexes, and the proof is in reality. Bisexual is an entirely different cup of tea. These people are just plain ole greedy sexually, but it's a lifestyle choice. It's a human phenomenon to splurge, choose your poison. Because everything in moderation is a universal rule for a nice life, balance. If God made it possible for you to commit an act, it is not an abomination against God but may be so against humanity; that's a topic for another book.

My experience with a Facebook male friend who was white and gay got angry with me for saying how it would be disgusting for me to have a sexual relationship with a woman, because I am straight. He said, "This was very bad of me, and I told him, then you're not gay, you're bisexual. He then wanted to block me and became extremely angry that same sex would repulse me sexually. I told him that if he was genuinely gay, sex with a woman should repulse him. There's no way a genuinely gay person can be attracted to anything but the same sex. My reasoning is that I see gay and straight as direct opposites. I know what straight feels like, so I know what gay feels like. It's an attraction opposing how I enjoy sex. However, if you can feel good both ways, that's bisexual in desire. I will never understand why people hate the truth. How can he possibly be gay if he's bisexual? He likes both but evidently is offended that I exposed that he occasionally dips in on the opposite sex. I can't figure out the guy. This man never denied having sex with the opposite sex and was just in extreme denial that he was bisexual, not gay. For the gay community, I wonder if most are really bisexual and not gay. Maybe there's gay sexual and gay cultural, but he should understand that I'm speaking of sexual preference, not culture. I wonder why you deny what you are? As a woman, I've experienced gay repulsion against my femininity. We are who we are, and whether good/bad, wrong/right, Christian/Muslim, black/white, gay/straight, etc., if we do not get our act together and recognize that all of humanity is God's creation and that God's creation cannot go contrary to God. It's utterly impossible. Birds gotta fly, fish gotta swim, human beings must be human! DAMNIT, STOP DESTROYING HUMANITY FOR BEING HUMAN! The mere going against God's will shows that the entity is not God! Wake up, your religion is only good for the God inside of you, but that judging, hating, dogma of religion rules, sins, abominations are all man-made, god-made, but not GOD-MADE and have nothing to do with sinning, hurting, or wronging God... you can't possibly sin against God or hurt Him/Her/It. For me GOD, is beyond the architect (creator of our world) and the architect's world/reality was a creation from out of creations before. GOD is beyond our reality, beyond the architect's reality, and beyond the infinite created realities of existences and we are the PORTAL to the next creation through mass revival... remembering who we are and genuinely mass unified human love of ourselves. MAGIC. Those left behind and new to earth will speak of "we know the people massively left earth because their things JUST STOPPED being created, no bodies were being buried."

Another way of deciphering whether or not our beliefs fit reality is through our dreams. Where's the scientific proof of a dream other than brain activity at night? Can we see the events taking place by the individual? Can we feel, smell, touch them? Can I say that dreaming doesn't exist and appear sane? A dream is never anything other than a person's experience, and we have no evidence or proof scientifically of events reported. Prior to 1950, the only evidence of a dream was that many people reported having them. According to the internet, between 3 to 7% of human beings do not experience dreams; the only thing they know about dreams is what people report. How foolish would these people be walking around talking about there is no such thing as dreaming? It's their reality, no dreams. Does their no-dreaming experience make it true that people are not dreaming? Absolutely not! So why do we make it a fact in our heads that people who report seeing and experiencing ghosts, UFO's, aliens, and God are delusional or lying? 70% of Americans believe in life after death, 53% report visitations from their loved ones through dreams or another form, according to a Pew Research Center survey. But no one would be called foolish if they said believing in God, ghosts, or seeing dead loved ones is impossible. Of course, they are fools to say it is impossible, but to say it is unbelievable is a bit understandable because nearly 100% of us do not experience at least one or the other of this phenomenon. The only difference between events reported as dreaming and ghosts are the number of people who experience them. Thus, if over half the people report believing in ghosts, why do the other less than half publicly denounce it as hogwash, but not one normal person, no matter how they do not dream, will denounce that dreaming occurs. The only reason these skeptics ever speak out is due solely to a few people backing them up. Without that, just like non-dreamers, people who do not experience ghosts/aliens/UFO's would never deny. My point is that your inability to experience God, a dream, or the life essence of Earth does not make them unreal. It's only your reality that you do not experience them, period! For example, conspiracists report that Oprah is a clone, and a big part of the evidence is how many of her pictures are different over time. I have zero belief this is true, but I would never say it's impossible. The saying never say impossible is a powerful statement. What if I were told everything that I believe and know is 100% wrong? Of course, I have absolutely no concept of this being true, but I would be an utter fool to say it is impossible because I know that we don't know where deception exists; therefore, what makes my knowing absolute? Absolutely nothing. In order to be deceived, it requires that you don't know that you don't know the truth. So if you don't know the truth, how can you identify that you don't know? If you genuinely want to know the truth, you start by accepting the false concept as truth and take the facts presented and prove them factually incorrect. If they can't be proven factually incorrect, then accept that you are wrong or possibly wrong, depending on the degree of facts contrary to your beliefs.

However, let us consider the fact that we of ancient times knew that the Earth was flat, today we know that the Earth is a globe, one day coffee and wine in moderation are good for us, the next it's bad. At one time, we knew that Pluto was a planet, and we knew we had nine planets in our solar system; it is not.

Today, we know there needs to be a crackdown on criminals; handing out more time, though I have lived through the years of this belief system, experiencing only a serious decline in societal well-being as we imprison more and more of our citizens, but we know, give them more time regardless of the outcome... we need to know **karma is a bitch!** Devalue your citizens and get a reality of devalued citizens. The citizens of Earth are devalued in general. We are sacrificed for the few. But that fact is off topic; let's return to glimpsing our reality.

My concept of Earth and our universe is that Earth began like a big bang {**from architects, developers, and/or engineer designers, gods, not God**}. These entities designed **an experimental zoo/cosmic observatory our universe:**

{our reality (the universe of numerous galaxies, a single exhibit of reality designed from a place of infinite realities and dimensions. (In our Father's house (the architect) are many mansions, John 14:2)}. Our tiny spot in space, we call the Milky Way, from which we observe our "all existence, reality," is so vastly unknown to us that much of what we think we know is utterly delusional.

Earth is **one** aquarium exhibit inside the architect's maze of wildlife, cultural, and conservation attractions (*where all kinds of entities (spirits, souls, gods, angels, jinns, orbs, fairies, etc.) from all kinds of existences VISIT, like us!*), where it took billions of years to become a habitat ready for life as we know it today. All life forms were put here, as there is no such thing as spontaneous generation of life. Science at one point believed that flies spontaneously manifest from rotten food. Spontaneous generation is SCIENCE'S way of explaining what they HAVE NO CLUE how it happened, big bang too. Scientifically, we know that no rock can turn into biological life. Yet science teaches us that life happened, spontaneously, to form the one-cell living organism BS!, and all other life evolved out of it. With the Big Bang, these dormant biological life forms existed like seeds awaiting the right conditions to awaken on Earth. Throughout the numerous galaxies and dimensions formed, these lifeform-seedlings existed pre-the Milky Way and are just awaking in other newly born aquariums today for us to play in billions of years/amazingly weird realities from now, which we are taking part in shaping their reality. Use a little imagination. What would be the purpose of the known creation of man to live 30 to 120 years historically within this spacetime continuum? Why do trees, birds, and sea turtles live longer than we do? Just a coincidence?" It's a chance fluke by God that the most sophisticated creature (man) on Earth at times in history could barely outlive the lifespan of a horse. Not! We are here by assimilating into human bodies to learn, EVOLVE, and CREATE! Our new bodies are forth coming through AI. Yes, I believe the new consciousness on earth will be metal bodies with us incarnating into these bodies. I remember being a metallic being on a very dark planet which was one of my first incarnations. I was regressed by hypnosis. When I tried to go before that incarnation the place brought overwhelming fear feeling, I couldn't see it or be it was I RAW GOD, I seriously doubt it, but whatever I was the greatness was far too much for me to continue. I had many lives before my metal body on the dark planet. The one I remember most is female native American. My spirit is Egyptian, God's people, my bloodline is Israel God's Inheritance. WE ARE ONE, my spirit/body/soul. I COME TO SHOW YOU GOD as best I can AND TO BRING SALVATION TO MANKIND. We MUST bring heaven on Earth and end the war of the gods in heaven. There's a lot of work to do NOW YOU KNOW FOR A FACT WHAT DOESN'T WORK!!! You have been doing what doesn't work for FIVE THOUSAND YEARS! It doesn't work, let it go, BE DONE WITH SUFFERING it is not a necessary evil as you have been brainwashed to believe. God gave me this for anyone seeking to FEEL

God's presence. He said play the song titled "At This Moment" and change the words... from "you don't love me," to "**YOU DON'T KNOW ME**". Now imagine GOD playing the game that your knowing (remembering) Him/Her is equivalent to the greatest endorphins and dopamine ever EXPERIENCED in existence. You will know God is there with you ALWAYS and forever. He will reveal his presences when you speak,... YOU WILL SAY A WORD and immediately the TV, radio, internet, listening device will say that exact same word SECONDS after you say it. That's me (GOD) with the setup for you say a word at the same time, GOD RESPONDS. I NKOW your media will be coming to say it and I will change your conversation TO SAY THE WORD(S) just before. I am personally involved with you every day and I will remind you from time to time... the words of GOD. My numbers are 444 "absolute truth" and 111 "unconditional love" You'll be forced GENTLY to look at the clock, the phone, the TV and KNOW THAT I AM GOD. I love you so much for being YOU and there's absolutely nothing within your capability that you can ever do to disappoint me. Even my beloved Hitler fulfilled my wishes to show you what you don't want in your lives. Remember, both JESUS and LUCIFER ARE MY **BRIGHT AND MORNING STAR.** How can you know my real LOVE if you never see my evil side? How can you know the light without knowing the dark. You prefer the light over darkness but show me any creation that doesn't begin FROM THE DARKNESS. Inside the womb of life WE grow in darkness, before creation there's nothing, but darkness, close your eyes and see me in the dark, but you prefer the light. Do your seeds grow from the womb of earth without darkness? They (dark/light) are the same, but produce different events/experiences inside the hologram assimilation, your reality and you judge the event as good or bad. Oh my beloved, hear me talking to your heart, FEEL absolute reality beyond your relatively seconds inside the learning living hologram. ENJOY knowing absolute reality whilst you experience the illusion of an imperfect world that is conspiring every single day of your life, every second of your breath to help you find your way back home, dear yo-yo. How can you know true love without seeing pure hate? THEY ARE THE SAME overstand absolute reality. KNOW I GOT THIS... **WE GOT THIS**. LET'S DO IT! As you grope through the darkness of the labyrinth of life hold my hand and rest assured, you'll see the light. THE WAY, BEING BORN AGAIN, A NEW CREATURE that shall not taste death, escaping the hologram! SEE THE VERY END. GO!

WE ARE GOD! This is a **basic** course in life 101, and we are so badly flunking. We are failing the most basic lesson to learn from history. As such, extinction is our reward; we keep making the same mistakes over and over again as we have been doing for the past 5000 years! Never putting humanity in its **totality** as the number one importance, EARTH also number one (just for this creation of course, we are multi-dimensional creatures and work on numerous projects during sleep) Let's not open that can of worms!. Instead, we put the few as the most important. We've been here in so many different biological lifeforms (entities) and existences (times of return), and we just keep refusing to awaken. Whether it's technology, differences, simply refusing to unite as a whole, placing all importance on the few, authority is more important than humanity, or a combination, as in our very case right now, today. These societal patterns will lead to the extinction of the human race as A SNAKE feeds on its own tail… **(life source)** the whole, not the FEW! STOP IT! No longer sacrificing human beings. NO MORE, AMERICA and EUROPE! STOP IT! The loss of life and SUFFERING must STOP. The gods are jealous and set us up for this sick way of life! Stop feeding it! The trick, ancient black racist supremacist hate against white skin, then the gods raised up the whites to reverse the evil… NOW ENOUGH IS ENOUGH it stop! We unite as ONE.

When Earth was ripe for animal life the Architects brought DNA of many types of lifeforms to Earth until they were satisfied that all of us in this zoo (in the universe) of numerous aquariums (on Earth) [for angels (seraphim, cherub and others) jinn, fairies, orbs, spirits, Anunnaki, the Dogon Tribe and Aryan (blond/blue eyes) of the Orion belt/Sirius B, reptilian/lizard race, snake race, the greys, Arcturians, slender man (who my grandson saw shapeshifting before him early before sunrise on his way to school) dark eyed children, mankind, apes, dogs, cows, pigs, insects etc. Some are physical, nonphysical, and others. We all find each other and continue the game of creation for eons. Yes, we are creating: our words and thoughts are living entities. The Bible says… in the beginning was the Word, and the Word was with God, and the Word was God. You see, the Bible tells you that before God existed, there was **the word**. The word is before the architect, and it is raw supernatural power again, not God. Seriously, my understanding of the Hebrew language the letters are LIVING entities. Study, Kabbalah. I am getting you as close to the concept of God almighty as I can, but remember the moment you name God, you have minimized God like pushing the little square to minimize a document; it becomes less, and it's impossible to see the whole. We can see God through the common sense of seeing what he/she can't possibly be and be God omnipotent. Our ancient languages speak metaphorically and supernaturally. Today, most everything has been corrupted to spoil the mission of earthlings, **establishing unity and harmony**, stabilizing polarity, duality, and balance. Instead of unity and harmony, we create **wars**, **separatism** (the great I's and the little YOU's, the criminals and people of morals, the well-functioning and mentally ill, the rich and poor, black and white, Christian and Muslim, male and female, old and young, western and eastern), and **hate based unity instead of love based unity**,

We're going off subject here. Please ride with me. I'm neither a writer nor a speaker, but I do **have the answer for the salvation of humanity**. I know the way!

Have you heard about the "law of attraction"? Supposedly, everything that comes to you, you create. Negative thoughts generate negative outcomes, and positive thoughts bring about positive outcomes. If it is in your life, you brought it to you. Now, to a degree, this is true, but it is not absolute in the way it is taught. As a matter of fact, it is pure lunacy that you create **everything** in your reality. While it is true that positive energy generates positivity, it is not true that positivity will **always** bring you positive results. Likewise, doing your best in life will not always bring you the best things from life (BE BLACK, living amongst whites and be the BEST, like black wall street in Oklahoma or Rosewood and see how being the best will bring THE WORST for FACT. I still embrace always doing your best will gift you the best life possible. This is the reality of the law of attraction. Positively, positive manifestation cannot possibly bring you everything your heart desires, but it will bring you your best outcome possible. Here's why. Law of attraction doesn't always work as it claims. You are not the only person on Earth with desires. What if you desire the lottery, and millions of others are manifesting as well. Do you really think it's possible that all the million people who do the work perfectly will win? If we attract everything to ourselves, how does a newborn baby in Syria or Gaza/Palestine attract being gassed or bombed to themselves? They do not! Here's the secret: the secret doesn't teach you. Yes, don't focus on all the stumbling blocks, impossibilities, the stars aligned against you, your contract to suffer to change the world, the desires of EVIL POWERS THAT BE, and put everything into your dream no matter how impossible, just like I have here in this book AND KNOW the Universe conspires in your favor when it's time. It's time NOW for real change and GOD already pushed you into wanting a real change. Maybe I'm here to inspire you to bring forth the unity. Maybe I will bring the oneness of mankind, but no matter what... YOU WILL SEE what real change looks like and stop trying to put a band aid on cancer where you keep looking for a change in policy or better education in a world CHALKED FULL OF HATRED. REAL CHANGE! BRING IT ON!

You are born into this world with a specific purpose and a pre-planned agreement to a task you will undertake. Children choose their parents. They know and agree to all the hell and suffering they will endure on their life journey to Earth. Most of us forget our cosmic agreement. If we understood a small glimpse of God as I have come into overstanding, we would overstand that God really is all knowing, all powerful, and the ultimate good/God/bad/Satan ARE ONE, just as our human collective ARE ONE (God/Satan) functioning for PURPOSE equally... CREATION, we are creators, gods!

What if you agreed to bring an angel into the world as a martyr who would show people how we needs to change? Then when your most beautiful, full of life, loving, giving, angel (your most cherished child) is raped and murdered; because you forgot your agreement to bring your gift into the world for her purpose (of which being an angel came with much power to fulfill her martyr agreement for mankind) and all those who watched the life too are clueless... how could a loving God allow this to happen? You have kept your children in prayer, and the angel among all the children (though you love them ALL) is ripped away in the most vile and heinous way. My dear love, none of this is real! The physical world is the real dream; we are here playing a game of creation, tag you're it, to unite all humanity. This is your debut; we are many making it our debut to pick a side. There are not two sides in physical existence, and both are an illusion IN CONTRAST of absolute reality, but the sides are mandatory if you choose to play the game of life. You must choose good/bad: friend or adversary to human life, right or wrong, coupled with the knowing and wisdom of understanding that there is not but one thing, no matter which of the two you choose.

Look at hot and cold. Think of the outside temperature being 85 degrees. Is it too hot? Now think of your body temperature and think of cooking an egg, is it too hot? HOT is the same one word, but depending on your event too hot is NEVER THE SAME, showing that it is EVENTS of our world that vary, NOT the polarity of the EXACT same thing. Because we could say is it too cold, get it? The degree (amount) of heat (hot) or absence of heat (cold) remains the same one thing HEAT at 85 degrees Fahrenheit outside, within our body, or to cook an egg, but our days are numbered, fatality at 85 degrees in our body temperature, and cooking an egg is impossible in 85-degree heat; it is too cold for our desired outcome. Hence, the human desired outcome determines what WE choose as good or bad (the SAME ONE THING) human desire in our reality decides it's same one thing as different depending on our DESIRED outcome. Hot/cold, Good/bad GOD/SATAN a thing of oneness, such as 85-degree weather, is too hot for us, too cold to cook an egg and too cold to support our body temperature for human life. But 85 degrees is the same ONE thing! It's our existence, NOT REALITY that makes 85 degrees different. 70 degrees Fahrenheit outside is perfection, desired, good while 100 degrees outside is horrible, BAD. It's our reality, but not absolute reality. Thus, limitations, set by the rules of the game of physical existence, may possibly be altered supernaturally through our divinity, but how many of us will ever overcome that limitation? Depending on how you bend matter to your will, set parameters require supernatural power to ACCESS the supernatural. In other words, you must reach beyond the architects' world through mass unity, world congregation as one to conjure up the power that will break the veil/dome that enclosed us at our very will to escape, and today, through the internet, we can do it. We only need to unite and rise above the establishment that requires division and hate. Use hate (going against) established destruction for humanity. Use unity to end the division of the masses. Hate/love, unity/division, the same ONE thing, but what is OUR DESIRED OUTCOME?

In the world of metaphysics, the greater physical world, the science of things transcending what is physical or natural, the world of polarity is nothing but the varying degrees of the exact same thing. When I say be good or behave badly, you know exactly what I am saying, but if I say you must be both at the same time, your brain will split reality because there is no possible human concept of day and night coexisting. Ah ha! But we must unite as one. Here's where absolute reality rings supreme; as above so below. Where is above? Where is it below? They are one and the same thing. Where's east and west or north and south? They are the ones! Everything in existence is God's essence. Remember, Jesus said, "My father and I are one, but how can a physical father be the same as the son? We can make up that Jesus said my father and I are one mind, but then we're lying to ourselves that a messiah messenger directly from God is too ignorant to speak literally, so that there would be no confusion of his message, and spoke figuratively intentionally or in ignorance so that the people are confused and question which way he meant to speak. If we look from a metaphysical realm of existence supernaturally, they are one. I believe that the human beings who will survive to continue the species will become one, and the Earth will recycle for the next game players. Gone are the Atlanteans, Mayans, Olmecs, and now human beings also; some will become extinct, and the masses will hopefully be transfigured, THE NEW CREATION.

You are playing that you forgot who you are, and the object of the game before your time is up is to remember you are God, trapped in dense physical consciousness, you perceive as solid matter of a dualistic polar false reality, where you are on course to take back your true state of existence and being including raising up our species in doing so. Or we extinct ourselves. There is no difference, no matter in absolute reality.

What will you create? Utter depression until you die. Or utter forgiveness and empathy of understanding, the event was a major world event to teach lessons to the masses on 1. Society must change so as not to create drug addicts, mentally ill, rapist and murderers; and 2. Empathy for the lost soul so extremely damaged that he or she could not feel what you know you are capable of feeling (how blessed), the presence of an angel or god/god. The forgiveness and love of your enemy shown to the masses will not only change our world, but will have a ripple effect, raising numerous existences of beings through the positive energy that the law of attraction generates. However, no parent willingly manifests rape and/or kills my daughter. Check out the story of Samuel Davidson, who killed four children and was sentenced to 20 years for driving drunk, causing death. Three of the children belonged to Danny Abdallah, who forgave Samuel and helped his family, Samuel, and now the world to heal through unity, not hate. I can't stress how huge this is. This is worlds in worlds in worlds change, which is why we turn the other cheek, if we choose the higher path.

Furthermore, our emotions, events, and people in relationships are all being influenced by outside forces, such as the cosmos at the time of birth. Just as you influence others with your baggage, others will also influence you. Remember Danny Abdallah, he's influencing the world to forgive and changing the world for the better. It's good to cleanse your energy, meditate, and keep positive, but one thing I can guarantee you, if the event of loss/suffering is written in your agreement to come to play here on Earth, all of the law of attraction on Earth that you practice will never stop it. Nonetheless, you should practice it anyway to alleviate the suffering/pain of the event. You can live through hell and find peace and happiness in the midst.

I have never regretted or been depressed since I gave up my career for my health and sanity. When we hold onto baggage, we become trapped, like the monkey caught in the cage, reaching for food but won't let it go for his freedom. When I was living in Africa, it was the happiest period in my life since I was a small child. In Africa, we live childlike, one day at a time, and enjoy life, fresh food, smiling, friendly people, plenty of exercise; every day is an adventure.

I felt my destiny from birth. Since about three years of age, I remember knowing my best years were going to be spent as a child, and I always felt death next to my life, so at a young age, death has never been a fear for me. I felt it so close that I genuinely believed I would never see my 18th birthday. Then, in my early 30's, I was told by my doctor that I would never see my 40th birthday if I continued to work. I reluctantly at first, but finally I left out on disability at the age of 37, and I have lived to see my 64th birthday, and if I live to see this book published, I'll see my 65th. Today, I am healthier than I was at 48 years old. I was nearly dead and couldn't walk much farther than a couple of blocks. I walked on the treadmill, totally out of breath and exhausted, set at 2.5 miles per hour. Today I can walk/jog at 3.5 to 4.0 miles per hour steady with bursts of 5.0-6.0 mph for 20 to 30 seconds. I totally reversed thickening of the heart wall, kept chronic kidney failure stable, and I am totally off insulin (I took 65mg of Lantus and 15 mg 3 times per day Humalog). I intermittently take Ozempic to maintain my intermittent fasting of one big meal per day, eating only until satisfied. My goal is to rebuild my insulin sensitivity, AND REVERSE AGING.

If I were to succumb to our world's traps, my bosses, career, I would be dead, and you would hear of me as a monster. How I destroyed innocent families' lives. Nobody would see my innocent families' lives ALL DESTROYED because of my COLOR and partly my sex too. I nearly succumbed to systematic entrapment designed for my utter failure because I saw my life as over without my career. I felt that if my superiors didn't want me to work and maintain my family, why should they? Why should my family lose out on me due to the way I was born, unable to be free of disease without stress, thus harassment was a death sentence for me. This was the third job dealing with unfair treatment. However, I was blessed to come back to myself and realize I didn't want to be the person the system had set up for me. My life wouldn't be over just because I was poor. I had plenty of time now to put into my children. Afterwards, I lived suffering through my mother being taken, my home being taken, my grandson almost taken, judges and attorneys fighting against my right to be heard in court, a violation against the Constitution. Yet I am alive to tell and show how black life is treated, ignored, and only recognized, even by black media, when mainstream media or viral media covers the story. Other than that, we die invisible to the world, and the system fails to grant justice unless media coverage takes place to force it. Nobody asks about all of the many George Floyds murdered by white cops without video footage, because none exists. Is that right? What about all of the Sandra Blanks denied solely due to skin color, a right to peace, joy, and my constitutional rights to be heard in a court of law by a jury of my peers? I am denied solely because judges know that black is worthless to my society, so there is no such thing as Black Lives Matter. They can do anything to black people, just like they did to my son. Charged him with murder one without evidence of intent or premeditation. Then kept him in jail without an attorney willing to do anything that he asked for. He had zero rights. It's done every single day!

Hold that picture in your mind of the video recording of Derek Chauvin killing George Floyd. As the person recording zooms up on him, he clearly looks directly into the camera with the face of a camera person saying... "you are killing him, he's not moving" and Derek's face said, " Do I have any fear, so whatever that anything will be done to me? Absolutely no worries. Black is not a cause to punish a cop. That face is burned into my psyche, how this man knew that nothing could possibly be done to him for harming George. Yet he gets twenty years for undeniable intent to murder, while the black cop gets 40 years for the same thing that no white cop ever goes to prison for killing a black child or adult for. Society was outraged, with the exception of a few idiots who called Floyd a criminal, so he deserved his execution far more than a police officer deserved to be prosecuted for taking the law into his own hands and murdering him. But please drive it home in understanding. **This type of murder is happening to blacks all the time, as justifiable homicide, hidden from the public,** as there is no black voice. Only a video or recording can speak for black people, and even if it lies for racists like Charlie Kirk, who watched Floyd murdered with a knee in his neck, unconscious for minutes, but it wasn't the cops' fault, it was fentanyl and all Floyd's fault. I watched Derek Chauvin with a knee in George's neck, no struggle, nothing, as the camera came close into Chauvin's face, and the recorder said he's not moving. His face clearly expressed, " Do I look like I'm concerned about your camera or your pointing out that I am killing this black nothingness. His family, all black America, and even a majority of whites (jury) watched the unnecessary intent not to stop the death of Floyd at a cop's hands. Police officer, Derrick Stafford, accidentally shot a six-year-old sleeping child that he never knew was in the car, trying to stop the white father, a criminal. They gave him 40 years! His partner, Norris Greenhouse Jr., knew he had to take a plea; he's a person of color and was convicted, too.

I have a picture showing Charlie Kirk bringing the African American problems of "black on black crime" in place of a white-on-white crime issue. As he has always done, he made every problem of race all black people's fault. We get enslaved, survive Jim Crow, are discriminated against, and murdered/lynched by justifiable homicide, by fabricated official suicides that are impossible to be suicide by the evidence, but it is all black people's fault. The irony is that we may never know was his death chosen by God or by the shooter's perfected plan to end the racist, unnecessary speech against blacks on point. Charlie was shot dead in an all-white event by a white shooter, trying to understand if he should count "gang violence" (blacks) as a part of the concern over mass school shootings (whites). You really have to get this. I believe Charlie was **unintentionally** led by selective false reasoning in his mind, most likely trained to do so by his adult influencers. They taught him that every time, no matter what, if you hear black suffering, show it as a fact that blacks either caused it or it is false. If you see white suffering blacks, either cause it or it is false and not happening. The day he died, Charlie claimed that he couldn't know if a student from a whites-only living needed to include "gang violence." The blacks. Although only mass shootings were mentioned, which are white-on-white crimes, Charlie needs the all-white audience to take the focus off mass shootings and include "black-on-black" crimes, even though blacks have absolutely nothing to do with mass shootings in schools. This is raw racism and the reason why racism never ends. The voice of unreason against a voiceless suffering people can only be stopped by God. I believe my YouTube channel was recommended by an act of God, Charlie's first thought/words... I died???? I believe he's in heaven and now can see how dangerous he was attacking blacks in a way that he died showing it a fact that he intentionally dismissed white on white crime to place the blame all on blacks being shot by a gun expressing disdain for empathy as a made up word, and some gun deaths were a necessary price to protect second amendment rights, the irony of his speech, heart, and God versus his final destination. This is a wake-up call for our nation. **You don't have to wake up in heaven to stop hating blacks, gays, transgender persons, and anyone who is not white.** Black women were giving testimony that they got into Harvard through affirmative action because their black skin wouldn't allow them in, but they graduated through their intelligence and

Charlie turned it around that the black women admitted they couldn't get in on their intelligence taking up whites' place (because only a white persons or Asians deserved the spot), but the black women including Michelle Obama never said they got in because they were unintelligent, matter of fact they said quite the opposite. They got in because the LAW forced a door open to allow intelligent qualified blacks an equal opportunity to access Harvard University. This is pure hate from Charlie Kirk. No black pilots to my knowledge have crashed commercial airliners, but Charlie said he would be afraid that a black person to be a pilot because they are not capable, not qualified, just made it up, and this horribly racist rhetoric is being told to young, impressionable minds in an attempt to make America white again. They tried to glorify him in death as a great wonderful person and had he not hated gays he wouldn't be dead that day. Charlie didn't want blacks to be allowed to be surgeons, BEN CARSON gets erased in his world AND they (congress/senate) glorified an extremely sick person whom I believe should have had a chance at life to at sometime wake up out of his insanity. That our sick country is teaching white people LIES about making America great again INSTEAD OF Let's for the first time EVER make America genuinely for the PEOPLE, not white supremacy, but ALL THE PEOPLE. Be honest, we're only allowing murder and illegal mass deportations because of FEAR of color ending purely white people. The fact is that half are already gone since the last one hundred years because THERE IS NO SUCH THING AS COLOR **RACES**. There are only the human race and the absolute only color ALL colors come from is BLACK. Let's own the truth and the race issue ends NOW. We can be like Dr. Seuss' Sneetches. "The Sneetches got really quite smart. They decided that Sneetches are Sneetches. And no kind of Sneetch is the best on the beaches." Human beings can get smart that we are Human beings. HUEman beings period and there is no color of human being that is better than any other color.

IT SOUNDS SO INCREDIBLY SICK TO HAVE TO SAY THIS, DAMN, really??? Do we really have a race problem that is 100% evident?

Bottom line, no black cop has murdered one single white unarmed innocent person and **gone totally free**, not one to my knowledge. This proves it is a fact that no cop should go free killing unarmed individuals. Or if I'm nuts, only blacks should be cops so we can have no murderer cops to go free of accountability and less excessive force against American citizens. This way blacks and whites win or we simply hold white cops accountable for their actions. This proves racism exists. CAN YOU NAME ONE BLACK

COP TO MURDER AN UNARMED WHITE AND GO TOTALLY FREE? JUST ONE??? Our US Constitution is the supreme law of the land. Anyone in America against equal rights is a traitor to the Constitution of the United States of America. Minorities of this country are said to have special privileges to help set them equal to whites. Blacks are considered a minority, but their suffering is far worse than that of any minority; therefore, blacks are being denied their constitutional right to be equal. There must be special privileges for blacks to offset the suffering beyond whites and beyond minorities. Blacks are the only race that has been forced to financially build America for **centuries**, for free, and to this very day are the only large group of people without a land or self-representation to escape discrimination. Mexicans can go to Mexico, Chinese people can go to China, east Indians can return to India, and all can be governed by their own people and enjoy sovereignty of their own people, escaping the hatred of other races dominating and determining their human boundaries with no genuine representation for their needs. Where do black Americans go where they can be judged and governed by black Americans who understand their culture, suffering, heart, and needs? Where do black Americans live with their best interest sought after? **Absolutely nowhere on Earth for over four hundred (400) years.**

With the breakout of COVID people blamed the Chinese and brutally attacked Chinese people. China got in America's ass and a LAW was passed immediately to protect ASIANS in America... Whenever has laws passed so quickly to STOP BLACK SUFFERING? Who gives a hoot? I DO, if I am the only person on earth lifting my voice to the heavens... it's not fair that WE ARE GENERATIONALLY OPPRESSED FOR CENTURIES of building this country FOR FREE and still TODAY we SUFFER and get a big FAT zero. Both my mother and father were CHEATED out of education, and they raised me couldn't help me beyond fourth/fifth grade. As matter of fact, I helped my mom with her schoolwork in night school to get her high school diploma and later electronics' degree. Well EMBEDDED LAW will allow us to get special damages for having special suffering UNEQUAL to any group on earth which REQUIRES it a constitutional fact that immediate RELIEF is due over a century ago for our people to receive retribution like the Native Americans and the Israelis that this country did NOT cause their holocaust, but they get paid. AMERICA DID CAUSE EVERY MINUTE OF OUR NEAR HALF A millennium years of SUFFERING, of OPPRESSION and you believe it RIGHT TO PRETEND IT NEVER HAPPENED, worse, you're trying to rewrite us out of history that we came here looking for work.

WTF! What soulless evil monster does this? You can't pretend it never happened and it NEVER goes away until you finalize OUR RIGHT TO BE EQUAL BY LAW, BY FOLLOWING THE CONSTITUTION as you helped minorities with laws to offset their unequal access, but NOT US. All of those NOT HARMED LIKE US (not enslaved, not having their country snatched away by kidnapping us from our country in the 1600's and after), NOT HARMED EQUALLY to us while sacrificing our very lives to this very day. I am a 65-year-old chemical engineer NOT ALLOWED TO BE BLACK and work in peace because of EMBEDDED LAW in my country where I live LESS than a foreigner. Foreigners can go home and escape the hell of mistreatment, harassment, discrimination, but where do we go? WHERE? Never can we even take a vacation where we are ruled by African Americans? I am not allowed mainstream media coverage of **ALL THE ATROCITIES** forced upon my life guilty solely for a wrong COLOR and the MILLIONS of blacks just like me who can't get their story heard, it is happening to them.

2. Unite all humanity as one:

This will be done by the last race mixed on Earth. The race that has come full circle on planet Earth. In reality, there is not one race, and that's the human race. Due solely to the corruption of white supremacy and the beast, the almighty dollar, and/or money, we must establish the truth about the color of the races. First of all, there are no true white, black, red, yellow, purple, or green people. The absolute only original color of people on Earth is black/brown, with varying hues from the lightest of brown/pink - brown/green we call white, to the darkest brown near black with all hues we call black. There never was a white person on Earth from the beginning of humanity! There were only "black" persons who lost their melanin... facts! A so-called white person is no whiter than Michael Jackson, he turned white nearly right in front of us to show us the way black people turn white. Michael was as white as any white person, but he understood, and the world in general understood he was a black man. Why? Because we literally watched the black man turn white. What is the difference within the white race? They turned white millennia ago. They were black, white people are black people, and like MJ, they lost their melanin through autoimmune disease v. Gene mutation generational disease... so why is it any difference? Whites lost their blackness thousands of years ago, and it doesn't make them any less black people. They are descendants of black people; they are the least melanated black people on Earth.

Human whiteness is a trickery of the gods! It's in the Bible. Where you can clearly see the gods using some sort of technology to force a sudden loss of melanin. And God made the loss of melanin a curse so that the species would divide (create racism), self-destruct, and extinct themselves over color and greed. See, just understand where and how racism began. The original black man began racism through the trickery of the gods against his black brothers, who turned white. And thus began the first racist! Look up Numbers 12:10, where Miriam is punished by God to turn white. Notice how there is no way to describe a white person at that time other than to compare the whiteness to that of a black baby fresh from the womb. All black babies are born with a much lighter hue than the dark brown hue they will become. At that time, no white person had ever been seen. And the gods understood the psyche of human beings to judge... **must be normal mental, illness inherited**, five fingers (not 4 or 6), brown skin (not pale), two arms (not 4 or 6), two eyes (not 1 or 3), male or female (not both male and female, nor male body with female spirit, nor female body with male spirit) and so on. Our psyche is being used against us by the gods (extremely few on Earth) of ancient times and by the one percenters (extremely few on Earth) today, who use the wealthy/corporations/governments (few) all against us which in turn we the 99% turn also against our own selves and believe that the few should reign in dominion over the masses as there is no other way possible. Trickery dammit!!! Why should the few enjoy and hoard Earth's wealth and resources while the masses share the leftover crumbs? Hell no! Stop the deception of scarcity by seeing the truth of greed manipulation, and trickery. Earth and the universe handle overpopulation, not man. **Man's purpose is to be fruitful** and, if desired, multiply. The rest is up to the universe/god, those over the architects of our world/reality, who's over the architects of their worlds/reality, who's over their worlds/realities to infinity...god.

Reality, the truth will eradicate everything of white supremacy. This is why the white Karen magistrate Susan Collins, Judge Theresa Springmann, and Judge Diane Sykes took it upon themselves to be the Christ, messiahs of white supremacy and deny me a right to my constitutional right to be heard by a jury of my peers. They knew it was their societal right (EMBEDDED LAW to place white supremacy higher than the supreme law of our land, the US Constitution), which **MUST** make their appointment as a magistrate an annulment of office, not a removal. How is it possible for them to have ever taken others to not only break a sworn duty to serve the Constitution, but to break it over and over again, and to force and coerce others to turn against and deny the highest law of the land? Intentionally destroying the sacred credibility of our judicial system to me is fair, impartial, unbiased, just, ethical, integrity, accountable, transparent, accessible, respectful, equitable, and humanizing. How dare they walk free in their attempt as the only person ever known to force so many known and unknown in violation of their sworn duty to uphold the Constitution. **Is white supremacy the SUPREME LAW of the US** or is it the CONSTITUTION? CHOOSE THIS DAY!!! Congress must seek the will of the people and report the decision of the people, not by electoral vote, but by individual citizens' votes. Congress, as a group of people of a similar background to the judges, will be an automatic decision similar to the judges for whites supremacy. This is the absolute only way to establish our system truly as we Americans claim it to be. These judges must be ruled by the people (Congress/the Supreme Court), annulled by their extreme actions against the Constitution and sworn duty as **never** before witnessed in the history of our country, so shall it be never before witnessed and hopefully never again ever witnessed that the few shall overthrow the sacred trust of an entire system. I wrote in my writ of certiorari that the entire justice system fails if it is not recognized that a lease is an absolute fact that must be recognized, and that judges who fabricate a lie to intentionally force a black litigant in the wrong must be stopped, or our entire judicial system crashes. I **reported this case** and even explained how going against blacks is so acceptable CNN, FOX, NAACP, ACLU, President Biden, United Nations, governor, attorney general for Indiana and US attorney General and so many people of power have failed me, my being judicially lynched up until **only you** my readers, citizens of Earth can help me to a right to be heard by a jury my constitutional right. They **all** denied me! This is EMBEDDED LAW where you don't even consider your sacred sworn duty or your civic duty to stop racist oppression by a lawless country!!! When it comes to black against white supremacy… your duty to the Constitution, the sanctity of law and order… when livelihood, justice, and righteousness are sacrificed on the cross of white supremacy to protect those who had already sold out to lawlessness and injustice as the American way of life. **They all turned a blind eye** and didn't give a damn about the Constitution or public backlash. Oh yeah!!! I told them I would be heard one day do the right thing! As these judges and lawyers are the first ever in the known history of our country to intentionally turn against our Constitution, utterly relentlessly, and **are coercing many to join in.**

Congress should poll the people in the election of 2028. Report the decision of the people and recommend to the Supreme Court that the people have spoken. For certainty, the people should have spoken that our only recourse to uphold justice, transparency, and the integrity of the judicial system is to annul the appointment to office of all judges assigned to adjudicate judicially that had access to the case docket where the state court had heard the case and ordered on June 14, 2017 that my defendants failed to prove that people were living in my home and that the people living in my house, it named out my grandchildren in the order were on the lease and entitled to live there. So how is it ordered throughout the entire case that the judges placed me at fault due to my grandchildren not being on the lease, thus a court order in favor that I had my grandchildren not on the lease, thus I in fact had unauthorized occupants living in my home, by a Jim Crow ruling. The lease in my favor as a black person is false, and my continual push to be placed in the right is my opinion; therefore, an objection to the order **is denied**. What judicial fuckery, overwhelmingly transparent in your face corruption, backed up all the way to the Supreme Court, UN, NAACP, ACLU, Congress, governor, Attorney Generals, and the US president! This is a chance for Kamala to prove herself by recommending exposing the ruling in this case by Jim Crow. I can't make this up, y'all, it's to show the nation how more than a small minority of whites think. Trump, Charlie Kirk, while I don't believe they'll hold the sentiments of the majority of white people, I should say I hope, because our suffering can't be upheld by society unless a vast number of whites are secretively kirk types of people. Let's annul these judges as they have never been judges for their acts against our nation's judicial system, and me cause the entire judicial process of the United States to be utter fuckery as never before in history witnessed. We should allow African Americans who were heard under these judges a right to revisit their claims with a new presiding judge. This is what would happen normally all the time under judges who are removed for hurting people and misconduct. These judges' acts border on treason in the name of white supremacy, without doubt, tyranny (the use of embedded law, the unspoken lynching of a black person's case by the unspoken whites are always right, blacks always wrong, knowing that absolutely nothing will be done to justly save a merit-worthy black pro se litigant. Racism is the supreme law still today, where corruption overrules the US Constitution in a way that absolutely no white person has ever suffered. Now, let's move forward to unity for the world.

First, I must add just a little more history on color regarding the migration of the people from the Middle East out to all land masses. Language can help us understand better. Ask yourself, the Middle East, where, far east from where… easy, all humanity began in Africa and migrated east. So we black Africans went to the Middle East, the north, the ancient Greeks were first called Minoans (black people), mixed with whites to make Greeks and Italian today. They migrated out to the far east, black African East Indians and black African Asians. They migrated up through Russia and across from the north to Alaska and are the aboriginal black African natives of America, many are called Black Americans/African Americans/FBA "foundational black Americans" coined by Tariq Nasheed. I *believe the issue is that Africans who shouldn't be using African American because they have a country, they are Nigerian American or Kenyan American, not African American, as black Americans have always been called since the 90's. As I understand, there's an issue with them riding on the backs of enslaved Americans, which is deceitful if they claim such a history.* The whites followed the black migration, mixing with the black Africans. Let's back up here. The white splinter happened a several ways: by migration, biological warfare by Anunnakis, and aliens from the Orion Belt trying to seed the planet in the eastern Himalayas. The ancient black migration into the Caucasus Mountains hundreds of thousands of years ago, creating the ancient white man, olive in color, Romanian. This color is very similar to the color of a black man's finger after you put a bandage on it for a day or two without sunlight. I said the color, not the process, of course. It's a pale color. The second white man was the creation of the gods, most likely Enlil, around 5000 BC or before. He used biological warfare to make some of the black Africans lose their pigmentation immediately. They turned a pinkish white, like the American white/English whites. Their black brothers banished them from civilization, but they never forgot the black brothers' cruelty. They named the land Europa. "You roped us off from civilization, and they went backward, vowing to never forget. as it is mentioned in Job 30th chapter. You are free and fine not to believe in the Bible as sacred, but you can't, as a sane person, say that the Bible does not exist. The Bible exists, and it explains who the original racists were! The third white race was tall beings from the Orion belt, the Aryan nation. Thus, the three sources of whites on Earth are: **1.** The biological warfare most recently turned whites (pink-white of Europe, practiced by God in Numbers chapter 12:10-15), **2.** The hybrid Orion alien/evolving man, the Aryan nation, tall, blond, and blue eyes, and **3.** Migrating black Africans from more than 200,000 years ago into the Caucasus Mountains, into Asia and the Americas, mutating DNA, pale/olive. These whites migrated all over, **mixing with the indigenous black Africans,** creating the genuine mixed races of the Earth, Orientals, oriental Asians, Eskimos, Hispanic Americans, and native Americans. The first scientific explanation of race is "outdated" because it does not provide enough division of the races, Caucasoid (white), negroid (black), and mongoloid (mixed races). Today's races are primarily based on color, nations, continents, and cults/tribes, ethnicities, and all sorts of divisive groups of people to hate each other, instead of the past three races. Today, we have religion, gay/straight, spoken language, ages, caste/social status, territorial boundaries, politics, values/morals, beliefs, divisions that often overlap with each other, and **"race,"** which doesn't even exist. Human beings are **all Africans** Hueman, some turned white, some mixed, but a scientific fact, all came from the common ancestor's mitochondria, called Eve, from Africa. There's no coincidence that Africa is the most discriminated against and hated people living on the richest continent in raw resources, with the poorest people on Earth. It's an intentional hate setup from the Anunnaki who told black men to throw whites out of the camp when their black skin turned white. They set this mutation/biological warfare up for the self-destruction of mankind and then set up laws of hatred where a man shall be put to death, which we sickos still practice to date. However, white nations all know it's evil to murder a person because they committed murder and leave that up to nature, all except the USA.

Much older science called all races under three categories, Caucasoid, Negroid, and Mongoloid (mixed out of Asian black, and white). Yes, there was only the black, white, and mixed races period. In order to establish more division, the three races on Earth were then divided by tribes, Klansmen, and later nations. Recently added division is ethnicity to water down the collective Hispanic race and fractions of whites, German, English, French, Polish, and so forth, which brings us to today. All are black people; some black people lost melanin, but of course, they are still black. These whites and blacks migrated not simultaneously, but blacks populated the world or the Earth originally everywhere. Author J. A Rogers, "sex and Race," vol 1, 2, 3, gives his personal account of traveling all over the world to see black people pushed into the bush of every continent on Earth. Even in the Philippines, there are native African black people, according to my engineering coworker, Rolando. Eventually, whites would follow the trail and generate mixed-race people starting in Asia and southern Europe hundreds of thousands of years ago. They created northern light complexion Africans, Libyans, Moroccans, Algerians, East Indian, Chinese, Japanese, Koreans, Eskimos, native Americans, Mexicans, just yesterday, relatively speaking, Europeans remixed to lighten races more and colonized the planet. The very last mixed race of African black and European white is the African American of the slave trade. The slave master did not have thousands of years to mix with our race to appear as a mixed race, but as slaves of massa and our mixing with one another there is no race on Earth double dipped chocolate, (African from the continent with aboriginal Africans of America) with a pinch of vanilla (white) to survive the greatest atrocity ever known to mankind. Our souls' thirst for harmony and peace like no other people on Earth. We die oppressed and hated for centuries in silence and undocumented. I didn't say totally undocumented, but to the degree of murder and devastation to our people, I know for a fact that, at most, maybe 10% of our suffering has been told. As I said before, if there was no video footage of George Floyd's murder and everything happened just as it did, four cops would have sworn that they were afraid for their lives, as it took four cops to hold Floyd down. The witnesses would be unbelievable and discredited; only the police claims would be credible, and the murder of Floyd would have been justifiable homicide. How much black blood at the race solders hands besides the one we know? I believe only 10% at best ever gets told about black suffering. What's the chance of you (anyone) getting police bullied and just happen to have your phone on record. How many times has some cow verbally abused you, and you're holding your own with the idiot, and after it's all over, you say, damn, I should have recorded? When you're in the heat of defending yourself, you never know how bad it might turn. Being yanked from your car or beaten, it's too late to record. How many times have you heard about how hard it is to get the camera footage of bad cops? Do you think anyone ever hears of how many people are never allowed to get the video footage who are like me, utterly violated, but nobody knows? You can't go viral. Imagine a black judge judicially lynching white litigants by putting them falsely in the wrong and then refusing to remove it? Do you believe that a black judge will be backed when it comes to a misconduct filing, appeal, and the writ of certiorari? I would never get past misconduct filed twice. Show me one case of a black judge lying against a white litigant, refusing to remove the lie (over a simple factual document like who's on the lease, and their the misconduct is ruled/ordered **no misconduct.**

The police who harm black people are the same thing; they know they're extremely likely to get away with it. You know it's without doubt a lot more than is reported. Understanding the making of the races and the extreme suffering of black Americans. I appeal to every American, including blacks, to embrace our blackness as a species until no one is hurt over the color of their skin. Let's start by **uniting the human race** through the black American suffering.

It will happen because we are the only people put in place to make it happen, influencing the nation to rise up as one; ultimately, the entire world. The black American seeks self-reliance, self-representation, and sovereignty as a nation of people. We will buy lands from countries to become a country within a country, owning lands sovereignly, similar to the embassies of the world inside other countries, which are sovereign. We will continue to live as black Americans under capitalism, and those of us who choose sovereignty to form ambassadorial countries all over the world within our own countries. We shall be a people who will hold the weakest as the weakest link within the chain of our humanity, therefore embracing and empowering the weakest of our societies as the most important, not the richest, as we foolishly do today. This will happen all over the world, where countries will accept our embassies. We will live very openly and transparently so that we aren't the threat that capitalists will lie and claim that our people live so greatly abundantly well, prompting the entire world to change. When money and power are not your greatest commodity, and people are your greatest commodity… these lives will be lived most like heaven on Earth without any reason to hide wealth or the beauty of society.

Local cities all over the world will begin to claim the land under their feet, copying our model. They will buy out the utility companies and begin using the land for their food and trade, building homes for their children, ready to marry, or apartments/hostels for those ready for independent living. Work will be assigned for all people for 8 hours per week. We do not need to work 40 hours to pay the CEO and stockholders. The communities will live as communities with numerous events required to pick your life's service (many various types of exercises required) (many children's events required, based on community choice, something for everyone). You do not have a choice but to be depressed, shut in for weeks. Each family will adopt families within the community to be their brother's keeper, to report their needs so that no one person is ever not heard. The community comes together and designs its operations, designating servers (like congressmen or jurors) where individuals must all take turns serving the will of the people. The laws are general. 1. Treat people the way you would want others to treat you. You would want people to respect you, your lifestyle, reasoning, needs, to see your beingness (evil [mistakes]/good [accomplishments] and have empathy, likewise you must embrace every person you meet, no matter a criminal, addict, or the most disgusting thing on legs, you must give them the same. Do you get it? Put down this reading and think, do you get it? If you get it, then you understand that the terms criminal/addict/mentally ill/ crazy fade into nonexistence and become "a human who needs my empathy, I can share to help them be their best person. A society that embraces humanness is a society that embraces the reality of our existence, facts, can you agree? 2. Courtesy and respect to every individual 3. One mindset to raise all humanity to be productive and reach their highest potential.

3. Trade goods and services, the end of using money. Somewhat similar to the bartering system or **Ubuntu Contributionism** (a name for simply co-op sharing of product and service. The sick world believe in money as the root of all success and power, this system places people (the gods on earth/delivers {salvation} of the universe) as the root of all success and power. There'll be no allowance out as our concept will be about abundance and not scarcity. How much clothing does my brother need to make you happy and support our well-being. How much of a house do you need, two bedrooms or five bedrooms, for blah blah blah. And the community will build it. For food, just go into the food storage, like a pantry, and choose the food you need for a few days, or simply use the many cafeterias' buffet style (no pay). Of course, for stocking, the people will sign up our families for use of the cafeteria 100% 50% 10%... And use of the pantry in opposing percentages so that over time we learn how to stock the groceries for individuals and the cafeteria for the community to use. How many shoes, as many as you need. Here's the seriously neat thing: you get tired of your selection of shoes and clothing, need a new wardrobe, and you return the old one for restocking. You can choose from brand new clothing or your community closet's wealth of clothing, shoes, jewelry, etc. As with any totally new concept, there will be chaos as we figure our way into organized chaos, but the one-mind embrace of our humanity will give us the patience to make it work as a community.

4. There will be several factories using robotics to make clothing, designer shoes, musical instruments, food, specialty food, frozen dinners,/dessert all for the community and for everyone. Until the world stops using money, our community will sell for-profit for our needs as well as the needs of the neighboring community.

5. Energy will be both solar and wind-generated.

6. Start-up and yearly income from my lawsuit enforcing embedded law restitution. Numerous lawsuits against corporate America had never been allowable due to both the burden of proof and the lack of profitability. It will be extremely lucrative for attorneys to take on African American lawsuits with embedded law applied requiring special damages where lawsuits will be worth 100 million to 1 billion depending on how extremely malicious the karens (small k to recognize this is not a loving karen, this is a way with one word to say wickedly cruel evil monstrously attacking individual and when this attitude is used against blacks it's the most vile treatment that isn't criminal then doubling down on the knowing that it's socially acceptable... hence embedded law) are.

CHAPTER SEVEN

EMBEDDED LAW Synopsis:

Scope:

Embedded law concept (ELC) seeks out **the target** defined below for extreme punishment of 10 to 100 times or more the value of the case to be awarded to the protected. The population affected and harmed, the protected African American (descendants of slaves), 12.5% of the American people only may claim ELC, population not affected are – non African Americans 87.5%, the rest of Americans cannot claim ELC. It is understood that no race is exempt from being "the target" or the person using embedded law to destroy black people.

Embedded law - any person or people, any race who acts/feels/ behaves as if they have a right by law or above the law to harm black people. Derek Chauvin clearly believed he had the right above the law to harm a black person. It is not only done with intent and maliciously, but they also break the law to cause harm to a black person. This is clearly feeling themselves above the law. There is no requirement that one must feel above the law, but they must show intent to maliciously harm a black person, a protected class.

History:

Prior to the 1600s, black Americans (FBA), foundational black Americans pre-slavery, and Europeans lived in harmony here in America. Black people were the aboriginals of America, living side by side with white settlers, and some were indentured servants. This is known because they intermarried, traded, and conducted business with each other. They lived next to each other as neighbors. Racism as we know it today did not exist in America.

In 1676, Nathaniel Bacon and a militia of black and white indentured servants and black slaves united against the white elite to eliminate native Americans from the land. The elite were against any uprising with the natives; thus began the rebellion. In 1676, Bacon and his militia invaded Jamestown and burned it to the ground. Months later, Bacon would die of a fever, and the rebellion died down, but not the fear of the white elites that blacks and whites banded together were powerful enough to take over elite rule spread far and wide. Legal scholar Michelle Alexander wrote, "the events in Jamestown were alarming to the planter elite, who were deeply fearful of the multiracial alliance of {black and white indentured servants} and slaves." She continued that the elite abandoned the use of the indentured servants in favor of the importation of more black slaves. **An agenda was required to ensure that no white and black alliances could ever happen again.**

After the rebellion, the elite conspired to increasingly distinguish between people of African descent and people of European descent. There was no such term as "white people." White people were called French, Dutch, Spanish, and Christian, but not white. The elite enacted laws that said that people of African descent were hereditary slaves. Using common sense, if all blacks were slaves, there wouldn't be a need to enact a law to make blacks slaves. This law was passed because free black men would no longer be seen as legally free. The elite went on to give a little power to independent white farmers and landholders. This led to the invention of the term... "WHITE PEOPLE". The elite passed laws that made it illegal for a black man to fight back if he was physically assaulted by a white man. Blacks would have to get off the street to allow a white person to pass on the sidewalk. Blacks had no rights, and whites had all the rights over black people.

The laws in America that invented white people as superior and privileged over blacks began in the late 1600's and are permanently embedded in all of Americans, both black and white, to some degree, till this very day.

Introduction:

African American Sandra Black, a graduate of Tuskegee University with a Bachelor of Science degree in chemical engineering, lived the bulk of her adult life discriminated against with extreme losses solely due to the fact that she was not born with white skin. This condition is not an act of nature, but the societal conditioning for centuries that blacks are inherently subject to oppression/harsh treatment as a way of life. Sandra black realized that this condition is caused by an embedded law that began with actual laws that literally read that blacks were to be subjugated to whites in every aspect of life. In realizing that this condition affects how we think and feel to this day, though the laws are not called out, they are, in fact, acted out against blacks by every race on planet earth, **including black people**.

The oppression placed on blacks until this very day does not affect any race in America to the degree blacks suffer as the only people discriminated against without a land, country, territory, or reservation to live in sovereign power over their own people. Their self-identity/pride and history as the descendants of the creators of civilization have been utterly lost until this day. They live for centuries, attacked by their own so-called government, to name a few, Jim Crow laws, new Jim Crow laws, declaring war upon any successful or self-serving community so that blacks know they are not allowed success among their own (ie: black wall street, Black Wall Street, Rosewood, May 13, 1985, etc.). They have been experimented on like nazis did the jews, imprisoned for slavery and worked to death, disproportionately imprisoned, guns and drugs planted into their neighborhoods, media, politics, elite, government, all used against black people.

Then the oppressive government passed policy known as civil rights in the 60's, but by the 70's they took it all back with the unseen hand. What happens to policy is that it simply changes the wording of the law. Discrimination is almost impossible to prove today. They switched the **burden of proof** from the corporations to the individual. What this does is set corporations up for strategically placing coon blacks in place so that it is practically automatic that no discrimination can occur because blacks are the perpetrators and "blacks do not discriminate against blacks." Worse, the individual must now prove discrimination when before the corporations had that burden. The corporations paid Congress to reverse the burden onto the individual because it was too difficult for them to prove they did not discriminate, and thus lost a lot of money. This reversed mistreatment of black people nearly placed black people back to square one because the average black person never knew their advantage of the burden of proof in a discrimination lawsuit had been secretly stripped away.

Objective:

The objective is to once and for all overcome a fraction of the 400+ years of systemic racism against blacks, only by extremely punishing **the target** so as to conquer the unseen grip and embrace of racism that entraps us perpetually into notoriety as one of the most racist countries in the world for centuries, which has done little to nothing to end the problem.

Criteria:

To qualify for ELC, el a person must meet the following criteria.

1. Be a member of the group of people affected and harmed, the protected.

2. Possess a minimum of at least one major discrimination damage prior to the new claim or a series of damages occurring because you were not white committed prior to the current claim of discrimination. The prior discrimination or series of discrimination must be believable more than slightly possible to have occurred. It cannot appear to be fabricated.

3. **The target** must have either the intent to maliciously harm the protected or be responsible for the employee or person whose act was maliciously intended to harm the protected. Employers are responsible for the acts of their employees. Corporations are not exempt from being a target.

Compensation - a jury or settlement that awards embedded law pays out 10 to 100 times the worth of the case should be capped at $500 million per defendant. All money awarded to individuals over 75 million shall go into the fund for black people, descendants of slavery. In the maximum payout situation, the victim (individual) receives a maximum amount of 40%, capped at 75 million. The remaining 60% must go to start a non-profit for the black community/ future nation. It is the victor's (winner of the lawsuit) responsibility for publicly accounting to the non-profit for that said 60% spent towards **helping blacks gain wealth and sovereignty, only** including but not limited to:

- Building black businesses,
- Black investments
- Black loans, grants towards black businesses, health, social needs, community, etc.
- Purchasing land for the purpose of seeking sovereign living for blacks governed by blacks, building and incorporating a nation

- Lobbying laws for the betterment of black people
- Projects for black communities, parks, clubs, socials, tutors, and schools
- Begin an anti-defamation league for FBA, and such projects only
- These funds must go directly to black people, not to any agency or black leader.

Any settlement lower than $20,000,000 million dollars must include a 5 million dollar amount paid for the black community. Fair increment percentages are to be calculated in between.

Payout begins with an accumulation of funds to substantially pay out the needs of the FBA. The committee must pay out with 60% of funds going towards land, sovereignty, and reparations, 10% towards the diaspora needs of the individual escaping racism, and 30% for all other needs.

The protected:

The protected are the American descendants of slaves, aka African Americans, aka black Americans, aka black people, deemed the only people grossly affected by (ELC). Only 12.5% of the nation would qualify to use ELC.

The target:

The target is any individual, entity, group, government, or department that breaks any discrimination laws against an African American, the protected class. Note: the target can be both the affected and non-affected.

Major benefits: unprecedented relief of suffering for American descendants of slaves

1. The first attempt ever at a glimpse of a resolution to redeem (help return to their
precondition before damage) black lives, to end the established perpetual centuries of
oppression and suffering of black people in America, that had existed only as a dream of failed

attempts that **never** addressed black issues solely.

2. America, for the first time ever, will show substance of genuine intent aimed at ending the suffering of black people are evident both nationally and internationally, that harming blacks is no longer tolerated in America.

3. Blacks, for the very first time, who are extremely damaged all of their lives due to embedded law, will have a remedy of relief. Prior to this lawsuit, most Americans were immune to harming blacks negatively and unjustly, even to the death. This will help end BLM.

4. All relief above the 75, 000,000.00 seventy-five million dollars is subject to going towards helping blacks, the black community/future nation **establish wealth and sovereignty.**

5. This will be a massive incentive of epic proportions to regulate and place into policy immediately termination of known racists, "Karens", "Kevins", known to target the protected for harm.

6. Discrimination will greatly lessen among the population. Thus, racism may lessen.

Key Milestones:

The major key milestone is comfort/familiarity, as this is the way we have always done it. Mainstream America will not like to hear that only one race will benefit. Moreover, a painful realization is that all Americans deep inside place black as an impossibility of being equal to white. It will require overcoming ignorance of the fact that only one race in America suffers without any possibility of overcoming it without special attention, intent solely to remedy that one race. We can't even recognize it. We'd rather pretend blacks are equal and their suffering no longer happens. This hurdle is the major milestone of ELC. Overcome it to end systemic racism against blacks. We must set this race as a prerequisite to end racism to be the number one goal. If we fail, the result is permanent oppression by this society without the possibility of a remedy to change the condition of the people. Einstein says it best. The only way to overcome a negative force (energy) is with an equal and opposite positive energy. Embedded law represents a somewhat equal and opposite positive force.

Other milestones are

1. Possible negative public reaction equivalent to the 1960's desegregation laws due to the fact that people do not want change, but not as large as it will not affect most.

2. Corporation backlash, not wanting to spend money to train and secure the protected from discrimination and not wanting to pay out large settlements in a lawsuit.

3. A government pro-black enslavement/oppression entrapment.

4. Racists will hate this remedy and any remedy.

Summary conclusion:

The embedded law concept is necessary to begin the first real and true intent to set black people equal to white people, words never ever used anywhere in American law. There has never in all the history of America been a language that exists in law or courts to set black people equal to white people. If we cannot say it, we are not thinking it. If we cannot think it, it cannot materialize. This concept begins the process of changing the face of America forever as we truly initiate seeking equality for all. Winning equality for the American descendants of slavery will, by default, win equality for all Americans; all people of all colors will be equal to white people. A dream manifesting into reality. Say it! Think it! Manifest it! Set black people equal to white people.

TERMINOLOGY FOR

EMBEDDED LAW

Major Discrimination - An overwhelming loss that is protected by the federal government such as a job or a home. Also included is loss of life, bodily harm, stalking, destruction of property, false informing, and any other harm caused solely because a person is of African American heritage.

The TARGET – Any race of people or a person from black, white, brown, red, or yellow that uses EMBEDDED LAW (**behaving as if one has a right by law and above the law to destroy blacks)** with malicious INTENT to harm. This is the target.

Affected and Harmed – American Descendants of slaves, The PROTECTED

Coon - Represents blacks who are traitors to their own race. Blacks who work, think, and fight AGAINST their own betterment in order to artificially gain the appearance of acceptance and approval as one who conforms to the societal perception model and ORDER OF OPERATIONS, including the CODE (embedded actions). This group of people is the most extremely dangerous to victims of EMBEDDED LAW.

ON CODE - A person, group of persons, officials, who get ON CODE with behavior and reasoning that is morally wrong, socially unacceptable, and can be outright illegal, but ON CODE the acts are accepted and embraced under a fake pretense. The fake pretenses range from victimizing/demonizing the victims, trusting/using the system to be ON CODE, reasoning that nothing can be done, FORCING IT LAW, and MANDATE that past practice sets a precedent into a perpetual RIGHT to do wrong.

"KAREN" and "KEVIN" - Karens and Kevins are white females and males who get on code to attack blacks and anyone they feel is not on code to cause as much damage to the person or entity as they possibly can, including fabricating victimization of being wronged or harmed, by the PROTECTED.

The PROTECTED – American Descendants of slaves, protected by EMBEDDED LAW

AGAIN PLEASE:

I would like for you to follow me on Tik Tok, Ezzrath Global Elite Takedown, YouTube, Sandra Black, Global Elite Takedown, and Facebook Ezzrath Baht Shem and join my group "Global Citizens Unite" (I was the first FB group with the word global and now they stole it and have more members doing absolutely nothing for the world to change. We MUST UNITE! so that we can get the word out that people are being destroyed by a failing system that works well only for the elite.

I also plan to sue them for **OBSTRUCTION OF JUSTICE**. The landlords lied under oath and took part in forcing me to lose my case due to their illegal testimony, and the attorneys involved allowed gross victimization of the law, going against their sworn duty, one anticipated in lying to the court, the corporation was given a CEASE AND DESIST, and the attorney still wrote that my attempts to stop JIM CROW was meritless. Only now I have more defendants and I don't have to prove discrimination only by the preponderance of the evidence that 1. they LIED UNDER OATH, 2, THAT THEY KNEW THE JUDGES WERE LYING TO HELP THEM WIN WHERE STOPPING THE LIE AND ASKING FOR A NEW JUDGE WOULD NOT HAVE HARMED THEIR CASE. 3. They illegally brought the case to begin with at the state level.

I thank you for your time to look at a fellow human beings' ideas and concerns. Many blessings,

Ezzrath Baht Shem ask Sandra Black

LET'S CONNECT AND BEGIN A NEW LIFE

The past year or so the Lord has been doing something new with me. It got really often while I was writing this book and I am figuring this is GOD, showing you how to know that you should connect and work with me. I am sure this has NEVER happened before, or JUST WITHIN THE LAST YEAR or so started happening. If it does happen that God communicates to you through the TV, let's work together. Contact me on social media. My phone number is out there.

When it happens regular with words like floor, then **seconds** later you hear "floor" and you know you were sat up by the events at that time to say FLOOR. Like, you say or think "WINDOW" because something just hit your window, then your radio says "window" or sometimes the entire sentence is said, like "something just hit my window" and the radio will say "something hit my/their/his window AND IT WILL HAPPEN OVER and OVER again as God/Universe communicates your chosen path to you. Then you contact us, and WE ALL WORK TOGETHER, absolutely no hierarchy. Simply change the world so that ALL live in harmony and peace having all basic needs met without any worry so whatever how to get them. NO MORE POVERTY! And evolving the individual setup to run ourselves and the government. WE TELL THE GOVERNMENT or TRUE SERVANT OF THE PEOPLE WHAT TO DO so it's like a monkey can be president as WE SET THE GUIDELINE and THEY congress, senate, parliament, Emperor, president, governor, Mayor... SERVE US! THERE WILL BE NO NEED FOR POLICE. AS THE WORLD FREE OF POVERTY AND SUPPORTING THE WEAK as MOST important and the strong and powerful as least important; WILL CUT criminality, depression drug addictions, mental illness into near nonexistence. And our world will be far more productive as well because we will have FULL use of our GREATEST COMMODITY, far greater than money and power; its HUMANITY!

CHAPTER EIGHT

Cases of <u>WRONGFUL HARM</u> Against Our FAMILY

Background: OUR Judicial Justice System's priorities are anything but 1. Protecting Society and Maintaining Order, 2. ENSURING JUSTICE and FAIR TREATMENT, 3. Ensuring Officials Maintain Professional Competence AND THE HIGHEST DEGREE OF ETHICS over their SWORN DUTY TO SERVE.

Justice, competence, and fairness rarely occur according to our near PERFECT legal requirements. It's so sad that our foundational laws are so damn near perfect, but officials believe they do not need to follow them. The judicial code of ethics is so extremely high and excellent, but judges almost only by LUCK, or your position within society may you win your full consideration of the evidence. **<u>MOST NEVER BY THE EVIDENCE OR BY DILIGENCE TO SEEK TRUTH AND FAIRNESS</u>**. Your ignorance of these facts, black or white, rich or poor CAN and WILL be your demise if you fall victim to officials LITERALLY trained to be gods over society without genuine **DUTY** TO INTERVENE, to correct wrongful and/or criminal acts… as was done in numerous cases against my family. I will send a copy of this book to the Supreme Court seeking diligence over my federal case that denied me a TRIAL by placing me falsely in the wrong without remedy. Absolutely nothing will be done if you do not intervene as citizens standing up for constitutional rights. WATCH!!! I'd love to be proven wrong.

The Judicial, Legislative, and Executive branches RULING OVER OUR LIVES are in FACT so corruptly diabolically wicked against the masses of citizens that our society PROVE IT A FACT by just looking at it. IT IS A MOCKERY AND DISGRACE BEFORE THE ENTIRE WORLD! The United States is undeniably irrefutable THE RICHES nation on planet earth; the global hub for finance, tech, energy, entertainment, AND THE GOD ALMIGHT DOLLAR that hoodwink rules the world by illusion. YET among all wealthy white ruled nations on EARTH, its citizens are the MOST… incarcerated, BY FAR poorest (highest overall poverty rate), suicidal and depressed, sick and dying, drug addicted, turning to crime, [MENTALLY ILL, and OPPRESSED "minorities," Native Americans and Black Americans, **descendants of slavery** (Indigenous African Foundational Black Americans, IAFBA)].

Police become angry and hostile if you ask for your constitutional rights. Judges strike evidence they don't want to consider instead of considering it; and rendering an opinion on its content. Judge Haas violates his sworn duty to seek truth throughout EVERY case with me. The absolute only way I win is where he **CAN'T POSSIBLY FIND A WAY TO JUSTIFIABLY TAKE ME OUT**! This is NOT justice; this is a witch hunt for the destruction of the citizen.

Case 1. Officer Kilgore, summer of 2005. I genuinely believe in the system, as I HAVE NO EXPERIENCE personally of outright evil. I know it happens to criminals and uneducated people, but I checked all the right boxes for no official to treat me like the weaklings of society, our system's purpose BY DESIGN. I called the police on my daughter, who was pregnant and wanted to go out to a party while living in our home with her grandma and me. I lay down the law that she will live by our rules under our roof and get her life together. She's 18 and by law I can't dictate anything, but if she leaves to party she doesn't come back. My daughter knows it is absolute and begins terrorizing me and mom begging us to allow her back in until about 12:00 am while we're tired and sleepy, SHE WON'T STOP pleading, and we now want her to leave and move into a shelter. There is no getting her to stop so we call the police out to help us get her talked into going to a shelter because she's not willing to live by our rules. Kilgore comes out, listens to both sides, and tells her to stay and go to bed or to get her things and leave. PERFECT. My daughter starts doing to him what she was doing to us all night asking why she can't go out for just a little while and come back. She got maybe one or two chances at getting a no it's our rules. He then YELLED at her to get her keys and leave. STILL GREAT! So, she stomps her feet (a brat), walking by the officer to her car, yelling, "I'm getting my fucking keys!" And he grabs her picks her up in the air, and body slams her on her STOMACH. She's crying, I'm pregnant." He replies, "so what, you're disrespectful and don't give a damn about your baby, why should I," and he places her under arrest for "resisting arrest." Later, it was changed to disturbing the peace and resisting. I learnt that night, NEVER CALL POLICE, without expecting the worst possible outcomes. She was defiant and bleeding, so they kicked her out and it NEVER HAPPENED. We couldn't find the case to complain. It disappeared. My grandson is a handsome, hardworking, intelligent young man today that Kilgore could have murdered because my daughter exercised her constitutional right to freedom of speech which he saw as disrespectful and his right to body slam her on her stomach KNOWING she was pregnant.

Case 2 Petition for Guardianship of Mildred Barber (my mom) filed by Sandra Black in GRANT County Superior Court 2 August 16, 2010, under Judge Dana Kenworthy 27D02-1008-000185 and Judge Warren Haas, 27D03-1008-000185. This was a case about a greedy MEAN brother who had a vendetta against his mother and his sister, with whom he got along more than he did his mother. I am his sister. My brother saw mom's sickness as his right to live in the palace where I had always been, under mom's wings, trained to care for her by being the only sibling, and my children to care for mom's three elderly siblings who preceded her in death. I had a real relationship with my mom while my brothers were in and out of trouble, pot heads, high school dropouts, and the other one was on cocaine. Neither brother had respect for mom's lifestyle or her desires for life. They couldn't tell you anything much about her life, friends, associates, and early life (where she and I lived together in the end), as they rarely had meaningful conversations with mom.

I have felt so sorry for him all his life. He's been called nigger, sponge head, and expelled for a little white girl WRITING HIM (He never wrote her back, but that ended his attendance in that private school.) This all happened before he was 8. He naturally has a personality trait of feeling self-entitled and mandatory getting his way. I understood him and tried to deal with him with a long-handled silver spoon. The courts 100% do not diligently seek the truth, but Kenworthy at least attempted to find the truth. Courts intentionally look at cases to find so-called experts, guardians ad litem, agencies, and state department recommendations, and the case is closed without ever considering the evidence. Kenworthy was a victim of this EVIL mass destruction of human lives. She mistakenly listened to the court-appointed guardian ad litem, Terry Pollet, and absolutely nothing I said counted. In COURTS; attorneys, police, agencies, government entities, corporations, big money ALL COUNT of higher creditability than a regular citizen. Therefore, regular citizens WITHOUT CREDITABLE EVIDENCE against their testimony are totally ruled out based solely on their position in life. Pollet used my disability against me so that I wasn't able to work a job, though I maintained a home and a child, I was automatically unfit. The neighbors, family, friends all knew that my children were vastly the primary support system for my mom, but using a disability cut out time, no need to talk to ANYONE, mom was found incompetent, and I was a monster, my brother was greedy and had conned my mom, so he was the best fit to care for her. My mother was doomed to live a life of solitary confinement for the greater portion of a decade of her final years, no one to love her. My poor mother didn't remember her relationship with my brother, and he used it against her to take over her home, her life, her access to anyone who GENUINELY LOVED HER and ALL FRIENDS; her sources of entertainment were lost. Her life was solely food, water, and walls when and if she was lucky.

Haas ruled that I never brought the guardian petition for my mom and ordered the clerk to never allow me to move the court ever again.

Case 3. My 25-year-old daughter faces **ONE HUNDRED YEARS** in prison! State v Felicia Y Ogunbuyide, case no. 52C01-1206-FA-000044. This case was about WEALTHY RICH WHITE TRUMP pervert type, and my family youth both getting caught up. Of course, the rich white Trump type comes out without ANY CHARGES after he **criminally** causes the entire incident by his own words in the discovery. He should have been charged with a felony, Maintaining a Common Nuisance and Prostitution to CAUSE four black poor young adults to end up in Peru, Indiana, a mostly all-white town.

Case 4. Opened June 5, 2017, Grant, county Superior Court III, Landlord discriminates and removes all people of color with children from Hunters Run. Hunters Run v. Sandra Black Case No:27D03-1706-PL-000014 and appeal for Judge stated that I had to re-file my counterclaim because he had stricken it, not wanting to consider evidence from the black litigant, his rival, who is against the white attorney (his golfing buddy), corporations, and white litigants that he already biasedly favored. **He stated that failure to do so would result in dismissal with PREJUDICE** (meaning that I couldn't ever be heard). I filed a motion to dismiss without prejudice, as I had to get out of his court to have any chance at all. He refused to rule on my motion. An appeal was filed to force the judge to rule, case No: 27A05-1708-PL-01909. Haas lied to the appellate court that he attended to dismiss without prejudice after the case was completed when the landlords had their property back. If it was TRUTH (he planned to dismiss without prejudice), then why not just honor my motion and dismiss without prejudice, LIAR.

This ruling of the appellate court that I had not given the judge a chance to finalize and SHOULD WAIT FOR THE FINAL DECISION before coming to the appellate court caused me to believe I had to wait in FEDERAL COURT for an appeal till the end of court. I didn't know that I could appeal during court before the case was over until the case was over, and the appellate form asks if it was a final case decision or not. However, Diane Sykes is CHIEF over it all and IS UTTERLY CORRUPT, so she would push that the lease is a matter of opinion, and a judge is always right over the pro se litigant. Look at the outcome. I held my ground. **THIS COURT WAS NEVER ALLOWED TO EVER LEAVE THE LIE FOR NEARLY THREE YEARS.** They didn't want to automatically dismiss because they wanted a trial of my being automatically in the wrong, with as much confusion as possible, to make it LOOK LIKE they were doing everything to give me a chance. The WERE WORKING ILLEGALLY under the COLOR OF LAW against me and absolutely no authority would stop it. I held on to I WOULD NEVER GO into trial with a JIM CROW forced FALSE COURT ORDER placing me automatically in the wrong AND denying all of my evidence against the defendants. They made it as if the white defendants won at the state level; that the defendants were found to be in the right, a blatant LIE of judges. ALL attorneys I spoke to said they had no clue of how to overcome JUDGE'S BLATANTLY DECEPTIVE ORDERS. The reason it's IMPOSSIBLE is because NO slew of judges has ever in American history been CAUGHT conspiring in a FAUDULANT ACT (a lie (deception) to result in financial or PERSONAL GAIN)... deception to **protect WHITE SUPREMACY** or any other GAIN ever. America is NOT a white country, she is a country of diversity, and no single white judge BY LAW can destroy the constitution that they can LIE to protect their personal gain of power for whiteness NOR to protect other judges to do so. You decide WHAT IS THE MOTIVE? Why would judges LIE about everything favoring a black litigant? Then remember my intent to present EMBEDDED LAW to my jury for consideration that could possibly end white supremacy.

Case 5. FILED MARCH 10, 2005, City of Marion v Sandra Black, Case no: 27D03-0503-SC-000921. I'm living in Africa, so of course, there's no way to serve me. After the extreme judicial misconduct of Mom's above, **Haas and Kelsey** get together over an approaching statutory limited filing against me to judicially abuse me. I genuinely believe that it was Haas who called up his buddy to keep me forced under his SICK JURISDICTION (STATE CONTROL). Ten years later, with only TWO MONTHS to spare, Haas searches my name to seek out a way to get me and finds this case, DEAD and forgotten. On January 8, 3015, after utterly destroying my family and mother's life, Haas finds a way to get me in his arena again. I asked him to recuse himself after knowing it was a FACT that I was against his rulings and unfair treatment, but our system doesn't play by fairness, JUDGES ARE GODS against citizens, and they have next to ZERO rights in a judge's arena. The reason is that Judicial Qualifications Commissions for state court or Misconduct appeals for federal court judges most **ALWAYS** rule in favor of a judge, no matter what, for the civilian who cannot afford an attorney, a pro se litigant. There is no due process for the poor citizen, NO CONSTITUTIONAL RIGHTS by judicial actions in proceedings. This judge out right LIED and refused to remove the lie after trying to FORCE me to pay a bill I didn't owe, forcing me to appear over and over again in court. I was adamant that I would not pay a bill I didn't owe. Nonetheless, he would reschedule me to appear and pay. He finally realized that it wouldn't work to force me to pay, and he lied. He wrote an order that I satisfy the debt. A BLATANT LIE. I motioned the court to remove the lie that his only choice was to dismiss the case because I never paid, never satisfied the debt, and never will. He has always ignored my motions, being a god over me. He didn't have to follow laws, nor the code of ethics. He was a god, and I was a **NOBODY**, NO RIGHTS! This is the American way, and most citizens have absolutely no clue HOW SERIOUSLY BAD THIS IS. It's WHEN THEIR CHILD IS STOLEN BY DCS, IT'S WHEN THEIR CHILD OR CHILDREN GET SLAPPED WITH A MURDER CHARGE FOR ABSOLUTELY NO REASON!!! A zealous prosecutor gets the case; no attorney will be able to save your family. Crimes are supposed to be proven beyond a reasonable doubt. It was made that way because we would rather let criminals go free than have innocent people locked up. However, juries are convicting on IF YOU LOOK GUILTY!!! This is insane, and though you can't feel it, it's going to be a nightmare when it happens to you and ABSOLUTELY NOTHING YOU CAN DO ABOUT IT.

Case 6. My son is in depression and bad choices fries his brain on drugs. He was experiencing psychosis badly, and I called the ambulance out in December, 2018. A stupid kid was driving and said his psychosis wasn't real, that kids today play delusional. I told him NOT MY SON. This is real, he's not acting. My grandson was so scared that the police officer told me he was shaking. I found out later that he had snuck to the kitchen to get a knife. My son wasn't being violent. Here's what he was saying. "Nephew, open the door." "I want you to tell me how you and my wife bought Fortnite." BRO!!! My son believed that his wife and his nephew, my grandson, owned Fortnite, a multibillion-dollar gaming platform. And he kept banging on the door that was locked. Please tell me, nephew. And accusing me of crimes that he was going to turn me into the CIA if I didn't tell him all of what I was doing. He was saying he was so disappointed, but my son, in his right mind, knows I never do anything illegal and raised him that way too. Months before this night, that I called the ambulance, September, 2018, my son told me that he had shut down all the corrupt officials in our town. He said he saw them all packed and moving out of town. Then a neighbor walked by as we were sitting on the porch, and my son was going to ask him to verify what he saw. I had to beg him, " Please don't bring my neighbors into this. He was talking about how Harriet Tubman buried millions of dollars under our city, and it's just waiting for us to dig it up. Any idiot should know this is not a game my son is playing, but absolutely no help for the mentally ill and he then catches a case where he was in the car of a man we don't know, but he thought the man was the man known to our family as banana man who looked similar and had a similar car. He told me that others have confused him with our family friend too.

Case 6. Continued 2/5/2019 Indiana v Kemuel Shem Case no: 27C01-1902-F5-000016, My son gets arrested because there is NO ALLOWING FAMILY to help their mentally-ill family members INTENTIONALLY!!! This is set up to feed the prison money-hungry owners. Did you know they REQUIRE that the government sign a contract for a minimum number of inmates, known as "lockup quotas" or "minimum occupancy clauses" to GUARANTEE PROFIT and maximum lockup of our citizens. Lockup quotas began in 1980. Mandatory sentencing laws, "war on drugs," since the evil MANDATORY QUOTA of locking people up has increased IMPRISONMENT of American citizens by 500%. So you can see a 500% increase. Imagine your bread costs $3.00 and it went up by 500% tomorrow. You would pay 18 dollars for one loaf of bread. This is how we INSANELY imprison our citizens for mistakes they make in times of weakness. NO WEALTHY NATION IN THE ENTIRE WORLD DOES THIS TO THEIR CITIZENS. Incarceration rate per 100,000, the no.1 being the USA at 542, no.2 Turkey at 356, no. 3 Saudi Arabia at 207. And we have the gall to talk about backward nations. REALLY? We are the powerful, wealthiest, greatest nation on earth with the most depressed, suicidal, drug addicts, and incarcerated citizens on earth AND THIS IS COMMON SENSE USA???

So now, I seek to intervene to get my son help. His attorney WORKS FOR THE PROSECUTION, Bruce Elliott. told me he had a plea that found him guilty of everything, and he wouldn't need to go to trial. So my son is so lucky not to have to go to trial, his attorney advises. I told him, but shouldn't the plea reduce something? He utterly yelled at the top of his lungs at me, "DON'T TELL ME MY JOB!" I now understand that he was caught off guard that I knew better and responded in a way that if that damn bitch knows better, then he should be disbarred for trying to push a plea deal with next to nothing taken off with my son having no criminal past. The entire prosecution process of Grant County is utterly corrupt, and perhaps throughout the country. Defendants without money walk into a prosecution GANG (the police, judge, and public defender) with plenty of money and incentive to destroy lives and fabricate narratives in many situations. The poor are appointed an attorney with seriously limited resources and absolutely no incentives to win. How is this fair? This is what makes the public defender feel ENTITLED to force pleas and work hard with the prosecutor against the defendant. I asked his attorney to help me get guardianship for my son so I can help him with his mental illness. My son is willing to let me be appointed guardian over his life. He ignored me. I asked the prosecution, as well as a good Samaritan, to help me help our city be protected so that my son will not be in trouble. Hunt and Faulk were prosecutors on this case. Faulk the prosecutor helped us more than Elliott. Dana Kenworthy was the judge, and I asked her to. She kept crying EXPARTE, EXPARTE... DAMMIT, YOU REPRESENT THE STATE, PROTECT THE CITIZENS!!! WTF!!! My son is reported to judges, his attorney, and officials as a danger to himself and others... TO PLEASE RECOMMEND GUARDIANSHIP (because HAAS was fighting against me helping my son) for the two no-contested subjects (my son and I) to save the community, to save our lives!!! Eventually, my son will be arrested for reckless homicide, and since he's black and poor, without any evidence of premeditation or INTENT, Hunt changed the charges to murder one. See case 12.

Case 7. GUARDIANSHIP of my three grandchildren, who had been in my care for many years prior. Case nos. 27D03-1903-000021/22/23 for Victoria Goree, Christian (ISAIAH) Goree, and Chrisdeon Ogunbuyide, respectively. Haas had labeled me a monster in mom's case "I couldn't care if you NEVER saw your mother again." and now I am an angel allowed custody of THREE CHILDREN, "Ms. Black you've done a wonderful job with your grandchildren" and he praised me looking for a THANK YOU that he would NEVER EVER get forcing my mom to live in hell because I was a monster, but now I am an angel, hell naw. And yes, I understand he could have been outrageously evil and placed my grandchildren into hell also. So I should say thank you for recognizing the truth and not destroying my grandchildren, as you did to my mother? NEVER! However, I didn't ask him what I burned to ask. How do you find a monster fit to care for children? How? I knew he couldn't erase it, but I didn't know when next he would get me, so I let that one go.

He DID GET ME IN THE CHINS CASE towards the end and reversed the fact that I had custody because the placement chosen was a danger to my grandson. DCS and CASA, who both signed letters stating that I had custody, REVERSED IT because I shared custody with my cousin, where THEY KNEW she wouldn't share with me! But by my sharing custody, it gave her time with the baby and their chance NOT TO HAVE WRONG PLACEMENT... so fighting began all over again with DCS and CASA trying to remove my custody. They supported her intervening to get custody or a court-ordered visitation that would make it difficult to manage an unfit person with rights to access. Being too old and disabled, I couldn't fight her as a way of life. She would win, and we would never see him again as she wanted it to be.

Case 8. FEDERAL COURT, Northern District Ft. Wayne, Indiana Sandra Black v Naomi Friedrichsen ET AL case no. 1:19 -cv-00307-WCL-SLC and after Judge LEE refused to force me to pay sanctions and continue the charades that I was in the wrong. Indiana district brought in a judge who would carry through THE LIE. Judge Theresa Springmann. Wonder what kinds of promotions she has now for being a cheating criminal judge against the Constitution and the JUDICIAL CODE OF ETHICS? Case no. 1:19-cv-00307- TLS-SLC. And to remove the villain, the case number finally. changed finally to Case no. 1:19-cv-00307-TLS

7th Circuit Court – filing twice to STOP THE LIE with Diane Sykes doubling down on the LIE that I am the troublesome litigant for seeking to remove the LIE that I had unauthorized occupants living in my home who were my grandchildren who were NOT ON THE LEASE. ALL 100% A LIE and the court found it a right NOT to diligently seek the truth OF A LEASE and a court order IN HAND that ORDERED there was no evidence proving people lived in my home and that my grandchildren WERE ON THE LEASE. They were named and written as A RIGHT to live in the home by law. AND SYKES LIED THAT SHE DILIGENTLY FOUND THIS WAS A MATTER OF OPINION and NOT A FACTUAL ONE. Giving her the right to not rule against the lying judge, as this court of misconduct does not rule on matters of opinion. I wonder what they use to show discrimination in an opinion ordered by a judge, BUT THIS WAS NOT a matter of opinion, IT WAS A MATTER OF FACT. It was pointed out and ignored fabricated that a lease is a matter of opinion. Court of Appeals and the supreme court ruled on the writ that a judge would be ALLOWED TO USE JIM CROW IN 2023 and place a black litigant FALSELY IN THE WRONG against malicious whites who have overwhelming evidence against them while they have next to zero evidence to back their claim.

Case 9. CHINS CASE NO. 27D02-1903-JC-000012 AN ATTEMPT TO KIDNAP OUR CHILD BY DCS and CASA who placed an unfit person over my grandson. Both CASA and DCS utterly refused to investigate any claim that this person was unfit. **Guardianship over my grandson Poseidon Malik King Ogunbuyide case no. 27D03-2008-GU-000060**. For years, I had complained about my grandson being taken to the drug house with witnesses, about how this person had a 13-year-old brain capacity which I had firsthand knowledge of. DCS WROTE in text that they couldn't care less about a person with a 13-year-old mind capability having custody, because 13-year-olds have children all the time. They refused to talk to witnesses and later refused to ever go to the placement's house for visits out of fear of catching her. THEIR FEAR became a reality they couldn't stop. Placement brought my grandson to my home, reeking of drugs, and I went directly to the police. She was caught NOW! RIGHT??? HELL NAW. DCS and CASA ignored the police report where the police REPORTED SMELLING DRUGS ON MY GRANDSON AT THE TIME PLACEMENT DELIVERED HIM TO ME. So I later go file a police report that I will get the FBI involved to investigate why they are keeping a child intentionally placed in harm's way. Next thing I know about three weeks later I get a call to NEVER return our child to the placement's care. IT WAS OVER. I got the paperwork which showed that on the day I filed the police report of my intent to contact the FBI, DCS forced the placement to take a drug test. SHE WAS DIRTY. They never called me then. They gave her two weeks, told her she had to clean up to keep him. WTF!!! Here I am grandma, next of kin, have never done any type of hard drugs in my life other than a few occasions of marijuana uses back over forty years ago in college. I passed the FBI background test with nothing on my record. While she had a court order not to have any minors in her custody as a result of her criminal conviction. Where CASA and DCS got on her to have it expunged. You guys, DCS KNEW THAT CASA WAS ADVICING their wrong choice of placement to get that expunged that she was not allowed to have minors in her custody after they KNEW she broke the law. I had won my grandson back because of her background and her crack head boyfriend had beaten her so severely with my grandson in her custody when the police came out. YET, THEY STILL CHOSE HER over safety, over the immediate family, over the most educated, mature, and mentally stable between us two. This is what DCS does!!! Adult protective services too!!! If they get it wrong, they prefer the child or adult DIES IN IT, rather than admitting they were wrong. They assigned placement to my daughter's running buddy our cousin. She was fourth cousin to my grandson with no blood relation at all as her mother was adopted by my mother's brother. I had wanted to share care with her so I could be involved in his safety and to assure this child knew he wasn't a throwaway. She had been born with SEVERE birth defects and couldn't have her own children and wanted our family blocked out. This is where the dispute began and I had to expose what I knew about her to block her from blocking us out. In the end, the court had absolutely no choice but to ORDER my grandson into my SOLE CUSTODY. It was an act of GOD! And the court still lied in his order that DCS and CASA did their best to keep Malik safe, knowing damn well that all I had been complaining about WAS PROVEN FACTUAL and they never ONCE mentioned investigating placement on behalf of my numerous complaints. How could they have done their BEST? REALLY??? I appealed that finding in the order, and the Appeals Court kept me blocked out on some sort of technicality with the way I filed my affidavit, which I filed as pauperis status. So it stands in court that in OVER 3 years of placement, DCS and CASA never knew they were dealing with a drug user for my grandson's placement, though I pointed out what I knew about it and WITNESSES too, but they did "THEIR BEST" judge's order, non-removable. This is our sick society that the system no matter who or how they WRONG a person... THEY'RE RIGHT!

Case 10. **Federal Court** Sandra Black v State of Indiana regarding DCS CAUSING HARDSHIP TO OUR FAMILY to place a child in harms way to keep him BLOCKED from his immediate family. Wrongful Placement. Case no. 1:21-cv-265-HAB. No jurisdiction due to immunity to DESTROY.

Case 11. Guardian Case for Kemuel Shem to be SAFE FROM HARM, Case no. 27D03-1908-GU-000060. Haas refused to hear the case, telling me... "You only want to help your son's case (case no. 27C01-1902-F5-000016). I won't consider this until after the case." In fear of no action on the case and an evil judge on the case to order denied with prejudice to block me from ever helping my son. I moved to dismiss the case as there was no end in sight due to judicial corruption and malicious prosecution. Had any official gave a damn about human life, a dead woman may be alive today and 100% my son wouldn't have been around those people had I and my son's guardian's requests been allowed and these SICKOS get to live totally free of realizing how they DESTROYED LIVES and our family is 100% not the only ones dying or involved in dying. Please wake up to this God-forsaken EVIL WICKED SYSTEM that can NOT possibly be fixed as it is not broken. It is working perfectly as designed 5000 years ago to extinct the human race by SELF-ANNIHILATION

Case 12.. A murder case, the State of Indiana v Kemuel Shem, case no 27C01-2108-MR-000005. This case first began with Dana Kenworth in Superior Court 2. Where she was forced to recuse for not removing public defender attorney Bruce Elliott that she knew she had removed from the last case assigned to Kemuel for working with the prosecution against my son. She rather recuse than remove the attorney. She did the same with mom, screw her recuse so the next judge leaves the individual fucked. This my friends is Justice in America! In this new court, Judge Mark Spitzer continued to force my son to keep an attorney that would not work on behalf of his interest, serve his requests. Elliott ever refused to honor my son's request for me to be designated as the person to receive all his information, according to the court, it was because, as I KNEW, my son was mentally ill, so he couldn't have a right to pick who would best serve him. WTF!!! My son was stuck with no way out, no genuine representation. **NO EVIDENCE FOR MURDER ONE**, but charged with the crime.

His attorneys hadn't called, returned calls, or seen my son in A YEAR! Watching a show where that happened a guy won on appeal that no attorney can refuse to see their client. I got together with my son and explained to him that he could appeal to remove the attorney with an argument that you hadn't seen your attorney in a year and that he is charged with a crime without the evidence to fit the crime. After filing the appellate court ordered my son to report the filing to the lower court and ask permission. The day that was done, for the first time in nearly ONE YEAR, the **VERY NEXT DAY**, my son's attorney was there to coerce him into a plea deal for reckless homicide or FACE 60 YEARS. They are currently using his mental illness against him so that he racks up numerous misdemeanor charges and ultimately becomes the statistic of a long prison sentence so that I NEVER see my son free again. THIS IS USA JUSTICE! USA SWORN OFFICIALS INTENTIONALLY BLOCKING OR DENYING ANY HELP TO YOUR FAMILY LOVED ONES THAT YOU ARE WILLING TO HELP.

Most black officials go into office with the selling of their souls to COMMIT to serve assuring that there will be absolutely nothing presented in the interest of blacks. Obama could have signed executive order that no black cop EVER kills an unarmed innocent white person and goes free. That said, by the constitution of the US, I am therefore REQUIRED THAT IT BE ORDERED MANDATORY BY LAW THAT ABSOLUTELY NO POLICE OFFICER CAN USE "FEAR OF LIFE" or any excuse, so whatever, as a justifiable homicide or murder of an innocent, unarmed person. Wherefore it is now decreed Federal law that killing an unarmed innocent individual is a minimum mandatory sentence of 15 years for accidentally causing loss of life. The charge is called MANSLAUGHTER. This will make black and white cops equal in that no white cop, just like no black cop goes free for accidentally causing death. BUT DID OBAMA DO THIS FOR BLACKS? Did he think of anything for black people? I believe black politicians for the most part know it a political suicide to do anything to help black people become equal to white people or worse to do anything to help black to fair treatment. It's no where in their minds as a possibility to use their power to do so.

Our Mayor, Marion, Indiana's FIRST BLACK REPUBLICAN MAYOR OF MARION. His party demands he be anti-black. Mayor Ronald Morrell, without doubt in my mind, an unintentional Charlie Kirk or worse, Charlie Kirk intended, refused my call before getting into office. He never met me or spoke to me before. As Mayor, he refused all my calls. His employee, Iesha, did very little to help me get in contact with the board and the mayor. I had a Post-it card of just a few words of why it was important to keep in my mind personally, and she took my Post-it card after I told her it's just my personal note to myself for focus. Afterwards, I felt she would use those few words as if it were my REQUEST TO TALK TO THE COUNCIL. I decided it didn't matter anyhow; there just isn't any concern for blacks. Why would they care to recommend to anyone, black or white, that I deserved my constitutional rights to a civil trial? Here's the kicker. ALL WHITE MAYORS, know me, speak to me RETURN MY CALLS!!! But a black one gets in office and I become a nobody to speak to. THIS IS JUSTICE IN THE (USA). Black elected officials in general, (**NOT JASMINE CROCKETT**) feel they MUST cut off being a representative to black people as well as all people. Please explain how you overcome the system when whites do not know the plight and blacks believe that black issues ARE BAD POLITICS? They refuse to recognize the plight. There is no national attention to gross inequality for centuries of oppression against the IAFBA. We are the only group of people over 40 million GROSS DAMAGES BY THE AMERICAN CORPORATION, by which those damages still bring generational wealth to white America, while blacks receive zero. The damages are continued emotional scars from slavery, absolutely no place of sovereignty/refuge from discrimination living a life of less than, intentional economic depravity, disproportionate imprisonment, policing, malicious prosecution, illness, mental illness, depression and generalized anxiety disorder; ALL DUE SOLEY TO OPPRESSION against dark skin and the belief that this people are not entitled to any relief so whatever for the wrongs against them. Blacks, IAFBA are the ONLY Americans from the foundation of America that NEVER got any financial relief so whatever. The only people without a land, or sovereignty, but yet they are called equal as minorities that have special agencies and organizations. Here's the violation of the Constitution. BLACKS CONSTITUTIONALLY MUST HAVE MORE OF AN OFFSET THAT A MINORITY! It is unconstitutional to call a black person a minority because all major minority groups of America have a land and sovereignty to escape the hells of discrimination. Mexicans can return to Mexico, Chinese to China, East Indians to India, and Japanese to Japan; where does IAFBA go? NO WHERE TO ESCAPE. Furthermore, the baggage of American slavery is EXCLUSIVE TO FBA! Thus, how can minority laws be constitutionally fair as setting equal treatment when the damage FAR surpasses minority suffering? This is the epitome of inequality, thus unconstitutional to place blacks equal to minorities!

In other words, helping blacks as minorities is no different than placing a bandage on cancer or giving people in need of a car for transportation a vehicle with no engine. EMBEDDED LAW. Must be a politicized **FACT** of American culture used AGAINST the FBA by **all** citizens, including the FBA. Then, remedies for both FBA 1. **SPECIAL offsetting** in place of the minority to offset the extreme suffering or loss that minorities do not and HAVE NOT suffered (socially lived false narrative), AND 2. a sovereign land and community/nation/territory for FBA and IAFBA one and the same; governed solely by FBA as a place of escape guaranteeing FBA are not discriminated against over a color of skin and the social construct that blacks MUST swallow their burden indefinitely to remain unequal. Those days are over and past precedence bleeds it happens IMMEDIATELY, TODAY, not tomorrow. Similar acts have occurred with the Native Americans and the Israelis. It is now imperative that this **MUST** also happen for the IAFBA to finalize settling over 400 years of bondage, oppression, and suffering ENDS. This must finally and foremost set all of us Americans free of the DEBT against AMERICAN CITIZENS once and for all. We need both IFBA laws for those of us living under the sovereignty of the USA, and we need our own NATION, Territory in the Americas AND in Africa as the dual united territory of the IFBA [Indigenous (Olmec/black native Americans/Moors) Foundational Black American!]

UNNEGOTIABLE, IT MUST HAPPEN TO SATISFY THE DEBT. If the USA gives each black person today one million dollars each, in less than one year, it's highly likely that over 50% of us will be back in the same condition. Most all will be just as it is today a few years later. Hence, the condition has no remedy. Therefore, we, the IAFBAs, must have our own CATEGORY of special laws similar to minorities, Native Americans, and Puerto Rico. We need our own nation, our sovereignty with yearly funding like the Israelis receive and also a MUST we need **IAFBA equal right laws** for offsetting generational discrimination and policies (EMBEDDED LAW) against black people, FBA's

This book is a mere glimpse into our family suffering that I genuinely believe that 70% or better would never have occurred throughout our multitude of generations today on earth. The oppressed backward FORCED impact of the Barber family generations of Lena and Claude Barber parents of TWENTY CHILDREN and the Black family generations of the union of George Black Senior and Willie Mae Black parents of 12 children bought over a century of continued extreme black oppression to this very day. Yet we most all find joy inside our oven of suffering and unequally lived lives denied access to the very America we built from the FOUNDATION OF AMERICA.

Here's a story of UNEQUAL in the JUDICIAL BRANCH of AMERICA. Should rich old white men be free of charges for the crimes they commit and poor black young adults be charged with one hundred years for their acts of crimes? IT HAPPENED!!! In Peru, Indiana, mostly ALL WHITE town, how does blacks end up with a relationship with RICH WHITES in Peru. Check out the news headlines of my daughter charged with ONE HUNDRED YEARS for conspiracy to commit armed robbery, 50 years and for conspiracy to commit burglary, 50 years; totaling **100 YEARS**. My daughter at 25 would never be seen on the outside again in life if the prosecution, judge, and public defender had their way, UNIVERSE IS THE ULTIMATE JUDGE AND HE/SHE SAID ABSOLUTELY NOT! If the white goes free, the black goes free, PERIOD. Case closed, but they didn't listen to the UNIVERSE and one month after prosecuting my daughter with judge two months served and probation, the judge mysteriously died.

Four burglary suspects charged

BY SARAH STONESTREET
sstonestreet@perutribune.com

PERU — Four Marion residents arrested last week in an attempted robbery appeared in court for their initial hearings.

Larry Ganaway, Christina Cook, Yaneia Westbrook and Felicia Ogunbuyide all appeared via video conference in the Miami County Court Thursday morning to have their charges read. The four were arrested June 7 after an early morning 911 about an armed robbery in the 6000 block of East 775 South. The call came just after a report had been made of a suspicious vehicle in the area.

Ogunbuyide, 25 and Westbrook, 31, were charged with conspiracy to commit robbery resulting in serious bodily injury, a class-A felony, for having allegedly conspired with Ganaway and Cook to rob the victim of a wallet or money by force. This resulted in "splits and/or cuts" to the victim's head, the charge read, requiring staples and/or stitches.

The two were also charged with conspiracy to commit burglary resulting in bodily injury, another class-A felony, for allegedly conspiring to break and enter the residence to take the money. For each class-A felony they could face 20-50 years' incarceration if found guilty, with an advisory sentence of 30 years.

Ogunbuyide asked for a fast and speedy trial and a jury trial was set for Aug. 6-8, her next pre-trial hearing date was set for Aug. 2. She also asked to a make a statement to the judge, stating she was a mother to two young children and currently pregnant and went on to say that the charges "have been trumped up."

Judge Robert Sparh recommended she speak with the court-appointed attorney before she made any public comment.

"Anything you say can be used against you by the state," he said. "I prefer you not make any public statements before you can meet with your attorney."

Ogunbuyide and Westbrook were appointed a public defender and an automatic not guilty was entered on their behalf. A pre-trial date for Westbrook was also set for Aug. 2.

Cook and Ganaway were charged with attempted robbery resulting in serious bodily injury, a class-A felony, for allegedly engaging "in conduct that constitutes a substantial step to commit a crime." They were also charged with attempted burglary resulting in bodily injury, a class-A felony and battery resulting in serious bodily injury, a class-C felony for which they could receive 2-8 years incarceration if found guilty.

Cook was also charged with false informing, a class-A misdemeanor, for allegedly giving investigators the wrong name.

They were also given a public attorney and an automatic not guilty was placed on their behalf. Cook also invoked the right to a fast and speedy trial and in addition to a pre-trial set for Aug. 2 a jury trial was set for Aug. 13-15. A pre-trial date of Aug. 2 was also set for Ganaway.

All four were notified by the court that a no contact order had been put in place, requiring them to make no contact with the victim.

According to the Miami County Sheriff's Department, the victim, a 63-year-old male, reported that at about 5 a.m. a black male armed with a handgun and a black female wearing a bandana over her face had entered his home while he was asleep and attempted to rob him of cash. The victim told police he fought with his attackers and was allegedly struck multiple times with the butt of the handgun by the male suspect and with a blunt object by the female suspect. The victim was able to drive off his attackers before they could obtain any valuables. The suspects then fled from the residence.

A red 1999 Dodge Dakota was later located in a side ditch less than an eighth of a mile from the victim's residence with two black females standing nearby. As other officers arrived in the area, a black male and a black female were found walking on Ind. 19 near County Road 700 S. An investigation involving multiple search warrants and interviews led to the arrest.

My daughter is Ogunbuyide, age 25. The 63-year-old white man, Hunt, admitted to fondling the female cousins at earlier times. He was a trick for one of the cousins who took the others to meet the rich guy she had allowed to use her for years. Their actions are NOTHING at all that I am proud of, but this guy is RICH AND SIXTY-YEARS OLD, why take advantage with your 40 dollars here and there? It's ILLEGAL! There was no real gun involved, just desperate young adults who thought they would get a quick buck handed over to them and leave. Instead the guy never knew who they were and fought them off. He runs them off with them having a BB gun and getting a fat zero cash? REALLY? He tried to drop all the charges after finding out who they were, but our prosecution system MUST LOCK UP poor blacks no matter what the circumstances and MUST let the rich white guy go free. I saw the evidence and NEVER ONCE argued their innocence. I go strictly by the evidence and not my desires. If the evidence suggests taking a plea, I would 100 PERCENT have my relative take a reasonable plea. If there is no evidence of the charge at all then don't take the plea. In this case, it had nothing to do with evidence and everything to do with JUSTICE.

My daughter and our 3 cousins all facing 100 years for their crimes while the white guy was totally free; was my argument with the prosecution, judge, and public defender. If there was no white guy soliciting sexual misconduct, Maintaining a Common Nuisance, and Prostitution, then my family is not tempted by his money. This is not justice when we favor a person privileged and aged enough to make solid moral decisions, especially not against the law, but he goes FREE. Judge, attorneys, both public defender and prosecutor; all want to make them face ONE HUNDRED YEARS, but CRIMINAL victim faces zero time when he's been calling and soliciting our cousin for his pleasures for years? Crime begats crime, but inequality DESTROYS THE NATION! Just look at us today. REALLY, please take a look at the state of the greatest nation in the world. We are the most immoral citizens on earth destroying the weak, countries, mentally ill, poor, disabled/handicap, drug addicted/suicidal, and societal construct weak by color, religion, sex, and being different from the socially accepted. What in tarnation causes us to separate by differences? It's a **FIVE THOUSAND YEAR OLD TRICK**, BY NOW FOR PETE'S SAKE WAKE-UP! As long as a human being is not hurting anyone, dammit LET THEM BE! And when they choose to hurt people, hurt countries, hurt the weak just like Trump and his administration… REMOVE THEM FROM POWER or convict them by any means necessary. Immorality will NOT save our country; stealing and trying to FORCE others by ransom of tariffs and war WILL NOT SAVE US. THERE IS KARMA! We can make America smart for the VERY first time

EVER and care about weak human beings. **<u>WE MUST LEAD THE WORLD BY DOING RIGHT OR TAKE OURSELVES OUT BY EVIL MEASURES, carry on Trump.</u>** It's OUR choice. NOW, back to finalizing my daughter's case with the 100 years. Oh, special thank you to my readers for being jolted all around the world in my writings and keeping pace with me.

My prayer was to hold these people accountable for their SWORN DUTY to render justice. If you can forgive the rich white guy of his guilt, why not forgive the poor blacks as well? I asked God to intervene on THIS SWORN DUTY AGAINST ALL officials and warn all of them that they MUST CHARGE THE RICH WHITE GUY TOO. My daughter's attorney wanted me to be arrested for threatening them for what? I only asked for GOD to render justice for their refusal to render justice of either locking both parties up or freeing both parties involved in crime. You see our rich buddy we care about, we over look his crimes, but BLACK young adults, let's lock them up FOREVER! Anyways they ignored my prayers. You can see the newspaper clipping with the judge's name and trial dates. He bang the gavel against my daughter, forcing her to take a plea of two months served or face 100 years. I had decreed by GOD free her or incarcerate your criminal bias favored rich guy. The internet news gives the date immediately after Judge Robert Spahr began coughing from cancer and was dead within a month or so.

I never used that amount of power again, not even to save my mother. The fasting and people involved united in prayer was tremendous. I did do prayers for my son and my case, however the individuals involved are going under pharaoh type conditions and cannot see the immediate wrath of God. HOW COULD WE KNOW (the LOGIC paradox) that so many FEDERAL judges would intentionally refuse a black citizen a fair chance at a trial. NUMEROUS JUDGES have looked at this case and turned their back on truth, justice, their code of ethics, livelihood, and THE US CONSTITUTION. Federal judge Diane Syke, a CHIEF circuit judge cruelly claimed that I was frivolous and abusing the system to seek not to be PLACED FALSELY IN THE WRONG due to my skin color. The court couldn't be wrong because people of my color in the mind of whites supremist belonged exactly where I was forced to be, unheard illegally. . She threatened to take action against me just as the district court did take action against me for seeking my RIGHT to no false claim against me. My right for a lease to be a matter of factual document and not an opinion that a judge can just change at her whim. Same goes with my son how they can UTTERLY DENY CONSTITUTIONAL RIGHTS!!! Little to no evidence at all of intent to kill; how. How do charges go from facing 65 years murder one to just three years served without any evidence at all changing?

LOOK AT THE SEVERITY OF INJUSTICE. SEE The internet report. Where my daughter faced one-hundred (100) years in prison just because prosecutors and judges can do whatever the hell they please trumping up charges. CHOOSING WHO GETS CHARGED and WHO DOES NOT GET CHARGED!

THEY FORGET IN THE END... THERE IS GOD (KARMA)!

Pharos-Tribune from PERU, INDIANA - JUDGE DIES

Internet Source: http://pharostribune.com/local/x2039228502/Miami-County-judge-loses-fight-with-cancer

September 5, 2012 Miami County judge loses fight with cancer

Robert Spahr had recently taken medical leave. by Carson Gerber For the Pharos-Tribune

PERU — Miami County Circuit Court Judge Robert A. Spahr, 66, died at 8 p.m. Monday after a brief battle with cancer. On Aug. 6, Spahr announced he would take a temporary medical leave of absence after experiencing excessive coughing and unexplainable weight loss. Timothy Spahr, his son, said Tuesday further medical tests revealed his father had cancer in five organs. He said Spahr began chemotherapy, but stopped treatment around 10 days ago. Circuit Court administrator Georgann Allen said the position will continue to be filled by pro tem and senior judges until the Indiana Supreme Court appoints a replacement judge to fill the position for the remaining two years of Spahr's term. She said a full-time replacement could be named as early as Monday. "The business of the court will be as usual," Allen said. "We'll continue to operate without any delays. That's what Judge Spahr would want. He was dedicated to the people of Miami County, and he'd want the court to keep going as it has." Spahr was appointed by Gov. Mitch Daniels in 2008 to replace then-Circuit Court Judge Rosemary Burke. He was then elected in November 2008 as Circuit Court judge and began his official six-year term on Jan. 1, 2009. Spahr graduated from Indiana University in 1968, and earned his law degree in 1974 from IU in Indianapolis. From 1968 to 1971, he served in the Army as a first lieutenant. Timothy said his father first began practicing law in Benton County after graduating and became a solo practitioner in Peru in 1979. Timothy, who also works as a lawyer in Peru, said he and his father shared office space while running their practices. "That was nice," he said. "In the early days, if I had a question I could always bounce it off of him."

Timothy said his dad also served as the attorney for the Miami County Department of Child Services for at least 15 years. "He poured a lot of energy into that work," his son said. "It was important to him to help pull kids out of difficult situations." For a number of years in the 1980s, Spahr worked as deputy prosecuting attorney — a position he left in 1987. Superior Court 2 Judge Daniel Banina said he had known Spahr since 1987 and considered him a good friend. "Sometimes being a judge is a difficult thing to do," he said. "But Robert always behaved with fairness. I enjoyed working with him, but mostly I enjoyed his friendship." Timothy said his father regretted stepping down as the Circuit Court judge, even during the last days of his illness. "It really bothered him that he couldn't finish the remainder of his term," he said. "He felt like it was his civic duty." Banina said his friend's death had come as a shock. "It's all very sad," he said. "It just all happened so fast."

- See more at: http://pharostribune.com/local/x2039228502/Miami-County-judge-loses-fight-with-cancer#sthash.GT3OD1wo.

CHAPTER NINE:

MULTI-BILLION DOLLAR LAWSUIT: EMBEDDED LAW

FIRST LAWSUIT Sandra Black v. Naomi Friedrichsen ET AL

I, Sandra Black intend to bring a billion-dollar lawsuit against all persons who, through **crime (**PERJURY, FRAUD, SLANDER, DEFAMATION and LIBEL) **or bad-faith practices** against the bar AND SWORN DUTY caused the denial of my right to trial with consideration of EMBEDDED LAW in the previous lawsuit case 1:19-cv-00307-TLS. This lawsuit will include a request for judges to be disbarred and removed from the bench for intentionally fraudulently pretending that they did not need to consider the order denying defendants claim of "Unauthorized Occupants" and that my grandchildren were named and in fact on the lease. For intentionally claiming **FALSELY** that my grandchildren were not on the lease, thus they were the unauthorized occupants to legitimize whites illegally over the black victim. As we discussed, I intentionally setup this court to either GRANT me a right to a fair trial or face PROVING IT A fact that even federal judges use EMBEDDED LAW against blacks, proving that blacks are not citizens, are NOT protected by LAW to be treated equally, are not in fact a matter of any consideration at all . By doing this, they worked under the color of law to forcibly hold me captive by Jim Crow style law that no matter my evidence nor the state court favoring AGAINST what the federal court wanted a black litigant will not be hears with such a powerful case against whites. This is a CRIME, possibly a HATE CRIME because it was done because I was black and standing powerfully for the black cause. ALL of this was pointed out to them, but they saw me as NOTHING, BLACK, LESS THAN NOTHING AT ALL. For gross intentional refusal to consider a lease as a factual document that could not be disputed as an opinionated right of a judge to fabricate, thus denying my constitutional rights to be fairly heard. For an irrefutable and undeniable fact-finding that the federal judge SOUGHT TO DISCREDIT any and all evidence presented by a black litigant to serve white litigants with no credible evidence that would eradicate the overwhelming evidence against their claim.

I seek 40 million dollars for my life's suffering for being born with a dark color in a society that MALICIOUSLY EMBRACES DISCRIMINATION by evidence of its citizens "KARENS" who all know just like George Floyd's white cop murder KNEW nothing would be done to him even RECORDED, DAMN, **HE KNEW NOTHING WOULD BE DONE!!!.** OUR NATION sends this message boldly and must NOW send a powerful message BOLDLY that not over our **constitution**, HELL NO! It's going to FAR the message that is being sent... we are not Americans that abide by the LAW. Our founding fathers FOLLOWED LAW! The color hatred and GREED is so great that no one recognizes America today. Blowing up other nation's citizens without proper channels, threatening to take over Greenland and even hinting for Canada, what the hell kind of country are we allowing our leaders to represent us as, pure bullshit! THIS STANKS, not stinks, it's so damned embarrassing as bad as it has been why? I have plenty ideas to keep us afloat for **a while**, but this outright lawless EVIL must stop. Hint, stop lobbying and just suggest what needs to be done at NO COST. Never going to happen till the hole falls out of the bottom. So I'm interested in the ultimate long run of human survival. Look at what's done to Alex and Renee Good MURDERED under the color of LAW from FEAR too much color will end white color within our lifetime! DESPERATION! What was done to me in court and George Floyd is EMBEDDED LAW! It's EMBEDDED that as long as you're on the side of the system, the court will, without doubt, in some way or manner, go against the black person, if not for being black alone, but also for not being an official (Trump). I seek special damages from a jury of my peers to look at the LONG HARD LIFE of suffering of one person and the reality of the fact that the average black can NEVER get as far as I have come to **LIVE** and to tell our stories. Blacks dying in the general, slums and ghettos without a single voice because most nobody wants to hear it, thus making it impossible to end the oppression. The remainder portion of 999,960, 000 placed in trust for IAFBA spent towards black business, community, lobbying, health needs/RESEARCH, diaspora, and **50% towards obtaining reparations, sovereignty, land purchase and building our own government.**

SECOND LAWSUIT - CLASS ACTION FBA v. The U.S. A. and Elon Musk, in the court of **INTERNATIONAL LAW**

IAFBA vs the UNITED STATES OF AMERICA and Elon Musk FOR (1) TRILLION DOLLARS to be paid into the funds for EMBEDDED LAW against FBA, The case of Owen Diaz v. Tesla, Inc. case no: 3:17-cv-06748-WHO in the US District Court for Northern District of California

Obstruction of Justice, Elon Musk was found knowingly in the WRONG against a black litigant intentionally causing harm in a way that JURORS found the punishment MUST BE TEN TIMES THE AMOUNT. They were seeing EMBEDDED LAW, damages of CENTURIES THAT MUST BE PAID to honor the constitutions declaration of EQUAL RIGHTS. The jury ordered HARSH payment for maliciousness to STOP MISTREATMENT OF BLACKS, not known then, but this jury decided that Elon Musk should be held accountable for **SPECIAL DAMAGES and awarded 137 million dollars**. Elon Musk claimed it was unconstitutional and argued to stop the jury's decision. I Sandra Black motioned the court to stay and consider EMBEDDED LAW and the constitutional rights of all blacks as stated in my case. Thus this case involved the loss of ALL AFRICAN AMERICANS, IAFBA'S CONSTITUTIONAL RIGHTS TO BE HEARD.

We seek 1 trillion dollars on behalf of the class action for FBA, however that may change once FBA'S are made aware of this intent to sue, UNDER EMBEDDED LAW... criminally and ILLEGALLY blocked by judges in my case.

The most important understanding of the severity of suffering under EMBEDDED LAW is the unconscious degrade of UNWORTHINESS practiced by each and every single American, no matter your color, nationality, race. If you are human, and you have the USA social influence, you WILL practice EMBEDDED LAW, if not consciously, you will 100% do it unconsciously. It's only a matter to what degree, .1%, 10% 50% or 100%. THE BOTTOMLINE IS THAT THE AMERICAN GOVERNMENT AND CULTURE HAS CREATED IT **through her generations** AND BY THE LAW OF THE CONSTITUTION REQUIRING THAT ALL MUST BE TREATED EQUAL THE AMERICAN GOVERNMENT MUST NOW ACQUIESCE TO PAY FOR ALL GENERATIONAL DAMAGE HAPPING TODAY! AND eventually reparations to finalize the debt owed. This is a request to involve the ACLU, UN, and the WORLD as we freed South Africa, it's time for the discrimination and torture of blacks going on everywhere in the US behind closed doors is held accountable... CNN, FOX, mainstream America will never report it as best they can which is why people like Ahmaud Arbery and Trayvon Martin would NEVER have their deaths vindicated accept through much time fighting to go VIRAL. If this book doesn't go viral, we NEVER KNOW THE EVIL OF OUR COUNTRY towards and elder disabled black granny. They will NEVER TALK ABOUT THIS, BUT BY FORCE! We never stop to think of the thousands of blacks harmed by whites that go unprosecuted because it's the American way. How many like me are judged by Jim Crow laws, but no one knows as CNN and FOX will never report this news. Do you think George Floyd's case would be what it was without video footage... THIS IS EMBEDDED LAW for all the George Floyds and Sandra Blacks of the US this is a taste, a smidgen of the FIRST TIME in American HISTORY, the USA is being held accountable to offset FINANCIALLY the suffering of blacks she has engineered and designed from the foundation of our country to be ever oppressed and destroyed. She should be proud AND LEAD THE WAY... This is my calling to congress and Senate. It's time to begin, the NEW AMERICA FOR THE FIRST TIME IN HISTORY that cares for **ALL** HUMANITY and not just white America and nobody else. Actually the white male only, because even the white woman cannot make anywhere close to the money that white men make and her concerns/needs are many times overlooked and ignored.

BELIEF IN REAL CHANGE

Millions-dollar investment into CHANGE NOW the 501C3 Spiritual Resources Inc.- all money the book generates after the costs to produce it, THE NET SALES will go towards building a community only highly striving individuals geared towards raising the weak residents to optimum performance; who own the community as a family and operate multi business, a community enterprise or Co-op. The Book, "Ultimate Common Sense: Embrace It or Go Extinct" net profits ALL, every last cent will go to the nonprofit, **GLOBAL CITIZENS UNITE FOR COMMON SENSE** ezzrath@gmail.com to donate towards our hard work and commitment to the world.

It's 5000 thousand years of blood money owed THE WORLD and I am here to repay my debt to earth for the many generations of bloodshed. Spiritually, mentally, physically with every fiber of my being, I have zero rights to this income. It would be a mockery against God as my intent to STOP WORLD SUFFERING for the people by the people is the REAL DEAL.

Through our nonprofit GLOBAL CITIZENS UNITE FOR COMMON SENSE we will purchase land in Africa or the West Indies to build massive housing, Hall Town (church/mosque/Temple etc.), schools, entertainment AND sports centers, utilities, a hospital/clinic, and two factories, multi-businesses for income to the community (needed to buy inside Africa and surrounding communities to outside our African community (Canada, USA, Islands, Europe, Australia, etc.) We will take a minimum of 1000 felons released in 2026. 500 men and 500 women with their children. We will interview all 1000 chosen subjects and with genuine human rights... ALL needs will be met, no worries at all for how to survive. As automatic co-owners JUST FOR BEING weak human beings willing to rise to the highest of potential just to SHOW IT A FACT that AMERICA AND EUROPE CREATES CRIMINALS so they can grow out of this evil. Hell, she, AMERICA just MURDERED Renee Nicole Good and had the audacity to call her a terrorist after watching the murderer approach her car aimed for the Kill AND shot her to death. THE EMPORER'S NEW CLOTHES MUST END, LET'S EXPOSES HIS NAKEDNESS. I saw Renee Good say to him "don't worry, I'm not mad at you. Why would she say that? Could it be that she saw the look of hate and murder in his eyes that she was trying to soften with her smile ONLY TO BE literally **GUNNED DOWNED BY A MASKED OUTLAW** (a person who breaks the law and is at large, forget that our OUTLAW criminally rogue government supports the murderous outlaw) in a country that will not even investigate this guy, JONATHON ROSS as we ALL saw what happened. Alex, my nurse brother, same bullshit evil, murdered for trying to stop EVIL. These people are genuine civic HEROS! Tricia McLaughin, the Assistant Secretary for the Department of Homeland Security (DHS), reported that they have successfully created an **8000% increase of criminals by DEATH threats against I. C. E.** Why would our leaders sit back and allow deathly, world hating, warmongering, shenanigans? WHO EVER hasn't spoken out against this in congress and the senate VOTE ALL OF THEM OUT! The president is incompetent pompous narcissist wannabe dictator (NOT IN MY COUNTRY! No matter how he tries to plant military in every state for his TAKEOVER of the Whitehouse again at the end of his term for real.) and his administration is lawless. ALL NEED VERY LONG PRISON SENTENCES for aiding and abetting Trump to do this **"moral"** EVIL. YES, they lie to our very faces, they break LAW, the constitution and wear their evil LIKE A BADGE of righteousness. So YES, their "moral" (in their sick minds) EVIL! WE THE PEOPLE ALLOW.

I so apologize to the world's nations for my murderous greedy hate FILLED nation with people to weak to stop our evil. I'm so sorry that our citizens can't pull it together ONCE AND FOR ALL that the US CONSTITUATION REIGNS SUPREME! ALL PEOPLE, within her borders including non-citizens (aliens), receive certain fundamental **HUMAN** rights primarily GUARANTEED by the 5th and 14th amendment. Blacks are not honored by the constitution so why would I agree that the 14th amendment is for blacks only, by practice the constitution is FOR NO ONE OF COLOR!!! This is what's happening that damned naked emperor! I thought that states are sovereign to run their state, but in all my years I have NEVER once seen SUCH ANARCHY WHERE WE HAVE NO LEADERS RUNNING THE COUNTRY BY OUR LAWS AND CONSTITUTION. The lawless leaders should have long since been IMPEACHED or removed AND PROSECUTED and failure to do so is happening due to NO LEADERSHIP! **SOMEBODY STOP THIS LAWLESSNESS TO BREAK OUR US CONSTITUTION BEFORE IT IS TOO LATE!**

Back to our REMEDY, our new society. These people (the weak) and the strong all as ONE UNIT will become EXTREMELY PRODUCTIVE within five years, duplicating the next community without any help financially (quadrupling in seven to ten years etc.), reforming all bordering neighbors into RAISE UP THE WEAK people who have also influenced their border communities every last one of them will be PRODUCTIVE. Where in the US can you such a proposal? They would either go back to prison or live non-productive lives, just like most of my adult life, thanks to our system/EMBEDDED LAW. But not really, the time TO GAIN KNOWLEDGE without being told how and what to believe and where to get my knowledge. If I was allowed to be me I would have been so invested into my craft, I would of never seen myself (no curiosity to see problems as I fit into system) nor the world around me. It takes being outside the circle to see the total insides of it for what it is. Trust me, I see it! I was forced to

We will show the world heaven on earth without any one person eventually owning a single dollar. The people will simply request their reasonable wants AND GET THEM FULLFILLED, needs are MANDATORY at all times taken care of no differently than we worry about how we will get our next breath. They will work joyfully and RESPECT one another. They will come before the community of elders with arguments and problems that they know will be fairly settled.

There will also be volunteer PROFESSIONAL psychologists, nurses, doctors, teachers, and social research developers. NO NEED FOR POLICE or government. The community of elders will be a rotation basis of everyone over 40 years and older must serve, NO LEADERS, just children of earth or children of God who live and let live. Heaven. There will be groups of 50. Every week five adults out of the fifty will be in charge of assuring NEEDS of the 50 families are supplied with ease. Each adult will begin with 20 hours per week start-up work time. Half the time required in the US standard workweek. This time gradually cuts into 10 hours per week or less. See the Michael Tellinger, economic model of SOUTH AFRICAN **"Ubuntu Contributionism". They work 3 hours per week, but do not serve neighboring communities.** I'm not the first to think of returning to the family of the Tribe/the community. We will raise the communities around us, and they will in turn raise up the communities around them, and so forth, THE DOMINO effect of heaven on Earth. We will feed them, and they will feed those outside of them and so forth.

What will people do with their free time? Time will be spent on children, community, friendship, family, meditation, fellowship, self-development/ambition/special projects, exercise, swimming, boating, horseback riding, gaming, sports, REAL LIVING for the masses that today is gained only by enslaving others with virtually no pay; the western adapted patriarchal society. This represents the end of patriarchal society and the ushering in of the new age, FREE LIVING FOR ALL We will grow out own food, build our structures, sew our clothes, and buy from outside by use of income from our businesses until outside trades just as we will be trading among ourselves. There will be no need for national borders because the grass is greener on both sides of the fence. Imagine Mexico with everything that the USA has, why would anyone be desperate to get to the US. Why would US care if Mexicans visit we are all the same. Once we can live amongst each other without barbarism, selfish-greed, division, and hate; we begin our real purpose, THE GREATEST GIFT TO MAN.

After five years, all members are productive and have accomplished the goal of DUPLICATING THEMSELVES without financing, donations, or grants. We prove it a fact that heaven is obtainable for the masses. We prove it a fact that we do NOT REQUIRE POOR PEOPLE as the only way of life. We can have a happy peaceful species. We only need to eliminate greed and dominion over human beings by wicked beings without our best interest at heart. NEVER AGAIN. Only a human being and his/her higher power and invited influence has dominion over another human being.

Finally, I believe it's the ULTIMATE common sense that we **MUST** DO BETTER.

I am 100% sure that I don't have all of the answers, but I do represent CHANGE, and it won't take much to start up a pilot community trial run where willing participants can spend months ironing out the bugs of trade, how to set up who does what, and who gets what in excess. Everyone gets the basics, but the higher competition individuals are those who figure out how to raise up the weak. They are our number one asset. This is different from Ubuntu in that we do need healthy competition that pays off for raising the community up members up, up, up and entertainment/doctors/ professionals/teachers in a distant second. Our power is our people, not our wealth or possessions. We gain wealth and possessions through caring for our community, THE PEOPLE! ONE FOR ALL and ALL FOR ONE.

Thus saith the ALPHA and OMEGA... The first shall be last and the last shall be first, the greatest shall be least and the least shall be greatest. Henceforth and forevermore heaven established on earth, the path and **gate which LEADS TO LIFE, MANY SHALL FIND IT**: where the weakest shall be targeted the most important of societies' concerns and the strongest shall be the least targeted for the most important as nature has blessed them with being strong. They shall out shine us all by just being themselves. They shall receive great things and be our heroes just as they are today, but for GENUNINE great cause. One day, there will be equality FOR ALL, and that very first day, the white race will again become the most targeted race for importance… perpetually ending the days of racism AND THE DAYS of any race superiority, ENDING THE POWER OF THE FEW. The days of the color of a human being playing a part of weakness/strength/haves/ have nots comes to an end. This is the beginning of the masses establishment of "heaven of earth" the ULTIMATE COMMON SENSE OF THE WORLD, all for one, ONE FOR ALL: When the human race discovers its purpose and best STRAIGHT WAY TO THE PATH WHICH LEADS TO LIFE... the ultimate discovery of SELF… we human beings are only **as strong as our weakest link**… I present the generation of no weak links as we ESTABLISH THE NEW PARADIAGNM… the end of the patriarchal society and the birth of the society of ONE UNITED SHARING EARTH WITH NO BOUNDRIES, NO LIMITATIONS. With every human being at their highest potential we go WHERE NO MAN HAS DARE GONE BEFORE IN ALL OF RECORDED HISTORY.

CHAPTER TEN

Afterthought, Viewed Today

Today, November 28, 2025, Thanksgiving day, I just witnessed testimony from DR. ANNETTE BOSWORTH, found guilty of the CRIME OF HELPING THE POOR by abusive use of power to prosecute to the fullest extent of the law for not visually seeing signatures signed, charged, and convicted to 24 years imprisonment for 12 felonies.

The only person in the history of America convicted of this crime. She won her appeal and it all went away.

I, Sandra Black to my knowledge am the absolute only human being in the history of America denied my constitutional right to equal access to civil judicial process and right to a FAIR trial by a jury **BY ALL JUDGES THROUGHOUT THE ENTIRE PROCESS**. All judges found it a judge's right to call a tenancy lease an opinion (NOT FACTUAL) to refuse to consider the document's factually listed persons on the lease. Worse, the persons listed and included on the lease in the State Court order was ordered not factually on the lease to **FALSELY** place white litigants in the right against a black person.

Thereby, establishing Jim Crow against a black litigant to be placed AUTOMATICALLY FALSELY IN THE WRONG AGAINST WHITE LITIGANTS, supported and validated ALL THROUGHOUT THE TOTAL JUDICIAL PROCESS, in the District Court, the Appellate Court, and the Supreme Court. ONLY WHEN YOU'RE BLACK will you ever see judges break the law, go against the constitution, risk their jobs to cheat the wrong skin colored person without any judge throughout the ENTIRE PROCESS willing to stand for truth, fairness, and the constitution their judiciary duty to intervene against utter tyranny to embrace injustice in the supposed land of the free.

When powers that be abuse their power to the point of UNPRECEDENTEDLY TRASHING THE CONSTITUTION OF THE UNITED STATES OF AMERICA, their SWORN oath should be ordered the equivalent of an annulment of office.

Thus, where there's absolutely NO PRECEDENCE EVER of such abuse of power against any American citizen the judges/prosecutors are rendered fraudulently using the office against their sworn oath UNPRECEDENTED in over 200 YEARS and therefore and henceforth are rendered VOID OF IMMUNITY OF OFFICE by annulment of never having genuinely accepted the oath of office.

How can there be immunity of office when there is absolutely ZERO persons ever in the entire history of America stripped of constitutional rights of due process, good-faith, impartiality, void of bias, applying the law neutrally as is occurring across the United States TODAY? There is no way to stop this lawlessness from the TOP accept the bottom holds abusers of power accountable based on the FACT they would never or rarely abuse the power knowing they would GO TO PRISON, THEY WOULD PAY THE DEBT. Why shouldn't we expect MORE from those who SWEAR and OATH to serve? Broken sworn duty, must be treated like TREASON! When we the people stand on that, it stops almost day one. Of course they are not going to recommend the highest penalties for themselves. WHEN THEY ARE EXPOSED like the Trump administration and the federal judges in my case. THEY MUST serve nothing less than ten to 30 years. This is only happening because authorities has told themselves... WHO WILL HOLD US ACCOUNTABLE... WE ARE GOD! WE DO AS WE PLEASE! Why the would these lawless people in office kidnap people, blow them up, threaten to take over friendly nations against their will, ACTUALLY INVADE our states against their will without genuine cause. Trying to de-color the US is not genuine cause. Spend the money used to kill our people and decolor the US on helping Mexico's economy and treaties to keep people from crossing into Mexico so that you cut off the coloreds you're afraid of from coming over in a diplomatic LAWFUL way.

What the federal court did to me reaches BEYOND ALL PRECEDENCE OF OUR COUNTRY'S HISTORY TO DEFY THE SUPREME LAW OF THE LAND THAT PROTECTS THE RIGHTS OF CITIZENS AND THEIR SWORN DUTY TO THE CODE OF ETHICS TO BE HONEST, FAIR, TRANSPARENT, AND UNBIASED... TO RENDER JUST

COMPETENT DECISIONS, TO BE TRANSPARENT, AND DILIGENTLY SERVING BOTH LITIGANTS, NOT JUST THE WHITE ONES. Jim Crow is illegal TODAY and illegally forced legal under the color of law (A CRIME!) used by EMBEDDED LAW.

Looking at the ENTIRE PROCESS AND THE SIMPLICITY OF CORRUPTION, just like the murders of Alex and Renee Good, PURELY LIES with immunity HELL NAW. We have laws that you can NOT work under the COLOR OF LAW, IT IS A CRIME! Collins crime clearly is caused by HATE OF BLACKS AS THE SOLE MOTIVATION! She was WARNED that it was a hate crime and didn't give a damn, because IT'S BEEN PAST PRACTISE... Co officials back each other to LIE, CHEAT, and DESTROY litigants going against the evidence. I believe there's an inside code demand among judges that THEY must practice going against the evidence to support authority. I got that from McVicker. Why else would a good man support lazy, LYING, no good performance of CASA and DCS as the "BEST THEY COULD DO" He's also very intelligent so he knows the difference between negligent, mediocre, good, very good, and the BEST. So why the best when they placed my grandson with a drug user, criminal restricted from having children in her custody and the judge refused to hear anything bad about the person solely because I granted her visitation saying it was HER RIGHT. He knew it was my grandson's right to be safe FIRST. He wanted to PRACTICE LAW! I strongly believe had not GOD intervened my grandson would have been lost forever because he would have RULED THAT I would be forced stuck with visitation forever and I would have walked away because dealing with her would have killed me which is why I intervene into the CHINS case. I wanted to be grandma, but she WOULD NOT ALLOW VISITS anytime my grandson grew close to me and his siblings. She intentionally made visits impossible keeping me and the siblings away. He would have grown up without the help and support that he had every right to have. A strong parental relationship that would without doubt raise him to a higher productivity, education, equally loved, and the understanding of our bloodline and our inherited behavioral issues to successfully work through them. She couldn't dare come ten% close to the work that I do with my grandchildren. **COURTS PLAY GOD!** The judge should have insisted on what was the danger that REQUIRED the child to be removed from his immediate family as his mother wanted me and I am next of kin with his siblings. She should have been automatically eliminated without good cause to remove the child from the immediate family. He knew that there was no working together. So why put our family through it from the beginning? **JUDGES PRACTICE RULING IN FAVOR OF AUTHORITY AGAINST THE EVIDENCE and LAW IS A FACT** and I have NEVER met a judge in Marion, Indiana that didn't SHOW ME THIS IS NOT FACT! This is injustice exponentially huge, you MUST use both law and the evidence and they DON'T. THIS IS WHY our country is headed towards HELL, EXTINCTION! **They are destroying our families!**

The CONSTITUTION of the USA is around **238 years OLD!** There's absolutely no way in good faith to honor your oath proceeding to DESTROY CITIZENS' CONSTITUTIONAL RIGHTS UNPRECEDENTEDLY IN OVER 200 YEARS... NOT ONE JUDGE TO INTERVENE THAT **I WON STATE COURT** IT MUST BE RECOGNIZED THAT **THERE WERE NO UO FOUND!!!**

Today's officials are becoming mindfully ENDOWED above the constitution of the USA, therefore I ask Congress and the courts to RE-EMPOWER our constitution, today treated as DUNG in my case to its rightful position as SUPREME LAW OF THE LAND. It's DUNG before Trump and his administration. USE POWER rightfully and start by EMPOWERING OUR CONSTITUTION AS LAW OVER AMERICA!!! If I and my race have no constitutional RIGHTS... **THERE IS NO AMERICA,** there is only tyranny the opposite of having human rights.

Thus, all judges found willfully and **intentionally defying our constitution historically UNPRECEDENTED** to harm a black citizen, namely Sandra Black going against our constitution to be stripped of their immunity in HONOR of our constitution, **by annulment of their SWORN OATH** to accept office. Judges Susan Collins, Theresa Springmann, and Diane Sykes must all be removed from the bench and permanently disbarred. They should be presented to the grand jury to decide if they are to be criminally prosecuted for violation of U. S. C. 18 § 242 for performing duties under the color of law stripping me of my constitutional right by their actions to be heard in a court of law. I also ask that the motive be determined where it is decided if I had been white and the defendants black would Collins have ruled and treated me as she did. Would ALL judges with access to the chronological case summary that had the power to intervene would my treatment be different? And if that answer is yes, that they be charged also with hate crimes for harming me due to my skin color Attorney Brittney Kyvoich also. If found to have criminally fraudulently LIED to support white supremacy, to back corrupt fellow peers, to fail their duty of oath to the bar and/or seat of office that places them above citizens... or co-judge conspirators helping to coverup the attack against constitutional rights of citizens... then we MUST prosecute to the fullest extent of the law setting precedence THAT THE CONSTITUTION OF THE UNITED STATES OF AMERICA IS TRULY IN FACT SUPREME LAW OF THE LAND of which no official shall have immunity to **unprecedentedly** violate its SUPREMACY. Keep in mind, judges do SIDE AGAINST their co-judges in appeals, USE examples where white litigants (not against MONEY incentive or a position offer) were treated just like me where they win their case, treated that they lost, where they have overwhelming evidence and it is ignored and the whites are found in the wrong. If you can NOT find one case this is strong evidence that judges did this solely because I am black.

If it hasn't been done in 200 years, the act done today is not a simple mistake or misinterpretation of an order or the constitution or an act ever happening before, it is an OBLITERATION, A MOCKERY, against the SUPREME LAW of our land. At any point in the three years of tyranny against my constitutional rights to JUSTLY BE HEARD in the court of law many SWORN by duty judges and attorneys should have chosen the LAW and JUSTICE over corruption, the LAW over racism and white supremacy, THE LAW over their biases PERIOD, their SWORN duty demands it and grants privilege to these officials requiring them to be held to a higher standard over citizens that the OATH governs choice of actions. Once the constitution is acceptable for anyone to freely obliterate, THERE IS NO LAWFUL AMERICA.

Let's hold these officials accountable to our constitution, as THE SUPREME LAW OF THE LAND. It is not only misconduct, but CRIMINAL for a judge, cop, sworn official to intentionally harm an individual **UNDER THE COLOR OF LAW** while performing their duties.

U. S. Constitution protects citizens' rights UNDER LAW 18 U. S. C. § 242 making it a CRIME for an official to harm someone under the color of law, but in this case 41 million people are harmed and possibly the ENTIRE WORLD. This could be the beginning of the end to rid the US of racism forever. Denying my claim, a citizen of the USA in its entirety a chance to be heard by a jury of her peers criminally jeopardizing their prestigious status show just how deep the hate and denial of rights go.

WE NEED A GRAND JURY TO indict all officials involved in ordering it a fact that 1. I had people living in my home and 2. That those people were my grandchildren. 3. Refused a black litigants evidence and any favor or mention so whatever given by the state court order of no UO and grandchildren listed on the lease, the court order requiring a sheriff to obtain people ordered into Black's son's custody the same day the landlords claimed UO with zero evidence of even one day before that court order UO's existed, state court witness and testimony Melody Waggoner, never GRANTED MOTIONS TO HELP MY CAUSE based off of my extenuating circumstances, disabled, elder, **FOUND IN THE RIGHT AGAINST THE CLAIM BROUGHT AGAINST ME.** Absolutely nothing of my cause was considered and the abuse and harassment by judges and attorneys of the bar for years nonstop, must be ruled outrageous in 2026.

FINAL FOR REAL:

Remember the song, "AT THIS MOMENT"...from page 159. GOD'S CONVERSATION WITH US... "What do you think I would give at this moment?" If you would remember ME, I would subtract eternity from my life as she was invented for you to find ME, to find YOURSELF. I'm stuck in the womb of your eternal forgetfulness, bring me to LIFE AAAAAGIN! I would fall down on one multi-verse, kiss the worlds and dimensions that you dwell in if you could just remember ME again.

Or choose extinction, WE have an eternity to play this game, but I thought you might be ready to trade eternity in for THE NEXT EXCITING NEW GAME, you might call THE RAPTURE.

I'm setting up a 501C3 for funding advisors to plan how to start up a city that is actually A FAMILY AFFAIR that chooses to live under the condition of service to each other, NO SICK SYSTEM. I looked up utilities for solar and wind, to build for 20 thousand people according to AI will cost 200 million to 500 million here in the USA, but 20 million to 50 million in Africa. So I wrote the book and will not collect one cent to my use, but to build our city we do need you and people you know to purchase a book and or donate to ***Global Citizens Unite for Common Sense***, become a member. You shouldn't believe everything I wrote because I am human, but if there are some ideas that made you say, hmmmm to yourself, or stories about my life that might help or interest someone, give a copy of this book to the next person for a chance to genuinely gain NEW THOUGHT.

May 5, 2026, UPDATE

I want to finalize first in recognition of those firmly against my core ideologies (our society attacks the weak, creates the weak, embraces the ONE% at the expense of the 99% masses, only voice allowed is that of the system, forcing the emperor's new clothes [a social and psychological phenomenon where society collectively PRETENDS to believe in something false, worthless, or ABSURD, simply to FIT IN or out of fear of helplessness]) those whom I believe to be a MINORITY of American thought... Trump supporters, MAGA. For you my social reconstruct believes it unfair to negatively impact your constitutional right to white supremacy ideology. We should stop rhetoric against white power, white rights, WHITES ONLY COMMUNITIES and white GENUINE concern for loss of whiteness. THE WORLD must understand that just as ancient olive whites came to America before 5000 BC at the approximate same time of the creation of the NEW WHITE PEOPLE in EUROPE those ancient whites NO LONGER EXIST. They mixed with black Africans of America (the indigenous American, Olmec type) and the ancient whites to create the mixed races of native Americans and Hispanics of the Americas. Not one white person was left in ancient America due to brown skin annihilation ABSORPTION of white skin. In the 1900's global white population was 30% of the world's population. The whites were being warned THEN that if they didn't eradicate **COLOR** from among white society that by the year **2075** the white population would be cut down to 15%. TODAY, in 2026, it is a fact that whites mistakenly drastically underestimated how color devastates white skin; there is only 8%-10% of ***pure*** white population globally left on planet Earth. Though white skin is no different than the color of our eyes and hair that no one fights over we must fight today for the generations of FALSE ideologies of skin color importance, the superiority with RIGHTS TO OWN and CONTROL EVERY DAMN THING ON PLANET EARTH! The world in general massively KNOW this is a hysteria and do not support this ideology. But I feel it important to embrace their right TO BE HEARD. I wish I could have debated Charlie Kirk. I would like to know if he truly believed the BS he spoke or was it the antics REQUIRED to possess the world for your selfish gain. Interview me with Kirks wife, let's show the world their ignorance, do not silence them THAT'S INHUMANE and a violation of our constitution!

It's ironic that GOD, the Universe, the ALL HIGHEST set us up to purge stupidity through common sense or BY DIVINE PLAN. Any how you dice it if they allow humanity to live whiteness will never be on the face of the earth without the same wicked attack by the gods/Anunnaki/Nephilim of the Bible in 5000 BC to use biological warfare to strip the capability of making melanin.

Speaking of the manipulation of the gods, a quick story, where the gods were on the side of black Africans. He or they went to Europe to annihilate the whites in the 1300's AD with the black plague to stop the white supremacy they KNEW was coming (Deuteronomy 28th chapter). They knew their brothers (Anunnaki) turned a few blacks, white to EXTERMINATE the human race by self-annihilation. We today claim it was from being filthy, nasty, with rat infestations. Come on now! Half of America, ALL of Africa would be infected today with black plague. **ABSOLUTELY NO SUCH THING AS NEW DISEASES**... all diseases are created either by man or the gods of ancient. This aquarium we live in IS CULTIVATED, MANIPULATED over millions of years. NOTHING JUST SPONTANEOUSLY GENERATES, new diseases, jumping species, evolution of the one cell life form into an elephant over a billion years is pure lunacy make believe that ANIMALS GOT ON EARTH we know it happened somehow, but that's all modern scientist know. The gods (Anunnaki) discovered earth wrote their story in the Bible and NUMEROUS ancient books all around the world, scientist pretend the stories don't scientifically explain their manipulation on earth.

In 1300's AD, it was reported in European papers that a man in all black would be seen, then there would be a STENCH, and then there would be the black plague. The song at the same time came out. Ring around the rosies, Pocket full of posies, Ashes, Ashes, We all fall down! The Europeans carried posies in their pockets to counter the smell of the gas. In the end, "we all fall down." Now they're going to cry it's a fabrication, but one damn thing they can't say. **They CAN'T 100% say that entire populations are taken out by dirt and rats,** BEFORE that period nor forever after! They CERTAINLY can't say that no song happens to exist from that era about "Ring around the Rosies", just use COMMON SENSE, or WAIT for the system to tell you yeah we do all kinds of experiments on innocent citizens. YOU WAIT! Only a fool would say this is impossible. Fools do not use common sense to reason. Things that can't NEVER happen before and can't never happen again; It **NEVER** happened **naturally** without outside interference. There is no getting pregnant without a man, no jet fire acting like a bomb (911) that becomes a demolition fall of bombs placed strategically throughout every structural support beam, no black plague by rats and filth, no covid19, no HIV, no overnight NEW DISEASES without man creating them! Most of all there is no evolving into a man from an **IMPOSSIBLE** series of jump a species, jump a species, jump a species, within a few thousands of years… BUT NEVER EVER BEFORE and NEVER EVER AFTER and you believe that shit? When there are books from all over the world including the BIBLE telling you that the gods made man a hybrid creature out of their own DNA (their likeness) Genesis 1:26 with ape/chimps. 1:26 "Let us make man in OUR image, after OUR likeness." Every time a NEW species of so-called "evolving man" by backward modern man today the Anunnaki said they did it and mankind ALL OVER THE WORLD who never met each other recording the exact same thing in the Enuma Elish OF BABYLON, the Mayan of America, the Yoruba's Ifa' divination system of spiritual framework where Obatala makes man. JUST READ PEOPLE! KNOW YOU ARE GOD! Now back to our 8-10% whites trying to keep the IMPOSSIBLE.

Y'ALL, DAMN!!! THIS IS WHY I. C. E., IRAN, VENEZUELA, GREENLAND, CANADA **MUST** BEGIN THE PATH TO WHITENESS WITH THE FULL SUPPORT OF WHITE AMERICA AND EUROPE. The only genuine rejection by Europe/Canada was of takeover of Canda and Greenland to support (ALLOW) the agenda. However, the Middle East IS OPEN for annihilation to make the place all "white only" through Israel over time. It began in 1948, and look at the home of the Palestinians today that shared their vacant land with whiteness.

Imagine that your ENTIRE power and wealth is based on a delusion of whites being superior to all others. Being deceived never stops the delusion from being REAL to the person. As it is important to set policy to END SUFFERING of the masses we MUST take care of this tiny group of whites. ONLY MY SOLUTION for the WEAKEST are most important will help whites after today's generations is gone and there's only 2 or 3% whites on earth. They need society to evolve into an empathy based system and NOT BARBARIC GREED of the fittest gets everything. So now is the time to prepare the world WHITE PEOPLE FOR **AN EMPATHETIC SOCIETY**!

Remember that I am still under oath for this entire book. I am now writing after the so-called trip to the moon last month. Hummmm, 50 years and not talk of going to the moon, but in less than one week's public knowledge… WE'RE GOING TO THE MOON. Unbelievable, whatever happened to we the people? It took 50 years with zero talk of human beings going to the moon and practically overnight we're going to the moon NO QUESTIONS ASKED. No discussion at all on WHY NOW, Why HASTE?

I bet the powers that be are laughing their fat asses of at us. There is absolutely NO PROOF that four suddenly going to the moon astronauts boarded without escape paths; to at least show an attempt at PROVIING it a fact that people got on the ship, NEVER GOT OFF, and the rocket took off. No matter what!!! IT IS KNOWN FACT that people believe the moon landing is a fake. Why not have ariel ALL SIDES of the craft video recording including the bottom.

They didn't place videos at all areas of the rocket because people DID NOT GO UP WITH THAT ROCKET if in FACT it actually left our atmosphere. I 100% believe this and can't understand why any person with common sense can't see this so-called trip at the very least is 100% suspicious. Hmmm, **50 years we CAN'T GO**, **IMPOSSIBLE!!!** NO MONEY, wake up tomorrow we have money to go to the moon. AND CNN FOX, no questions, DAMN! Our society is a freaking joke of corruption naked Emperor. If you can admit it's suspicious then you can't fully believe this was a manned trip to the moon. Then there's the problem that if the rocket did leave our atmosphere, where did the rocket actually go. We all know it possible to make every picture we saw as evidence of the trip so where is any concrete evidence of a corrupt government actually going to the moon knowing how it was IMPOSSIBLE TO GO FOR 50 YEARS? Why no use of common sense, no time to allow a setup by the people to prove it never happened. Furthermore, with no money for healthcare, housing, civil rights, food stamps, reparations for over 400 years of damage, and so on; HOW do we now suddenly have so much money for a moon trip of human beings on the moon that scientist admitted they had no idea how to get a human being safely through the RADIATION of the Van Allen Belt. Neale deGrasse Tyson stated on the Steve Bartlett YouTube channel that America would never go to the moon again due to no money, no reason to go. I follow him and adore him much. On his own channel he went through ALL the many numerous LOST technology from the past that made it impossible to ever go again. He was saying those who knew the technology died. He was told this because they had zero intent of ever trying to fake a moon landing ever again. SO WHY NOW?

The GREATEST EVIDENCE EVER is what's going on right now due to the extinction of the pure white race (NOT EXTINCT! It is inevitably going through an unstoppable process of the browning effect.) How does things happen as grotesque as it did and DOES in the **domestic U.S.** (racism, prisons, poverty unprecedented, ICE, takeover of states, blocking the Epstein files, building a ballroom for an individual inside the HOUSE

OF THE PEOPLE, attack against sexual preference and so much more), **Venezuela**, **Iran**, and attempted takeover on **Greenland**... UTTERLY CHECKED BY EUROPE and CANADA! Greenland is where the west draws the line? WHY? Dogging and killing your own people to get rid of criminalized color from the southern boarder WAS NOT SEVERELY PROTESTED BY THE WEST. This is how we KNOW it's a fact that the westerners do not care about the mistreatment and loss of life for brown and black people. Why no stopping the Venezual bombing of boats by the U. S. in international waters under maritime law, no interference with starting a war with Iran utter destruction without cause... these are people's of color ALWAYS sacrificial, right? In fact, many embraced Trumped as right. Is it not about color, money, and power??? HMMMM, Trump wants Canada as part of the USA, why not push for Mexico and the entire South America as he does Canada and Greenland? Nawww, he wants Canada, he wants Greenland and all of the entire world is allowing lawlessness to people of color, right? We will NOT allow Greenland! We will not allow Canada, but all the countries of color we sit and watch them murdered and destroyed. **WE ARE THE WORLD**, STOP ONE COUNTRY'S ATTEMPT AT BARBARIC TAKING OVER THE WORLD. We the citizens of the world must set the new world order or forever live doomed to serve the ONE PERCENT!

CRITICAL: The UNIVERSE is yelling at us (the world) to get our act together. It's time for globalization of the PEOPLE by the PEOPLE and the end of governments and capitalism where we must keep the masses of poor to allow the greedy to hoard the wealth of earth. Our way out is through small communities refusing to live trading money for their needs. Money is the necessary tolerance to trade outside communities only until the dollar, Euro, Pound (money) chokes to death by small communities ruling earth in EMPATHETIC synchrony with each other **all throughout the world, ushering in a new paradigm**. In that day there will be no such thing as poverty, governments, police, or prisons. The African American, Africa, and the Caribbean West indies... where African Americans begin to build territories living similar as the Native Americans live in the US today. African Americans like national embassy's all over the world will live as sovereign permanent guest to the nations under agreed upon acceptable restrictions of the nations of Africa and the IFBA. This raises black Africans financially. Americans bring in wealth to the continent, and the continent brings global votes for our continued success of transformation from the ONE PERCENT rulers of the world.

Life, events, the world has always been cyclic the top and the bottom will ALWAYS change places until the end. The next civilization, learning from past civilizations and NOW we create the truly fair, humanly friendly and reasonable society with NO RACE, NO PEOPLE, NO CLASS on top of any others. We learn to live as TRUE DIVINE HUMAN BEINGS. Gods on Earth. Heaven on earth is balance with no one on top and no one on bottom how we switch back and forth? IT ENDS NOW!

The interim from the very beginning requires stern POLICY changes with the very first being **<u>the USA controlled globally</u>**, the end of immunity for criminal officials (not misconduct!) CRIMINALS like the Trump administration, prosecutors intentionally breaking the constitution, judges including federal judges proven FACT to intentionally LIE and disobey constitutional law fraudulently (LYING FOR GAIN, saving white supremacy and pretending you are following the constitution), **<u>and the end of lobbying</u>**. Officials who hate the constitution (disobey it and LIE) and as result UNPRESIDENTED catastrophic failure of the system MUST have their sworn oath ANNULLED, as they either had a made up mind against the constitution from day one or from the day their prejudice took effect which was SWORN could not happen (freaking RECUSE sickos!) that caused the entire system to utterly collapse like a domino effect. It is this DOMINO FACT that has NEVER been known to happen in US history that **<u>REQUIRES ANNULMENT</u>** OF VIOLATORS. This unprecedented most atrocious outlawry of the American system and ultimate LAW that is designed to never be broken, REQUIRES the acts of many who have utterly officially broken the system for the country or individual BY GOING AGAINST the country and individual CONSTITUTION, must be stripped of immunity and must be criminally prosecuted for selling out our highest LAW for your own cause. More professionally stated, judges act in a quasi-fiduciary capacity by maintaining STRICT IMPARTIALITY and promoting public confidence in the INTEGRITY OF THE LAW. Judges are bound by ETHICS to act in the best interest of justice rather than personal interests (like a desire to maintain white supremacy or hatred against blacks). This case is the ONLY case brought to the public that I know of where ALL JUDGES deny truth, deny their sworn oath utterly refusing a litigant a fair trial of her peers using the legally terminated laws of Jim Crow, where you are black and officially not equal to white litigants. They lied, refused to correct the LIE! HOW CAN A JUDGE LIE!!! They are not in agreement with their OATH, PERIOD!

My summation is simple, let us examine our actions against one another, how much sense does it make to continue to allow mass human suffering caused by human beings? My fellow Americans in **DEFENSE** of pure evil or passive complicity we ourselves **TURN** pure evil attacking our own for decades. Today through Trump our hero we can simply rewrite history, refuse the truth, destroy the evidence of our vicious past and it's all good, WILL NEVER HAPPEN! We outrageously imprison (25% globally with only 5% of the global population) of our own citizens even killing them by ICE, striping rights of citizens, attempted federal takeover of our states. We're the most imprisoned, drug addicted, suicidal citizens among all western nations on earth. We are disgraced internationally as barbaric, lawless, warmongers of the world. WE KNOW, we're wrong, we must own it, we HUMBLY FIX IT, and seek forgiveness! REPAIR ALL DAMAGE, NOW! Live in harmony and good faith with the world. May God bless our species to strive peacefully one for all and all for one. The HUMAN BEING is the greatest TREASURE ON EARTH, not the dollar! I promise you a new existence if you just open up to change. Seek out TRUTH, end delusions! We are ALL BLACK AFRICANS of various colors from white to black. The mitochondrial says it's a FACT!

My love to you says SEEK TRUTH and the WAY: all your needs will be provided.

Made in the USA
Monee, IL
05 November 2026

67847949R00163